CASSELL STUDIES IN PASTORAL CARE AND PERSONAL
AND SOCIAL EDUCATION

THE PASTORAL AND THE ACADEMIC

CASSELL STUDIES IN PASTORAL CARE AND PERSONAL
AND SOCIAL EDUCATION

THE PASTORAL AND THE ACADEMIC

Conflict and Contradiction in the Curriculum

Sally Power

CASSELL

Cassell
Wellington House
125 Strand
London WC2R 0BB

215 Park Avenue South
New York
NY 10003

British Library Cataloguing-in-Publication Data
A catalogue record for this book is available from the British Library.

ISBN 0-304-33223-2 (hardback)
    0-304-33225-9 (paperback)

Typeset by Action Typesetting Limited, Gloucester
Printed and bound in Great Britain by Biddles Limited, Guildford and King's Lynn

Contents

Series Editors' Foreword

It is natural that publications in the field of pastoral care in education should primarily be concerned with the development of professional practice. Indeed, this series of books has as a major *raison d'être* the promotion of precisely such development, since it is by this means that the education system may more fully provide the entitlement of each child. That said, the distinction between theory and research on the one hand and professional practice on the other is in some ways a false one. All practice is informed by theory, whether implicit or explicit. All theory and research in education is directly or indirectly about practice. The purpose of this series of books is to exploit this interface in order more fully to strengthen practice through better theorizing and more relevant and applied research.

Despite the tradition of vivid and insightful case studies of individual schools – for example, Richardson's (1973) study of Nailsea School, Hargreaves's (1967) study of 'Lumley Secondary Modern', Lacey's (1970) 'Hightown Grammar', Burgess's (1983) 'Bishop McGregor School' and Ball's (1981) 'Beachside Comprehensive – Best *et al.*'s (1983) study of 'Rivendell School' remains the only major published case study with pastoral care as its focus. A survey by the National Association for Pastoral Care in Education (Lang and Marland, 1985) established that a great deal more research was being undertaken in this field by the mid-1980s and this included a number of case studies. However, it would be true to say that much of this research remains unpublished and is somewhat restricted in both empirical scale and theoretical breadth.

In this book, Sally Power brings together case studies in two schools – 'Elmfield' and 'Kings Marsh' – with sociological analysis and an application of the theories of probably the most influential British sociologist since World War II, Basil Bernstein. Her analysis is contextualized in a carefully documented account of the development of pastoral care in 'the comprehensive spirit', identifying and critiquing the bureaucratic pastoral structures which emerged. Throughout, we are reminded of the relationship between educational provision and social inequalities and are invited to re-think the moral and political values which underpin the pastoral endeavour.

The ways in which the tension between the pastoral and the academic, and between hierarchies and the egalitarian spirit of comprehensive schools, are addressed (or not) in 'Elmfield' and 'Kings Marsh' provide interesting and contrasting substance for the more theoretical discourse.

Sally Power has written a book which is theoretically sound and intellectually challenging, while rich in implications for educational policy and practice. In an era when both pastoral care/personal-social education and sociology are too often undervalued (if not denigrated) by the critics of the Right, we make no apology for including a sociological study of pastoral care in this series.

We believe it makes a major contribution to the body of academic work in this area.

References

Ball, S. (1981) *Beachside Comprehensive*. Cambridge: Cambridge University Press.

Best, R., Ribbins, P., Jarvis, C. and Oddy, D. (1983) *Education and Care*. London: Heinemann.

Burgess, R. (1983) *Experiencing Comprehensive Education*. London: Methuen.

Hargreaves, D.H. (1967) *Social Relations in a Secondary School*. London: Routledge.

Lacey, C. (1970) *Hightown Grammar*. Manchester: Manchester University Press.

Lang, P. and Marland, M. (1985) *New Directions in Pastoral Care*. Oxford: Blackwell.

Richardson, E. (1973) *The Teacher, the School and the Task of Management*. London: Heinemann.

Ron Best
Peter Lang

Acknowledgements

There are many people who have helped me with this book. First of all I am indebted to the staff and students at the two case study schools, Elmfield and Kings Marsh. I am also grateful to the Economic and Social Research Council for the funding which enabled me to undertake this project.

I would also like to thank those people who helped me develop my ideas. In this respect, I am particularly grateful to Geoff Whitty and Len Barton. Many others, however, helped in all kinds of ways from critical comments to friendly support. Of these, I would like to mention: Stephen Ball, Basil Bernstein, Ron Best, Bob Burgess, Anne Chappell, Paul Croll, Gill Crozier, Brian Davies, John Fitz, Sharon Gewirtz, David Gillborn, David Halpin, Trish Harding, Chris Hood, David James, Peter Lang, Andrew Pollard, Una Power and Barry Troyna. And also, of course, my family.

The author and publisher wish to thank the following for permission to reprint copyright material.

Stanley Thornes (Publishers), for Figures 3.1, 3.2, 3.3 and 5.1, which are taken from J. Baldwin and H. Wells, *Active Tutorial Work Books 3, 4 and 5* (1980 and 1981).

Much of Chapter 2 appeared as 'Pastoral care as curriculum discourse: a study in the reformulation of academic schooling', in *International Studies in the Sociology of Education*, **1**, pp. 193–208.

List of Abbreviations

BEd	Bachelor of Education
BTEC	Business and Technician Education Council
CDT	craft, design and technology
CertEd	Certificate of Education
CPVE	Certificate in Pre-Vocational Education
EPR	education in personal relationships
EWO	Educational Welfare Officer
GCSE	General Certificate of Secondary Education
HE	home economics
LEA	local education authority
OCEA	Oxford Consortium of Educational Achievement
PE	physical education
PGCE	Post-Graduate Certificate of Education
PSD	personal and social development
PSE	personal and social education
PTA	Parent–Teacher Association
ROSLA	raising of the school-leaving age
RE	religious education
RS	religious studies
SE	social education
TVEI	Technical and Vocational Education Initiative

For Matthew

CHAPTER 1

Reconceptualizing pastoral care

This book explores the development, practice and significance of something called 'pastoral care'. Although the arrangements for its provision vary from school to school, it is usually held to be that part of the curriculum which caters for the social and emotional needs of pupils, as opposed to the subject-centred side which provides the academic cognitive dimension.

There is, as yet, very little empirically based critical analysis of the growth and institutionalization of pastoral care. Such analysis is badly needed, for it has potentially important implications for curriculum theory and professional practice. However, this book argues that pastoral care should not be considered in isolation. The 'pastoral' does not stand on its own. Indeed, it is impossible even to articulate the phrase without invoking that other dimension of the curriculum – the 'academic'. It follows that any adequate analysis of pastoral care must take on board its relationship with the academic.

This chapter begins by looking at the various ways in which pastoral care has been perceived and investigated. It argues that existing research tends to overlook the institutional and social context of the emergence of pastoral care, its oppositional relationship with school subjects and its significance for organizational differentiation and educational transmissions. The chapter concludes by suggesting that these issues can be fruitfully investigated using some of the insights frequently associated with the 'new' sociology of education. The work of Basil Bernstein, in particular, can help us begin to address the question 'How does this management of knowledge institute a complex pattern of cultural difference?' (Donald, 1985, p. 238).

THE RISE OF PASTORAL CARE: A NEGLECTED AREA

One of the most widespread changes in state secondary schools over the last thirty years has been the expansion of 'pastoral care'. Previously weak and disparate organizational features, such as form groups and houses, have increasingly been formalized into pastoral systems, through which specialist pastoral staff provide various forms of pastoral attention. However, despite its relatively recent appearance and the considerable personnel resources with which it is invested (Maher and Best, 1985), pastoral care tends to be a neglected area in the field of curriculum theory and research.

Such attention as it does receive is frequently hostile or scornful. Educational commentators from the right see pastoral care as misguided or even damaging. O'Hear (1991), for instance, claims that the increasing focus on pupils' social and personal needs is 'anti-educational', and passes scathing comment on the 'do-it-yourself self-esteem kit of popular American psychology' (p. 19). Such 'fads' are seen to be both a reflection and a cause of the perceived erosion of standards. Timothy Eggar, as Conservative Minister for Schools, argued that 'too many teachers … emphasize "caring" at the expense of attainment' (Eggar, 1991).

While pastoral care is dismissed by those on the right as some sort of woolly-minded liberal do-gooding, it fares little better under critics from the left. Sarup (1982), for instance, states that the growth of pastoral care represents increasing intervention of the state, inasmuch as 'what may appear as compassionate concern for the individual child is really an attempt to socialize the "deviant" ' (p. 14). Wolpe (1988), in similar vein, claims that pastoral care is 'a major vehicle for dealing with the many social problems encountered in large metropolitan schools, and an integral part of the control system' (p. 23).

Whether pastoral care constitutes some deluded attempt at 'social engineering' as maintained by the right, or fulfils the 'social control' functions attributed to it by those on the left, is largely a matter of speculation, for there is certainly little empirical research to underpin any such claims.

The reasons why pastoral care has been so overlooked can only be conjectured, but might be connected with a number of difficulties over its standing and structure. The lack of research could reflect lack of status within schools. To the extent that the prestige bestowed on research mirrors that of its subject matter, lowly pastoral care may provide little attraction for high-brow curriculum theorists. Less cynical explanations might account for the neglect in terms of the growth and form of pastoral care. Being the product of neither government legislation nor reformist zeal, it has crept in almost unnoticed. In addition, its rather amorphous structure makes it difficult to delineate both empirically and analytically. While school subjects can be represented as clearly bounded areas with recognizable contents, progression and assessment procedures, pastoral care cannot. As discussed later on in the chapter, these contrasts in both form and content may have led to the impression that pastoral care comprises something fundamentally different – rendering it exempt from the same kind of scrutiny which the academic dimension has undergone.

Whatever the reasons for the paucity of research, the growth and significance of pastoral care merit empirical investigation and critical analysis. At a theoretical level, its development provides an opportunity to investigate the processes of change and continuity within the curriculum. Exploration of its institutionalization engages with long-standing debates within the sociology of education which were inaugurated over twenty years ago concerning the relationship between school knowledge, educational identity and social structure.

However, it is not only on the grounds of theoretical illumination that pastoral care deserves serious consideration. It also has important implications for those who believe that the curriculum can be an important vehicle through which to effect changes in schooling. Such aspirations are not just the prerogative of irresponsible left-wing 'sociologico-critics' (Flew, 1976), but are also clearly evident in much of the writing of proponents and practitioners of pastoral care. There is within these texts (discussed more fully in Chapter 3) an implicit, and sometimes explicit, belief that pastoral care can counteract some of the apparently undesirable effects of the academic dimension. Duncan (1988) outlines the channels through which pastoral carers can recognize and challenge the stigmatizing and negative impact of our Eurocentric curriculum. Peter Lang, in his introduction to another book in the same series that is devoted entirely to issues of gender (McLaughlin *et al.*, 1991), talks of the 'major role' which pastoral care can play in addressing gender-related problems. Watkins, in that same text, outlines how pastoral care can provide a 'genuinely empowering' curriculum. Faith in the potential of pastoral care to tackle other issues such as sexuality (Ferguson, 1990) and disability (Beasley and Quicke, 1989; Quicke, 1987) is also apparent.

There is, however, little evidence to indicate that pastoral care is having any impact on these fronts. And the fate of other curriculum reform movements would suggest that any such aspirations are unlikely to be realized through good intentions alone. Whitty's (1985) research into various social and political education initiatives reveals how they failed to make any significant difference inside the school, let alone beyond the gates. In part their limited impact can be attributed to the processes involved in 'becoming' a school subject (Goodson, 1983) within the traditionally hierarchical English curriculum. While this might suggest that pastoral care has more potential to reform because it stands outside the academic domain, any such simple conclusion is likely to be misleading. Recent work on the implementation of cross-curricular themes reveals that legislated initiatives face difficulties of marginalization (Whitty *et al.*, 1994). These illustrations endorse the need for prospective reformers to recognize the complexity of the context within which they are working. While enhanced awareness alone may not be sufficient to effect change, it is surely necessary. What is certain is that without taking on board both the professional and political dimensions of the school curriculum into which pastoral care has been inserted, any alternative educational strategies are doomed to fail.

Lack of contextualization is not only likely to limit the effectiveness of future pastoral interventions within the curriculum, but has also been a characteristic feature of much of the existing research into pastoral care. The next section provides a brief overview of some of this work.

EXISTING RESEARCH ON PASTORAL CARE

Writing in 1977, Best, Jarvis and Ribbins drew attention to the paucity of critical analysis of the construction, organization and significance of pastoral care. They argued that most literature on pastoral care was located within a framework of 'conventional wisdom' where pastoral structures are assumed to be 'support-giving, reassuring and convivial institutions whose functioning makes possible the fullest and happiest development of the individual pupil's school career(s)' (Best *et al.*, 1977, p. 128). A glance along the library shelves would certainly endorse this impression. Up until 1980, when Best *et al.*'s critical collection *Perspectives on Pastoral Care* appeared, the only major publications in the area were 'how-to-do-it' manuals. Michael Marland's (1974) general guide to good practice, Keith Blackburn's (1975) advice for tutors, and Baldwin and Wells' (1979, 1980, 1981) tutor work schemes are typical of the kind of writing available. Empirical research into pastoral care at this time was extremely limited and focused unproblematically on the formal arrangements for its provision. Early investigations are composed almost entirely of broad surveys of the national distribution of organizational attributes (e.g. Monks, 1968; Bates, 1970; Benn and Simon, 1970). But, as discussed in the next chapter, features such as 'houses' are not synonymous with 'pastoral care', and nor do such surveys tell us about their implications for social relations within the school.

Since Best *et al.*'s (1977) call for greater critical investigation, there has been a growing body of research into pastoral care. The early to mid-1980s, in particular, saw a large increase in such work. As Ribbins and Best (1985) point out, however, much of this takes the form of student dissertations submitted towards Master of Education degrees. Not only is such work extremely difficult to access, resulting in a corpus of disconnected, small-scale studies, but it tends to lack sufficient critical distance, being generally undertaken by practising teachers who have a high level of personal and professional investment in the area.

Despite these limitations, the 'conventional wisdom' no longer constitutes the only genre of pastoral care literature. There is plenty of material which demonstrates that the 'reality' of pastoral care is not as benign and altruistic as the official rhetoric suggests. There is increasing evidence that there is tension and conflict between the academic and pastoral dimensions, exposing the myth of fruitful complementarity and co-operation. In addition, as Best *et al.* (1977) predicted, much research now shows that pastoral care 'may be less concerned with the problems of pupil welfare than with the problems of social control and administrative expedience' (p. 134).

In the only major funded study to take pastoral care as its central concern, *Education and Care*, Best *et al.* (1983) use ethnographic data gathered at Rivendell School to illustrate the gap between the rhetoric and the reality. Transcripts from pastoral staff meetings reveal more interest in empire-building and professional status than 'genuine' concern for pupil welfare. Pastoral procedures, such as induction, supposedly aimed at 'helping' new pupils adapt to their surroundings, are little more than a guise for staff to exert greater control.

Woods (1983) also considers the discrepancies between policy and practice and shows how institutional imperatives distort good intentions.
Eastgate (1982) and Buzzard (1983) look at the inefficacy of pastoral care
in intervening for the pupils' benefit at the 'options' stage when they select
subjects for GCSE.

Other research concentrates on pupils' perceptions of their experience
of pastoral care (Tattum, 1982, 1984; Lang, 1983, 1985). These accounts
illustrate that for many pupils pastoral care is seen as simply another form
of control. Taylor (1980) and Ribbins and Ribbins (1983) have looked at
the language of pastoral care. Taylor argues that, despite the less formal
context signalled by the tutor–tutee relationship, the unequal power status
of teachers and pupils is not overcome, leaving the tutor as 'interrogator'
and the pupil as 'agenda-guesser'.

Such studies provide a useful antidote to assumptions that pastoral care
must be unproblematically benign. In parallel with other accounts of
schooling which expose a 'hidden' curriculum (e.g. Apple, 1979a), they
suggest that the reality of pastoral care might actually run counter to the
official rhetoric. But they offer few analytical tools to help us conceptualize
the nature of 'rhetoric' and 'reality' or the processes which might lead to
such a contradiction. We need to move beyond them if we are to understand more adequately this apparent discrepancy or consider its
consequences.

In terms of existing research, such a move is frequently hampered by
limitations arising from the prevailing theoretical framework. Apart from
general surveys of organizational features, nearly all the empirical work on
pastoral care is conducted and analysed using a loosely interpretative
approach. This provides a welcome and necessary break from representing
pastoral care in terms of its formal arrangements, but it also restricts
analysis. While complex processes of schooling cannot be comprehended
without taking on board aspects of subjective experience, the interpretative approach evident in most pastoral care research places too much store
on participants' accounts and not enough on the setting in which they are
articulated. The lack of focus on context makes it difficult to explain some
of the key issues of pastoral care's institutionalization, particularly those
relating to its apparent control attributes and its conflict with the academic
domain.

The concentration on subjectivity rather than context means that
discrepancies between teachers' motives and the 'reality' of pastoral care
can only be conceived in terms of the institutional corruption of individual
intention. The regulatory and disciplinary aspects of pastoral care are
explained in terms of school requirements superseding 'genuinely' educational objectives. We are often asked to discriminate between practices of
'care' which are for the child's benefit and those of 'control' which fulfil
institutional functions. This not only presumes that 'care' and 'control' are
empirically distinguishable entities, but also presents a false dualism
between the 'individual' and the 'institution'.

Because the interpretative framework makes it difficult to bridge the gap
between individual and institution, it cannot adequately account for the
curricular opposition. At Rivendell School (Best *et al.*, 1983), for instance,

the tense relationship between the pastoral and the academic is addressed in terms of contrasting teacher perspectives, with conflicts portrayed as the result of clashing personalities.

Some studies do try to incorporate an institutional dimension. Burgess (1983), for instance, in his initial ethnography and later restudy (Burgess, 1989) of Bishop McGregor School, portrays the school as 'an arena for struggle' and attempts to locate the tensions of pastoral care within a context of materially driven interests and power relations. He shows how the division between pastoral and departmental staff becomes the source of an undercurrent of tension and hostility as staff groups seek to define and defend their interests at a time of contraction and uncertainty. Corbishley and Evans (1980) look at how the organizational aspects of pastoral care become a focus for professional discontent when they threaten the autonomy of the subject teachers.

But while the above research clearly demonstrates the existence of tension between the pastoral and the academic, there is little apparent explanatory linkage between such perspectives, interests and the institution, giving the impression that teachers' allegiances are idiosyncratic and free-floating rather than embedded in a social context. We are given no analysis of the nature of each dimension, or of the relationship between them, beyond the way in which they have been manipulated by teachers to further their own careers within the school. Curricular classifications are more than empty vessels which teachers can steer for their own purposes; they position people according to particular principles.

The connection, for instance, between academic specialization and professional development which has led to the less qualified staff seeking promotion in the pastoral side also has a significant gender dimension.[1] Over twenty years ago, Elizabeth Richardson commented on the differential appointment of men and women at Nailsea Comprehensive where '[t]he welfare role ... has embodied in it the imagery of the family, headed by a father who is seen to be supported by a wife and mother' (Richardson, 1973, p. 109). As in other areas of school management, men are likely to hold most positions of pastoral responsibility (e.g. HMI, 1989), but pastoral care has tended to be seen by women as their main route to promotion. A study by Lyons (1981) revealed that while there is a marked correlation between non-graduate teachers and pastoral ambitions (49 per cent non-graduate teachers had pastoral ambitions as opposed to 9 per cent of graduates), the correlation between women teachers and pastoral ambitions is even more striking. Only 9 per cent of male teachers had pastoral ambitions, but 55 per cent of female teachers saw their careers as developing along these lines.

This relationship between curricular division and gender differentiation illustrates the importance of locating analyses within the institutional and wider social setting. The tendency to overlook the broader context means that existing research on pastoral care suffers much the same weaknesses identified within other 'micro-studies' in that 'it reduces social relations to interpersonal relations and dissolves social structure into a series of settings for interaction' (Edwards, 1980, p. 69). While the interpretative approach tends to portray teachers as the architects of their practices, we need to understand how they themselves are organizationally positioned in relation to each other. The nature of juxtaposition is especially crucial for looking at the significance which pastoral care, and its relationship with the academic, might hold for pupils. Existing research which focuses on this aspect tends to portray the relationship as distinctly one-sided. Williamson (1980), for instance, suggests that 'pastoral structures actually prop up and conceal the ailing academic work of the teacher and the school' (p. 180). Hopper (1986) and Chadwick (1986) claim that pastoral care supports the academic side through 'isolating' and 'treating' children who are perceived of as a 'threat' to school order. But arguments that present pastoral care as simply servicing academic needs overlook the underlying conditions and resulting significance of the tension between the two domains, a tension which may be at least as significant and consequential as any convergence of aims.

In summary, before we can explore the institutional significance of pastoral care, we need to question its institutional formalization and location. In addition, until we can place the construction and transmissions of pastoral care within a framework which problematizes its structure and oppositional relationship to the academic dimension any research will remain over-simplistic and conjectural.

RECONCEPTUALIZING PASTORAL CARE

The construction and significance of the school curriculum have received widespread, if intermittent, attention from sociologists of education for over twenty years. The publication in 1971 of Michael Young's edited collection of critical essays *Knowledge and Control* (Young, 1971a) is often seen to herald this 'new direction' in the sociology of education.

Although a diversity of intellectual traditions and sociological perspectives is represented in the text, the contributions focus on a common theme – 'what counts as educational knowledge?' (Young, 1971b, p. 3). In critically examining the curriculum, the papers, together with the many other studies which appeared around this time and subsequently, sought to problematize an area which had hitherto been largely unexplored; for an analysis of this period see Whitty (1985). Many writers looked for, and found, bias in school knowledge (Nash, 1972; Millstein, 1972; Davies, 1974; Hoffman, 1975; Gleeson and Whitty, 1976; Anyon, 1979). They frequently argued that, either through omission or misrepresentation, the curriculum provides pupils with a distorted view of the world. Other work was undertaken on the boundaries which divide 'school knowledge' from 'everyday knowledge' (Young, 1976; Layton, 1973; Vulliamy, 1976; Hunt, 1972), and the boundaries between subjects (Hine, 1975; Jeffrey, 1974; Wexler, 1982). Some analysts, most famously Bowles and Gintis (1976), looked beyond the form and content of school subjects and focused attention on the social relations of the curriculum. However, despite the wide variety of approach and focus, little work over the last two decades has explored the constitution of pastoral care, the social relations which it embodies or its apparently problematic relationship with the academic dimension.

This neglect is particularly surprising in the light of the early writing of

Basil Bernstein, himself a key contributor to *Knowledge and Control*. As early as 1966, he had drawn attention to 'two distinct ... complexes of behaviour which the school is transmitting to the pupil: that part concerned with character training and that part which is concerned with more formal learning' (Bernstein, 1977, p. 38). The former he character-ized as the 'expressive order', and the latter as the 'instrumental order'. Although Bernstein is referring to contrasting systems of control rather than curricular categories, the distinction has relevance for reconceptualiz-ing pastoral care and its relationship to the academic. Pastoral care, in common with the expressive order, is explicitly concerned with social/moral attributes. It too strives to integrate, while the instrumental order, in parallel with the academic dimension, tends to segregate and stratify. Within the expressive order the emphasis is on the personal rather than the positional. Similarly, despite the apparent complementarity of the instrumental and expressive orders, Bernstein (1977) notes that 'the rela-tions between these two orders are often a source of strain within the school' (p. 38).

This early exploration of an 'expressive order' may subsequently have been neglected by researchers in favour of the 'instrumental' domain because it was perceived as distinct from the curriculum itself, and/or fundamentally different. 'Curriculum' is, of course, a slippery concept. On the one hand, there is the frequent assumption that it is composed only of school subjects, in which case pastoral care would lie outside the domain of curriculum theorists. On the other hand, narrow definitions are often replaced by those which are too comprehensive. This tendency is particu-larly evident in some of the existentialist approaches of the 1970s and early 1980s. Grumet (1981), for instance, argues that 'curriculum' 'can refer to a discussion at the dinner table, a sailing trip, the first day in kindergarten, the death of a parent' (pp. 124–5). There is a danger here that the term becomes redundant, its all-embracing nature offering little precision. While not wishing to extend the concept to these inoperable limits, it seems unnecessarily narrow to restrict it to subjects alone. Even within the conservatively academic National Curriculum, the cross-curricular elements represent acknowledgement that distinctive forms of knowledge and pedagogy exist outside school subjects. Moreover, the curriculum is more than just lumps of facts – it is a 'system of choices' (Bernstein, 1977, p. 80), in which the increasingly formalized pastoral care now comprises one dimension. As with subjects, there are pastoral specialists, pastoral time and space, and pastoral resources. Inasmuch as Musgrove's definition provides an adequate foothold on the nature of 'curriculum', pastoral care can be represented as part of that 'contrived activity and experience – organized, focused, systematic – that life, unaided, would not provide' (Musgrove, 1968, p. 7).

The concept of pastoral care as 'contrived activity' also helps to take us beyond another possible misunderstanding that may have inhibited subse-quent research. Bernstein's separate, and oppositional, representation of the expressive and instrumental orders might be taken to indicate that they are fundamentally different; the instrumental pertaining to the transmis-sion of neutral knowledge and the expressive dimension being concerned with moral and social values. This misrepresentation might be further endorsed by later work from Musgrave (1973), who identifies two components of the school curriculum which he terms 'academic' and 'behavioural' stocks of knowledge. The academic side is catered for by subjects, while the behavioural side covers other 'normative' transmissions and comprises 'moral' education.

However, drawing the distinction between pastoral care and school subjects on the basis of their moral content is misleading for it bypasses the moral and social character of *all* educational practices. Furthermore, it would be a misreading of Bernstein's own position. Firstly, the two orders are not isolated units but interrelated. And secondly, they are both cultural artefacts. The tension between them can be interpreted in terms of their different moral bases. As Bernstein comments in a later paper, the battle over curricula is 'a conflict between different conceptions of social order and is therefore fundamentally moral' (Bernstein, 1977, p. 81). The distinction between the pastoral and the academic does not lie in their respective degrees of morality or value-neutrality, but in their contrasting principles. An adequate analysis of pastoral care, therefore, needs to look beyond the practices to the principles through which they are generated.

THE ANALYTICAL FRAMEWORK

This book takes as its starting point Bernstein's early exploration of two distinct but interrelated modalities of control and draws on his later work on curricular properties and pedagogic discourse to unravel some of the issues surrounding pastoral care and its possible contribution to the construction, maintenance and reproduction of educational identities.

Bernstein's work on the relationship between education and social and cultural reproduction spans over forty years, during which time he has moved his attention from language and socialization to the structuring of educational transmissions. Although these shifts can be interpreted in terms of progression rather than discontinuity (Atkinson, 1985; Davies, 1994), it is his insights into curriculum and pedagogy which will be raided to provide the main theoretical framework of this book.

I do not intend to outline the key aspects of his sociology in any depth at this stage, as they will be introduced as the analysis progresses. Briefly, though, the book will be using his insights into the arbitrariness of curricular organization, the importance of the relations *between* elements, the structure of pedagogic discourse and the way in which power and control are inscribed within such relations.

There are dangers in relying overmuch on any single approach. And while it is Bernstein's work on social class and language codes which has received the most hostile attention, his writings on the curriculum have not escaped censure. Some critics focus on the way he uses particular concepts (e.g. Bisseret, 1979), or the lack of empirical support (e.g. King, 1983). Others believe that his entire approach to the curriculum is flawed. Pring (1972, 1975), for instance, claims that Bernstein's concepts of curricular classification and framing provide little that is new or helpful. Gibson (1984) and, more recently, Harker and May (1993) accuse

Bernstein of a form of structuralism which ignores the socio-historical processes of knowledge production. It is not my intention to address all these arguments, nor to defend Bernstein *per se*, but some of them need to be considered in order to justify the value of the framework and resulting analysis. The next section, therefore, briefly considers some of these criticisms. In particular, it looks at those which are directed towards his claims that social forces determine the organization and distribution of school knowledge, his insistence that we focus on relational properties, his alleged lack of historical specificity, and the relative absence of empirical validation.

One of the starting premises of Bernstein's approach is a recognition of the essential arbitrariness in the organization and content of the school curriculum. Overriding the long-established assumption that the division of school knowledge into different categories reflects the various properties of its subject matter, Bernstein (1977) claimed 'there is nothing intrinsic about how educational time is used, or the status of the various contents or the relation between the contents' (p. 80).

For our purposes, then, we should not start with the assumption that activities defined as 'pastoral' are intrinsically different from those classified as 'academic'. We do not have to preclude questions about what pastoral care 'is' in any ontological sense, or how it 'ought' to stand in relation to the 'academic'. It is more appropriate to bracket such issues and focus on what 'counts' as pastoral care – on those processes at work in its separate and distinctive construction and transmission.

This 'subversion of absolutism' (Davies, 1994) has attracted criticism from philosophers and sociologists. Gibson (1977), for instance, claims that 'sociologists neglect the intrinsic logic of differences between contents at their peril' (p. 36), arguing that school subjects are more than simply social constructs. Similar arguments have been put forward by Flew (1976) and Pring (1972, 1975). Others feared that such relativism would lead to a paralysis of any critically informed judgement with which to determine the contents of any curriculum, or, indeed, the research that addresses it (e.g. Bernbaum, 1977; Wexler, 1982).

These criticisms are not, however, fatally wounding either for 'new' sociologists of education in general, or Bernstein in particular. As Whitty argues in defence of a relativist approach:

> Even if it were the case, as philosophers would argue, that there were some features of knowledge not subject to relativization in any conceivable circumstances, there would clearly be others that varied in differing socio-historical circumstances. Certainly there are aspects of the way in which *school* knowledge is constructed, selected, organized, represented and distributed that are by no means absolute or beyond the realm of social action for change. (Whitty, 1985, p. 14, his emphasis)

Whitty suggests that relativization should be viewed not as an 'epistemological position' but rather as a 'procedural device' with which to problematize the self-evident status of knowledge categories. Furthermore, in Bernstein's work, school knowledge is not some free-floating entity which can be endlessly reformulated through being redefined. It is highly structured, but the structure derives not from essential properties of the subject matter but from the social context. In his now seminal words: 'How a society selects, classifies, distributes and evaluates the educational knowledge it considers to be public, reflects both the distribution of power and principles of social control' (Bernstein, 1977, p. 85). This important statement takes us firmly beyond some of the phenomenological and existential approaches exemplified earlier by Grumet (1981), and evident in the work of many contemporary curriculum theorists.

The emphasis on the structuring of school knowledge and educational transmissions is fundamental to understanding and using Bernstein's framework. Indeed, the importance of abstracting relational properties is written into his definition of the curriculum. It is to be understood in terms of 'the principle by which certain periods of time and their contents are brought into a special relationship with each other' (Bernstein, 1977, p. 79).

Not surprisingly, this refusal to give primacy to the contents of the curriculum has been subject to the same kind of reprimand directed at his relativization of school knowledge. Critics claim that boundaries reflect 'natural' divisions of knowledge rather than social forces. It is therefore pointless for us to problematize the relationship between the pastoral and the academic, or to give it any significance other than that it is the inevitable reflection of two different kinds of educational practice. It is, indeed, Bernstein's insistence on the importance of taking on board the relationship *between* curricular elements which makes his work so useful for this analysis. It is in the classification of curricular categories that social processes become visible. This is particularly true in relation to pastoral care. It is impossible even to think about what counts as pastoral care without invoking its oppositional relationship to the academic domain – and at the heart of this relationship lies a boundary. As existing work suggests, and this book supports, the opposition derives from a deep-seated struggle over the control and regulation of 'valid' educative practices. The drawing of a boundary between the two areas does not represent mutual acknowledgement and accommodation, but constitutes a battle-line. Moreover, to focus on contents at the expense of the way in which they are juxtaposed is to miss the signals which emanate from the juxtaposition itself. As Bernstein (1977) argues: 'The relationships between categories is itself a crucial message, perhaps the most crucial if these come to be considered inevitable and legitimate' (p. 198fn). As we shall see later on in the book, this process is particularly salient to pastoral care.

In addition to providing a theoretical framework through which we can explore the classification of knowledge, Bernstein (1977, pp. 116–56; 1986, 1990) has developed an analysis of the principles through which it is framed and transmitted. As mentioned earlier, many studies generated through the 'new' sociology of education focus on the way in which both the content and organization of school knowledge transmit distorted or reproductive images. Although useful in looking at the way powerful voices penetrate the 'text', they ignore the nature of the medium through which they are conveyed. As Bernstein argues:

It is as if the specialized discourse of education is only a voice through which others speak (class, gender, religion, race, region). It is as if pedagogic discourse is itself no more than a relay whose form has no consequences for what is relayed. (Bernstein, 1990, p. 166)

Just as Bernstein rejects accounts of the construction of the curriculum which neglect social forces, so too he challenges those which represent it solely in terms of external voices.

The unwillingness to analyse educational practices *only* in terms of the outside interests they carry is particularly important when thinking about pastoral care. As we shall see in the next chapter, its emergence and significance are often explained in terms of social control – the means by which threats to authority are contained and powerful interests protected. It is frequently hard, though, to see what was so inefficient about what went before.

It is Bernstein's insistence on specificity which undermines accusations that his approach is ahistorical (Williamson, 1974; Harker and May, 1993) and empirically unsupportable (Pring, 1975; Gibson, 1984). While Bernstein's early work may not explore historical dimensions in any detail, their importance is clearly signalled and developed in his later writing (Bernstein, 1990, 1995). Indeed, it is capable of more historical sensitivity than many accounts of the reproductive tendencies of the curriculum in which 'change is relegated to the millennium' (Bernstein, 1990, p. 170). As he argues in a later paper: 'any theory is only as good as the principles of description to which it gives rise' (Bernstein, 1992, pp. 5–6).

In terms of lack of empirical support, it is certainly the case that until recent years there has been only limited research using his theories of classification, framing and pedagogy. Bernstein himself rarely offers more than anecdotal illustration of this thesis, and early work by King did little to support his position (King, 1976, 1981a,b). But, in addition to the research conducted within his own immediate circle of research students and researchers (e.g. Diaz, 1984; Jenkins, 1989; Daniels, 1988, 1989), there is now a resurgence of interest in the empirical application of his theories (Davies, 1995).[2]

One reason for the relatively limited amount of research could stem from the approach itself. Tyler (1988) suggests that the kinds of argument which Bernstein develops are difficult to evaluate in the field. His framework 'generates its own methodological principles which make any "objective" empirical test to some degree self-validating' (Tyler, 1988, p. 159).

It is certainly the case that his analysis tends to be built around oppositional distinctions and paired concepts (Atkinson, 1985). With reference to the curriculum, for example, we have *instrumental* and *expressive* orders, *collection* and *integrated* codes in which the contents are *open* or *closed*, the boundaries *strong* or *weak*, the knowledge types *pure* or *mixed*, the pedagogies *visible* or *invisible*, and, more recently, discourses which are *vertical* or *horizontal*. Pring (1975) claims that analytical categories such as these are empty in that they do not represent real oppositions. He argues that Bernstein fails to appreciate that binary oppositions 'must assume that the differences within the types are less important than the differences between the two types' (Pring, 1975, p. 71).

An easy answer to this criticism is to say that all analytical categories must gloss over differences, but this is rather glib. The complexities of the curriculum are to be found not just in the tensions between different types of curricula, nor even between subjects, but also, as Ball and Lacey (1980) demonstrate, within subjects. There is, as we shall see, variation within the pastoral dimension. Moreover, the pastoral–academic opposition is just one of many around which the curriculum is structured. There is, for instance, the mental–manual divide, the academic–vocational rift. There are dangers of caricature in characterizing all school subjects from PE to physics as the 'academic' dimension and then setting them up in opposition to a homogenized version of pastoral care. But such caricature can be heuristic. What Bernstein is trying to do is not to describe real curricula, but to generate concepts which are capable of so doing. And his dichotomous distinctions, while clearly oppositional, are not absolute but relative. They indicate the principles by which knowledge is classified and framed which make it possible to compare and contrast diverse practices, principles and social processes. The trick is to recognize the dangers of circularity. As Tyler comments, Bernstein's approach

> is so differently conceived from other theories of the school, it does not lend itself easily to conventional empirical testing... The main danger with such structuralist theories is that they are not testable by the usual empiricist methods which deal by definition with 'surface' appearance or phenomena. (Tyler, 1988, pp. 159–60)

Although it is difficult to know precisely what Tyler dismisses as 'the usual empiricist methods', this book attempts to delve beneath the surface through the use of qualitative data gathered ethnographically. Drawing on two case studies, it explores the way in which pastoral practices are variously defined. It considers whether there is a distinct pastoral pedagogy, and how this stands in relation to school subjects. It concentrates on this relationship to consider the ways in which pastoral care reflects, reinforces and/or interrupts the distribution of power and principles of control.

At the start of the chapter, I began by outlining the key characteristics of existing research on pastoral care. While such research is undoubtedly better than none at all, I have argued that we should not look at pastoral care as an isolated area, but as part of that 'constellation called a curriculum' (Bernstein, 1977, p. 80). However, in order to do this we need to look at the socio-historical circumstances of its emergence and expansion. The next chapter looks at some of these issues.

NOTES

1. Although Burgess (1989) draws attention to the gender dimension in pastoral care, through reporting the staff discussions that surrounded the assumption that the head of first year should be a 'mother figure', its implications are not pursued. Gender is often implicit rather than made the subject of analysis. For instance, the gender dimension of pastoral care is reflected rather than problematized in Best *et al.*'s study (1983), where references to the 'teacher' use the male pronoun, and those to the 'form tutor' adopt the female pronoun.
2. As an indicator of this resurgence, two books on Bernstein's sociology of education have just been published (Sadovnik, 1994; Atkinson *et al.*, 1995). Unfortunately, these became available just as this volume was going to press and it has not, therefore, been possible to incorporate their contributions to the discussion on Bernstein.

CHAPTER 2

The emergence of pastoral care

As we saw in the last chapter, one of the reasons why the significance of the relationship between the pastoral and the academic is either over-looked or only superficially considered stems from a lack of research into the emergence of pastoral care as a distinct category of secondary school provision.

This chapter looks at existing accounts and argues that they too tend to see its development in isolation from the rest of the curriculum. Through a brief historical overview of aspects of curricular classification, this chapter shows that the opposition between the pastoral and the academic is a rela-tively recent construction which has resulted from long-term changes in the content and organization of school knowledge. However, the pace and direction of the incorporation of pastoral care needs to be explained in terms of more recent factors – in particular the widespread introduction of comprehensive education.

LOCATING THE EMERGENCE OF PASTORAL CARE

Locating the emergence of pastoral care as an organizational feature of secondary school provision is an uncertain enterprise. The incorporation of many school subjects can be traced through the implementation of formal assessment procedures. Other changes, such as the introduction of the National Curriculum, are set in motion by government legislation. There are, though, no such benchmarks to locate the appearance of pastoral care.

Ribbins (1985) claims that the term 'pastoral care' has been in use in secondary schools since the late 1940s. However, such early usage may not be representative. Oral evidence from long-serving teachers at the case study schools, Elmfield and Kings Marsh, places the widespread use of the term to refer to a multitude of 'non-academic' activities within the 1960s. Precise dates are, of course, impossible to establish and the situation is further complicated by the prior existence of features of school organiza-tion which have only subsequently been categorized as 'pastoral'. Thus, although many teachers have early recollections of taking form groups or school assemblies, the classification of such activities as part of a 'pastoral system' took place much later. House systems, in particular, have a long history. As discussed later, though, the 'house' of the comprehensive school bears little resemblance to its old public school counterpart. That pastoral care is no more than thirty years old is endorsed by Hughes's (1980) assertion that the term did not begin to appear in educational literature until the 1970s. It is certainly only since this time that the widespread growth of pastoral publications has occurred.

EXPLANATIONS OF THE GROWTH OF PASTORAL CARE

While there may be relatively little disagreement about the period during which 'pastoral care' emerged as an institutional form, there is significant divergence over the reasons why. Some accounts are highly generalized. Craft (1980), for instance, takes a functionalist perspective and claims that pastoral care developed to fulfil a variety of social needs, such as therapeutically reducing the personal anxiety endemic within advanced industrial societies. Other accounts are more complex. Lang (1984) rejects any unidimensional approach and points to a wide range of influences which include the move away from the traditional need for schools to instil deference and the growth of progressive educational practices. Generally, however, explanations of the emergence of pastoral care can be categorized into those which focus on long-term social processes and those which stress specific institutional imperatives. Accounts which centre on long-term social processes can be further classified into those which present pastoral care as the result of progressive enlightenment and those which perceive it in terms of increasing social control.

Hughes (1980) provides a clear example of the 'benign' version, where the emergence of pastoral care is explained in terms of changing social attitudes. Although he claims that the term 'pastoral care' has a moralizing and repressive legacy, he argues that current practices have been influenced by the spread of child-centred education and the child study movement. The development of the former is largely to be understood as 'a reaction against the crude and depersonalized atmosphere characterizing school methods' (Hughes, 1980, p. 27) which has contributed to our awareness of the child as an active agent rather than passive recipient. Likewise, he claims the child study movement has increased our knowledge of the significance of environmental factors relative to innate determinants of child development. For Hughes, therefore, the emergence of pastoral care represents the culmination of a variety of enlightened philosophies and their subsequent institutional implementation.

While Hughes is surely correct in drawing attention to the importance of these movements for the way in which pastoral care developed (see Chapter 3), they do not satisfactorily account for the specificities of its uptake. This is largely because Hughes does not adequately link education theories to the social context in which they were set in motion. For instance, his account provides us with little purchase in explaining the contrasting uptake of progressive ideologies by primary and secondary sectors. Secondly, because of his evolutionary perspective, he fails to avoid the danger of what Giddens (1984) refers to as 'normative illusion', where change is inevitably progress and development implies improvement. Walkerdine's (1984) work provides a useful antidote to any such illusion. Her analysis of developmental psychology and the growth of the child-centred movement suggests that, far from being unambiguously 'enlightened' or 'humanizing', such developments have led to increasing regulation of the child.

In contrast to the enlightenment theories of the rise of pastoral care are those which stress its social control function. Follett (1986) looks at the development of pastoral care 'genealogically'. Using Foucault's (1982) analysis of changes in the relationship between authority, religion and self-discipline, Follett attempts to show how pastoral power invested in religious authority became transformed into the individualized power of the more secular paternalistic state. The education system, he argues, provided a central site for the linkage between the state and the individual. In order to decipher the rise of pastoral care we should look to the forces behind mass schooling in the eighteenth and nineteenth centuries and the way in which various movements, such as the 'Civilizing Mission', were used to penetrate and control the working class at times of increasing political awareness. Drawing on Shaw's (1981a) work, Follett argues that pastoral care represents increasing encroachment of the state whereby

> the parental role was transformed into the legitimacy of the school authority through the term 'in loco parentis' via the original notion of paternalism of the authority of the state. This notion of paternalism itself became embedded in the role of the good school teacher and has been used as a strategy of social and cultural domination and transformation. (Follett, 1986, p. 9)

Far from signalling enlightenment, the rise of pastoral care represents oppression. His account, though, in common with many others which explain the characteristics of mass schooling in terms of the needs of industrial capitalism, suffers the dangers of 'excessive abstraction' (Edwards, 1980). Moreover, the kind of historical illumination which Follett gives us implies that the underlying functions of social control remain unchanged; we have just got better at disguising them. But even if we accept that change is merely illusory and represents only the modification of a legitimizing device, we would still need to know why the old one wore thin; what made it transparent, at what juncture, and why? What made the already 'regulatory' surveillance of school instruction (Donald, 1985) inadequate?

In short, explanations which emphasize long-term social processes, be they presented in terms of 'rational enlightenment' or 'social control', provide few clues to understand the specificity of the emergence of pastoral care. It might be more appropriate to discard these accounts in favour of those which focus on the fine-grained detail of the context in which pastoral care emerged.

There can, for instance, be little doubt that the emergence of pastoral care coincides with the growth of the comprehensive system of secondary schooling. The relationship between comprehensivization and pastoral care has been accounted for in a variety of ways. The need to subdivide the large new schools is often seen as significant (e.g. Best *et al.*, 1977), whether this is couched in terms of 'getting to know' the pupils (Marland, 1980; Burgess, 1983) or 'getting to control' them better (Lang, 1977; Tattum, 1984). Other accounts concentrate on the dilemma of what to do with displaced secondary modern staff (Hargreaves, 1980; Sikes, 1984). The difficulty of containing the increasing number of pupils who were forced to remain in schools as a result of ROSLA (the raising of the school leaving age) has also been seen as a contributory factor (Best *et al.*, 1977).

No one of these explanations seems adequate for the task of explaining the rise of pastoral care, however. Comprehensive schools were often larger than their predecessors, but this can be overemphasized. Pastoral care systems have been established in schools of all sizes (e.g. Halsall, 1970). Neither is it the case that the house or year systems, with their respective 'family' tutor groups, were the only means of splitting up these large cohorts. There is no reason why groups could not have been divided on the basis of perceived ability levels, as in the tripartite system (Hewitson, 1969; Lacey, 1970; Partridge, 1968). The need for a means of organizing pupils along lines other than those of academic differentiation can only be understood with reference to the 'comprehensive spirit'.

Similarly, the argument that pastoral care structures provided the route by which displaced secondary modern school teachers could be accommodated is, in itself, insufficient explanation. As mentioned in the last chapter, it is certainly the case that non-graduate teachers are more likely to see pastoral care as the vehicle for career development (Lyons, 1981; Hargreaves, 1982). It does not, however, seem likely that the need to accommodate these teachers would provide the sole driving force behind the emergence of pastoral structures. Teachers have always been differentiated and stratified. There is no reason why these teachers could not simply occupy the 'lower' positions within the new secondary schools.

The claim that pastoral care arose as a strategy to deal with the problems raised by ROSLA (Best *et al.*, 1977) is particularly weak. One of the key features of pastoral care is that it is inclusive rather than selectively distributed – that it is there for *all* pupils from their first days to their leaving.

This is not to say that the need to break down large schools into more manageable units, the drive to find positions for secondary modern teachers and the dilemma of what to do with 'ROSLA' pupils were wholly insignificant. Such factors may well have contributed to the speed with which pastoral care structures were inaugurated. It is unlikely, however, that such institutional imperatives provided sufficient impetus.

The difficulties of finding an adequate framework with which to explain the rise of pastoral care are no different from those which beset all attempts to account for educational change. For instance, in terms of Musgrave's (1970) framework for analysing educational change, has the emergence of pastoral care been major or minor? Is it sudden or gradual? Such dimensions are hard to establish. How can we know how significant the change is? While writers such as Follett and Craft imply that the growth of pastoral care is a function of the development of capitalism, others claim that it arose as a convenient way of accommodating a group of displaced teachers. Similar difficulties arise when trying to establish the origin and pace of its introduction – is pastoral care an inheritance of Victorian schooling or a post-war product? These questions have no single unambiguous answer, for both enduring properties and short-term contingency appear to have been significant. What is needed is an explanation which takes both dimensions into account – one which can encompass long-term social process without ignoring specificities.

In terms of the specificities of the appearance of pastoral care, we need to look at both the detail of the context in which it emerged and the features of the discourse. As Donald (1985) argues, it is only through looking at both external forces and the internal properties of ideas that we can more fully understand not just why change takes place at a particular time, but also the direction and nature of that change. The conjunction of the extensive and relatively rapid appearance of pastoral care with the widespread introduction of the comprehensive school has to be more than coincidental. Indeed, I shall argue that pastoral care developed in response to the need to resolve tensions embodied within the new system of schooling. In particular, the discourse and features of pastoral care, with its emphasis on individual differentiation and uniqueness, provided a means by which the segregative, hierarchical 'academic' dimension could be reconciled with the integrative egalitarianism of the comprehensive spirit.

However, both of these aspects, the tensions within comprehensivization and the particular properties of pastoral care, need to be accounted for within the wider context. They are part of larger histories. We need, for instance, to understand how changes within the 'academic' made the construction of pastoral care possible. Discourses do not appear out of nowhere. The next section explores this background through providing a brief illustration of some of the ways in which what counts as school knowledge has changed and, in particular, how the academic dimension has been reformulated.

REFORMULATING THE 'ACADEMIC'

It becomes clear, from reading contemporary curriculum and school texts, that in the early nineteenth century 'education' meant 'moral education'. It should, of course, be remembered that this does not necessarily imply that schools were in reality 'moral' institutions. As Donald (1985) points out of such accounts: 'We should be careful to treat them as what they are – which is less descriptions of existing institutions than prescriptive statements about why schooling should be provided and how it should be organized' (p. 216). Nevertheless, just as current educational debates are centred on issues of academic standards and institutional efficiency, those of the early nineteenth century were dominated by concerns about morality.

Although much has been written of the contrasts in educational provision available to the wealthy and the working class throughout the nineteenth century (e.g. Simon, 1974; Marsden, 1987), there were also similarities. For both the pauper and the young aristocrat, the discourse of education was constructed as a moral enterprise, whether through acquaintance with the classics or from the sparse instruction of Bell and Lancaster's monitorial system.

The classical curriculum of the public and endowed grammar school can be perceived entirely as an exercise in elitism. While there is no doubt that much of its status derived in inverse proportion to its usefulness (Wiener, 1981), it was also at the time widely accepted to be morally beneficial (Mack, 1938; Bantock, 1980). The following claim, for instance, is typical of many justifications: 'The merit of Latin prose literature, as exhibited in Caesar, Cicero, Livy and Tacitus, is that it teaches the intrinsic importance of human affairs, and inculcates dignity of character and conduct' (Browning, 1969, pp. 86–7). The classics were held to provide a moral basis for life. They would, through the emulation of 'greatness', provide the cornerstone of a civilized society. Although other subjects may have been taught in the public schools – some English, French, drawing or mathematics, and for girls, of course, home tuition in the less arduous social graces of music and dancing (e.g. Cobbe, 1904) – these too were presented as vehicles for the expression of 'worthiness'. There certainly appears to have been little tension between academic development and personal welfare in the public school curriculum at this time.

While classics and divinity may have been seen as civilizing the public school pupil, more overt moral instruction was available to those working-class children who attended voluntary school (see Donald, 1985). Whether through learning the alphabet, singing, or simply playing in the school yard, these schools would instil in their charges 'a consciousness of the true basis of moral obligation ... of conveying to them a sense of the importance of mutual forbearance, of the duty of protecting the weak, of the necessity of self-denial, of the inviolability of property not their own &c' (Kay, 1970, p. 27). As with the public schools, although a variety of other subjects began to find their way onto the school timetable, their value was also couched in terms of moral worth. In the early years of school science, for instance, the mental faculties to be developed through observation were always of secondary importance to the goals of religious understanding and moral improvement (Layton, 1973). As Kay puts it:

> the youthful mind will recur, with increased curiosity and intelligence, to the great facts and truths, and precepts of holy writ, if it be enlarged and enlivened by an acquaintance of other branches of knowledge ... It is desirable also that they should not be accustomed to consider that there is anything like an opposition between the doctrines and precepts of our holy religion and other legitimate objects of intellectual enquiry. (Kay, 1970, pp. 33–4)

Again, there appears to be no discernible split between 'cognitive' aspects and 'moral' values. For both rich and poor, 'character' was the ultimate purpose of education, and to be of good character, to set an example, was the prime task of the early-nineteenth-century pupil and teacher. In the public school, where the social status of the master was likely to be less than that of his charges, the example for pupils to emulate derived from the classical greats. For the working-class child, the teacher or monitor provided the character template.

The importance of moral worth and religious commitment is further supported in the criteria which have to be met to enter teacher training establishments. For instance, selection procedures for prospective teachers at St Mark's College were based on the following testimonials: (1) a certificate of baptism; (2) a declaration from the parents or guardians of the youth, stating that they have attended church service regularly; (3) a medical certificate; and (4) a recommendation from a clergyman on the nature of their character (Allen, 1843).

By the end of the nineteenth century, however, the tension between secular knowledge and moral objectives appears to have grown. The public schools, voluntary schools and newly established board schools still articulated the importance of religious and moral education, but it had become separated from other forms of knowledge. The position, for instance, that science would fulfil religious objectives became harder to uphold (Layton, 1973). A subject's merit was more likely to be couched in terms of its intrinsic value at the expense of any extrinsic moral purpose. School knowledge was becoming increasingly secular, while issues which were explicitly moral were compartmentalized and marginalized as being to do with the 'emotions', the 'heart' and, ultimately, the 'irrational'.

As with most change, the process was not smooth or uncontested. There were various attempts to 'turn the tide' and reassert the importance of moral education, either in conjunction with, or distinct from, religious education. The campaigns of the Moral Instruction League (Gordon and Lawton, 1978) provide a useful example of such rearguard action. Founded in 1897, the League campaigned through meetings and manuals to increase the amount of moral instruction, and to make 'character' the chief aim of school life. Although the campaign had limited success throughout the early years of the twentieth century, its impact was short-lived. Despite various changes of title, culminating with the Civic Education League, the movement had petered out by 1916.

The process of increasing secularization of the curriculum appears to have continued through the first half of the twentieth century. Where moral and religious objectives had dominated and permeated the entire curriculum, they were now contained, and to some extent marginalized, as discrete concerns. This does mean, though, that the 'moral' content of the curriculum was negligible at this time. Although there may have been little sermonizing, some subjects can still be clearly identified as having the 'ennobling' objectives of classical humanism. Up till the 1950s both English and history, for example, can be represented as moral enterprises. The concept of English literature as the repository of nobleness, with its emphasis on 'high culture', is also echoed by that of history as the means through which 'civilization' can be appreciated and 'great men' emulated.

However, even these more implicit moral dimensions were to be diminished through a further 'purification' of school subjects. Indeed, the separation of academic outcomes from social and personal objectives became scientific 'fact' with the publication of Bloom's *Taxonomy of Educational Objectives* in which the separate domains of the 'cognitive' and the 'affective' are unambiguously identified (Bloom, 1956). As Bantock argues of recent curriculum change:

> Classical humanism finally suffered defeat and a new type of knowledge, one directed to empirical actuality, gradually assumed a cultural predominance: thus it has gradually imported its quantitive methods into traditionally humanistic subjects like history and geography; even literature is regarded as revelatory of process rather than as a depository of didactic, moral wisdom. (Bantock, 1980, p. 24)

The growth of the 'London School' of English (Ball, 1986), particularly in its attempts to radicalize learning, relativize culture and introduce social realism, effectively divorces the study of English from any value position other than that associated with autonomous self-directed learning. Likewise, the prevailing discourse of history no longer touches on fundamental truths about 'great civilizations' or seeks to imbue respect for culture, but rather stresses the need for pupils to 'think historically', to empathize or to question links between evidence and account. The transformation from scripture knowledge to religious instruction and, lately, religious education, reflects the move away from a didactic and proselytizing subject to a more nebulous and uncontestable area. Instead of learning religion, pupils learn *about* religion.

These moves are not uncontested or resolved. Indeed, the introduction of the National Curriculum and the ongoing debates over its content represent struggles to 're-value' school knowledge. History and English have been particularly prone to attempts at such 'cultural restorationism' (Ball, 1990). Despite these moves by policy-makers, there is little to suggest widespread reconstruction at the level of the school. Professional orientations to school knowledge still prevail in many areas of the curriculum (Ball and Bowe, 1992).

The reasons why the nature of academic knowledge should have undergone such a reformulation are highly complex and will relate to a variety of factors – economic, technological and cultural – which cannot be explored here. What is important for our purposes is that, at the level of the secondary school, explicit objectives of moral, social and personal development have been divorced from the 'academic' domain and incorporated as a distinct curricular concern – pastoral care.

This could be taken to indicate that pastoral care developed to fulfil a functional need for moral regulation which was no longer provided for by school subjects. Indeed, this is the kind of reasoning behind Craft's functionalist and Follett's state-centred accounts of pastoral care. However, as mentioned in Chapter 1, the commonsensical perception of the academic as value-free and the pastoral as value-laden is misleading for it bypasses the moral and social character of *all* educational transmissions. These accounts also embody the weaknesses of functionalism generally (e.g. Giddens, 1984). In particular, they are based on the assumption that there is a correspondence between societal need and educational transmissions which is highly questionable. As Bernstein

(1977) states: 'only a very small fraction of the output of education bears a *direct* relation to the mode of production in terms of the appropriateness of skill and disposition' (p. 187, his emphasis).

This does not mean that there is no relationship between the school curriculum and political and economic spheres, but rather that it is dangerous to presume any simple direct one (e.g. Whitty, 1985; Dale, 1989). Rather than fulfilling any particular societal need, the rise of pastoral care can be more adequately understood in terms of overcoming specific tensions which became manifest with the introduction of the comprehensive system of secondary schooling. The next section looks at the background to some of these tensions and considers the contribution made by the emergent pastoral care towards their resolution.

PASTORAL CARE AND THE COMPREHENSIVE SPIRIT

Schooling, as Bernstein (1977) argues, is a class-allocating device. It involves the acquisition of relational identities; the reformulation or preservation of boundaries between groups. It is essentially a process of differentiation and cohesion, integration and segregation.

In the early nineteenth century, social class position was relatively fixed, being legitimized by birthright. Schools were explicitly segregated along class lines, structured around underlying concepts of the 'noble statesman' or the 'honest worker'. While the rise of the meritocratic ideology made it unacceptable to restrict access to schools on explicit social criteria, the correlation between social class and school type continued well into the twentieth century with the tripartite system. While the growth of the middle class, together with increased educational opportunities, ensured some upward mobility, social destination tended to reflect social class origin (Halsey *et al.*, 1980). Despite its formally open access, the tripartite system was still organized around stratified intakes and outputs: the academic scholar, the skilled artisan and the competent citizen. Educational identity was demarcated by clear-cut boundaries. It could be argued that it was the increasing mismatch between educational and class identity which led to dissatisfaction with, and eventual replacement of, the tripartite system. The rising number of middle-class children who were denied grammar school places through the post-war 'baby boom' was, claims Ford (1969), one of the driving forces behind comprehensivization. Whatever the reason behind its eventual introduction, the 1960s and 1970s saw the expansion of comprehensive education on a massive scale. By 1981, 83 per cent of pupils attended such schools (Reynolds and Sullivan, 1987).[1]

That the expansion of provision was not matched by clarity of objectives is now well recognized. But while the precise aims of a comprehensive system were never clearly articulated, they were underpinned by some loosely connected propositions about the relationship between segregation, justice and achievement. Ball (1981) identifies three possible principles along which comprehensive schools could be modelled: the meritocratic, the integrative and the egalitarian. Although, claims Ball, particular schools can be alternatively characterized in terms of these models, it is the meritocratic model which prevailed. Within each school, however, there will be elements of both the egalitarian and, in particular, the integrative, for the principle of integration lies at the very heart of the comprehensive school. It was broadly believed that early segregation not only sometimes narrowed educational and occupational horizons, but also instilled a false perception of the social structure as essentially dichotomous – 'us and them' (Ford, 1969). Through desegregating, not only could incorrect assessments be avoided, but pupil mix would alter perceptions and ultimately contribute to a more flexible social structure.

The proposition that comprehensives could integrate and widen educational opportunity and, in particular, access to the scholarly academic tradition was fraught with inconsistencies. Schools are not just about widening opportunity and breaking down barriers; they are also, as Bernstein (1977) reminds us, about establishing boundaries and highlighting difference. It was imperative that the comprehensive took over the academic tradition of the grammar schools. But this tradition remains powerful only insofar as it remains exclusive. Comprehensives could never be 'grammar schools for all', not simply because of the old argument about differing ability levels, but more fundamentally because the prestige of grammar schools was defined principally in relation to the 'non-grammar' properties of other schools. How could schools integrate, as the comprehensive spirit demanded, and yet at the same time preserve the exclusivity upon which the hierarchy of the academic tradition is founded?

This is the historical moment where pastoral care makes its appearance. The incorporation of the discourse and organizational features of pastoral care provided one of the ways in which the comprehensive school could be an integrative institution without compromising the exclusivity of the academic. It provided a necessary counterpoint to the grammar school legacy. If the academic tradition can be characterized as 'exclusive', pastoral care is 'inclusive'. Rather than stressing 'standards' and hierarchy, pastoral care emphasizes uniqueness and individual equality, in terms of relationships both between teacher and pupil, and between pupils. If the academic tradition divides and categorizes pupils for homogeneity, pastoral care does not. Its discourse and organizational features strive for heterogeneity.

While the following chapter explores the discourse of pastoral care in more detail, this next section focuses on its organizational properties. In particular, it looks at the significance of the dual structure of the comprehensive school, in which the carefully mixed tutor groups and house or year systems of the pastoral sphere began to appear alongside the carefully graded bands and sets of the academic dimension.

THE DUAL STRUCTURE OF THE COMPREHENSIVE SCHOOL

The house system

The school house, and its constituent tutor groups, has a long lineage in British education. Developed within the prestigious public school, it has been incorporated into almost every kind of secondary school. That the public schools should have provided the model for general school organization is, argues Wardle (1976), hardly surprising, given the scarcity of alternatives and the background of senior teachers within new school systems.

However, as well as the lack of well-established alternatives and the influence of the public school advocates, there were also ideological reasons that made the adoption of these features attractive for state schools. Newly established grammar schools, for instance, were keen to develop connotations with the most prestigious schools. Secondary moderns and, more recently, comprehensive schools may have found the philosophy behind the 'house system' a useful antidote to criticisms of largeness and impersonality – drawing upon what Lang refers to as 'the myth of the caring small school' (Lang, 1984, p. 143). It could also be argued that this vision of a bygone England has been a significant factor in the adoption of the term 'pastoral care' itself – conjuring up rural associations that were, in opposition to the world of industry and commerce, so well cultivated by the public schools during the nineteenth century (Wiener, 1981).

However, this long lineage should not be interpreted as indicating continuity. While it is possible to trace features of pastoral organization from public schools to grammar schools and ultimately to comprehensive schools, this does not mean that the functions or effects of these features have remained unchanged. Comparison of their changing nature and scope can be used to illuminate the different conditions under which they emerged.

The public school house system

For the public school, houses were initially arbitrary accommodation units. Boarding pupils would actually live in the houses of their masters, who would use the lodging payments as a means of supplementing their teaching income. The largely selective and narrow intake of the public schools originally made further internal segregation unnecessary. Even within the socially narrow range of intake, the geographical mobility created through boarding meant that further specialization and segregation between public schools could take place. Marlborough and Rugby, for instance, were popular with clergymen's sons, while Cheltenham was preferred by the military (Simon, 1975) and Westminster and Harrow were renowned as Whig schools (Bryant, 1936; Carleton, 1965).

Although most schools had an element of provision for the education of local children on a charitable basis, these pupils were excluded from the main part of the school. Not only were they taught separately, often by 'dames' rather than 'masters', but they were officially excluded from entering inter-house competitions and subjected to systematic exclusion and bullying by the rest of the pupils (Bryant, 1936).

With the reformation and expansion of the public schools throughout the nineteenth century, houses took on greater significance as the means by which pupils could be classified. The house became the main method by which pupils identified themselves, and the house-master gradually acquired the standing of 'a medieval baron in his castle' (Walford, 1986).

Within the public schools, the house system was underpinned by principles of segregation. Because of the economic pressures under which public schools were struggling in the middle of the nineteenth century (Simon, 1974), they were obliged to admit a wider range of pupils and curricular subject matter. These new pupils and subjects were, however, screened and segregated. The old established houses on the 'classics' side took on greater prestige and entry was tightly controlled. Boys who had come to benefit from the 'Modern', 'Army' or 'Military and Engineering' provision being made available in public schools were put into different houses. Clifton College opened a 'Jews House' in the 1870s.

Much has been made of the house system as the basis for sporting rivalry. However, while this certainly seems to have been a significant feature of its adoption within the grammar and secondary modern schools, it was not an aspect of the nineteenth-century public school. 'Inferior' houses were excluded from school sports. At Clifton College, for instance, it was some time before the 'moderns' were allowed to compete, and the Jews House was excluded from playing inter-house cricket until 1912 (Clinstie, 1935). The tutor or form groups were also an extension of the house system, and were primarily for the extension and evaluation of 'academic' rather than 'social' concerns (Browning, 1969).

In summary, within the nineteenth-century public school, houses provided the means by which the 'unclassical', and therefore 'vulgar', pupils and masters could be contained. And while such explicit social demarcations are no longer as visible in today's public schools, it is still the case that pupils are nominated and selected for houses (Walford, 1986).

The house system within the comprehensive school

Although other kinds of secondary schools have had 'houses', they retained nothing of the segregative significance of their public school counterparts. The relative lack of importance given to these features is evidenced through lack of reference in the literature (Davis, 1967; Edwards, 1969; Partridge, 1968). In the grammar schools, houses were certainly used as the basis of intra-school competition and extracurricular activities, but they appear to have been less significant than the plethora of non-house-based school 'societies' (IAAMSS, 1963). And while they may have been useful for generating types of loyalty, they do not appear to have been especially significant in the formation of staff or pupil identity (King, 1969). Likewise, in the modern schools, despite their 'incorporative collectivist' principles (Reynolds and Sullivan, 1981), houses do not seem to have been important, again receiving little mention in the contemporary literature (Partridge, 1968; Farley, 1960).

It was not until the introduction of the comprehensive school that the house again becomes a socially significant feature of school organization. However, in this new type of school, the house derived its significance from a quite different source. While in the public school the 'house' was a means of segregation, its function within the comprehensive system is almost entirely integrative. Pupils are not nominated or selected for houses, as at the public schools, but are deliberately assigned to houses so that 'social mix' might be achieved (Ford, 1969). Tutor or form groups are then worked out to repeat this diversity. Various accounts of setting up comprehensive schools make reference to the importance and difficulty of achieving this mix (e.g. Hewitson, 1969). Some schools went for purely random methods of selection (Climo, 1970; Burgess, 1983), while others deliberately tried to select for social diversity (Shield, 1970). Barnes (1970) explains how at Ruffwood School an elaborate house system was established that sought to preserve neighbourhood ties and at the same time create a mix of social class.

Unlike in the public schools, however, these 'social' units were not the prime means of classification – they were to run alongside other means of segregation, notably streaming or banding. Whereas for the public school pupil the house was the unit for both social and working relationships this was not the case for the comprehensive school pupil:

> There are the 'working' relationships of the form in which he is placed, and in which he will find children of roughly similar ability to his own. And there are the 'family' relationships formed in the House Tutor Group composed of children with all degrees of natural ability. (Crown Woods School Report, 1957, quoted in Blackburn, 1980, p. 56)

No matter how strongly the desirability of 'social mix' was stressed, this mixing of categories was not to interfere with the 'working relationships' within the school. For the main part of the day, pupils were still segregated on the basis of academic ability. Although some schools removed the rigidity of cross-subject streaming, pupils were divided through systems of banding and setting. Pedley's (1963) survey shows that out of 102 comprehensive schools, 88 streamed at point of entry, and 11 waited till the end of the first year, with only the three remaining schools delaying academic streaming until the end of the second year.

Lowe (1988) claims that the use of streaming as an internal selection device was found in all early comprehensive schools. Indeed, '[i]t was unthinkable that they might have done otherwise' (Lowe, 1988, p. 148). Even for ardent advocates of the comprehensive spirit, there was little doubt that 'work groups are the most natural, cohesive social units' (Pedley, 1963, p. 127). It was not the task of the comprehensive school to interfere with such 'natural social units', but rather to establish 'an alternative and parallel social system (houses with tutorial groups) which will bring pupils of all kinds of interest, background and ability together' (Pedley, 1963, p. 127). It is through this alternative and parallel social system that pastoral care ensured comprehensive mix without diluting academic exclusivity. It is perhaps ironic that the house system adopted from the élitist public schools should provide one of the only truly 'comprehensive' aspects of comprehensive schools.

Pastoral care offered more than a parallel system of organization. It provided the comprehensive school with a central organizing principle – that of the 'whole child'. Every curriculum is an organization and, as such, has internal coherence. There is always an underlying concept that makes sense of it all (Bernstein, 1977, pp. 79–84), whether it centres on the academic excellence of the 'scholar', or the 'competence' of the 'citizen'. The comprehensive school could never have such an unambiguous underlying code. As discussed earlier, the code of the grammar school is defined in terms of its exclusivity and could not be transferred to the comprehensive, where the rationale was based on inclusiveness. Although it is often alleged that comprehensives have been 'grammarized' (Elliott, 1983), this is only partly true. Comprehensives may have accommodated the scholarly tradition, but they had to locate it within a central organizing principle. The organizing principles of the secondary moderns and technical schools were equally unsuitable for, historically, such vocationalism is the cultural antithesis of the scholarly tradition (Wiener, 1981). The discourse of pastoral care, with its emphasis on individuality, provided the vehicle for an organizing principle based on unique differentiation. Rather than standing in opposition to the scholarly tradition, pastoral care enabled academic stratification to continue and survive within the comprehensive school as only one aspect of many that make up the 'whole child'.

In moving beyond the assumption that the emergence of pastoral care can be adequately accounted for in terms of either benign intentions or sinister functions, it has been possible to show that its uptake stems from crises inherent both in the reformulation of the academic curriculum and the introduction of a comprehensive system of secondary schooling. The oppositional categorization of pastoral care preserved the exclusivity of the academic tradition within the inclusivity of the comprehensive ethos.

Are we to presume from this that pastoral care serves a rhetorical and legitimatory function only? Such a presumption would be dangerous. Not only is it foolhardy to predict outcomes from imperatives, but it also makes no sense of the tension that appears to exist between the pastoral and the academic or of claims that pastoral care distracts from the 'real business' of education. To argue that the pastoral serves to preserve the academic is only part of the story. All curricular components have their own discursive structure and before empirically illuminating the relationship between the pastoral and the academic we need to understand this structure.

NOTE

1. It should of course be remembered that we have never had a 'true' system of comprehensive schooling. Private schooling, for instance, not only takes 7 per cent of secondary age students (Independent Schools Information Service, 1994), but also has a significance beyond its numerical frequency, for it is one of the ways in which the continuity between educational and class identity can be arranged. Furthermore, as Lowe (1988) points out, geographical differentiation has also ensured that those state schools which are comprehensive are socially selective. Comprehensivization is, he argues, a 'revolution postponed'.

CHAPTER 3

The discourse of pastoral care

This chapter examines the discourse of pastoral care. Chronologically it is a chapter that looks both backwards and forwards. In the last chapter, I argued that the properties and discourse of pastoral care provided a means by which the exclusive and hierarchical nature of the academic tradition could survive within the inclusive ethos of the comprehensive school. While we have already looked at the contribution of its organizational attributes, particularly house systems and tutor groups, we now need to understand what was distinctive about pastoral care itself.

This chapter focuses on the concepts which underlie the discourse of pastoral care. Through using Bernstein's characterizations of 'visible' and 'invisible' pedagogies (Bernstein, 1977, pp. 116–56; 1990), the structure of pastoral transmissions is analysed and compared with that of the academic dimension.

DISCOURSE OR RHETORIC?

'Discourse', like 'curriculum', is a concept which has undergone ever-expanding reference, and, similarly, is in danger of losing definition. However, it still retains advantages over the alternative terms 'rhetoric' or 'ideology'. Rhetoric is almost always considered to be 'empty' and set in opposition to 'reality'. Ideology, too, has associations I wish to avoid. As Foucault (1980) points out, it tends to be used in opposition to 'truth' and stands in secondary relation to some other force – it usually has to 'serve' broader functions. Now, while it may well be the case that the discourse of pastoral care and its oppositional relationship to the academic curriculum do serve broader functions, this connection should be demonstrated rather than assumed. Furthermore, the pastoral discourse is more than a transparent channel through which messages can be relayed; it has its own roots and structure. It has been suggested that discourses are analogous to 'ships in bottles' (Collins, 1985). While such an analogy is useful for drawing attention to the invisibility of the way in which discourses are assembled, it can create difficulties. The discourse of pastoral care is a recent construction, and one, I have argued, that has enabled a particular set of practices to be preserved, but this does not mean that it is a conspiratorial exercise – that, like a ship in a bottle, its method of assemblage is deliberately disguised.

In order to tease out the roots and structure of the discourse of pastoral care, pastoral publications have been analysed as 'social texts ... in their own right and not as a secondary route to things "beyond" the text' (Potter and Wetherell, 1987). This does not mean that the discourse is taken on board uncritically, but rather that it is analysed in terms of its underlying principles and organizing concepts.

PASTORAL CARE: A DEVELOPING DISCOURSE

Initially the term 'pastoral care' appears to have been used to categorize any task that did not fall within the confines of the academic (Ribbins, 1985). It was constituted in terms of what it was *not* – those 'non-instructional', 'non-academic' aspects that are dealt with in 'non-teaching' time. As it was defined primarily in negative terms, it lacked internal coherence and organizing principles. However, as pastoral care developed into a distinct area with the widespread growth of comprehensive schooling, so a body of pastoral literature began to emerge. There has since been a vast increase in what can loosely be described as pastoral publications. In 1983, a specialist pastoral journal was established – *Pastoral Care in Education*. Two years later, Ribbins and Best (1985) reviewed the literature and claimed that more than 800 texts had pastoral relevance. This growth in the literature of pastoral care is significant in terms of understanding the increasing professionalization of the area, and can be analysed to reveal not only the organizing principles of its discourse, but also how they stand in relation to the academic.

In the mid-1970s a cluster of pastoral publications emerged (Marland, 1974; Blackburn, 1975; Haigh, 1975; Hamblin, 1978) that concentrated on the development of 'good' pastoral practices. Haigh's *Pastoral Care* (1975) constitutes a shining example of this 'conventional wisdom' (Best *et al.*, 1977). The text is a compendium of 'common-sense' advice – drawn from the 'firm but fair' school of teaching. The book is full of anecdotes of 'humorous' situations, littered with sexist and racist allusions to 'lusty lads', 'dumb blondes' and the 'embittered parents' of 'coloured children'. There is no bibliography, and no references throughout. While the other texts of this time are more sensitive to these issues, they can still be loosely categorized as 'how-to-do-it' manuals lacking critical comment or analysis.

Recent publications, however, are more sophisticated and exhibit the adoption of a specialist language based explicitly on particular psychological approaches. It is hard to envisage current texts being illustrated, like Haigh's book, with cartoons by 'Larry'. Many texts and articles have large bibliographies and there appears to be a narrowing down and refinement of socio-psychological theories that are perceived as significant. There is more consistency within the discourse, and a considerable amount of cross-referencing between publications.

Although there are differences and debates within the literature, it is possible to identify a distinct feel to these publications that can be said to constitute a pastoral discourse. Drawing on Kuhn's theory of the social process of scientific endeavour, Ribbins and Best (1985) suggest that pastoral care research and writings have entered the phase of 'normal science'. Although the discourse of pastoral care must still be interpreted in terms of its relation to the academic, it has developed identifiable organizing principles and internal coherence.

This development can be interpreted as an increasing move towards the 'professionalization' of pastoral care. There are now opportunities for teachers to train and receive qualifications in this area (Maher and Best, 1985), providing pastoral teachers with their own professional status and passport to career promotion. A key criterion of the establishment of a 'profession' is the articulation of a systematic and specialized body of theory (e.g. Millerson, 1964). While specialization is an important element of career status, it also enables pastoral carers to evaluate and propose practices within their own terms of reference rather than simply servicing the concerns of the academic dimension.

KEY CONCEPTS: COMMUNITY, ADOLESCENCE AND SELF

Like all discourses, that of pastoral care is constructed from a variety of sources which are themselves contextually located. Throughout its development it has increasingly taken on board theories from other disciplines, particularly those of social psychology. In this respect, as we shall see later, it bears a close resemblance to the child-centred model of education which has been characterized by Bernstein (1977, pp. 116–50) in terms of its 'invisible pedagogy'.

Pastoral care also draws from other kinds of imagery. In particular, the concepts of 'community', 'adolescence' and 'self' are threaded together within the discourse. In tracing through these strands it is easy to see how pastoral care became so relevant for the newly established comprehensive school. It also makes it possible to understand the direction in which pastoral care has subsequently developed and the reasons why it now increasingly challenges the principles on which the academic dimension is structured.

Community

'Community' is central to the discourse of pastoral care, providing a powerful source of imagery which also evokes the parallel ideas of 'naturalness' and, more specifically, ruralism as 'refuge'. Lang (1984), in his attempt to trace through the influences behind the emergence of pastoral care, refers to the 'myth of the small school'. This might be more accurately identified as the myth of the small *village* school. Dooley's (1980) analysis of the philosophical and etymological roots of the term draws attention to the concept of 'pastor' and its evocation of images of shepherding. He interprets this significance, however, in terms of the authority relations that are implied and marginalizes the rural connotations.

The very term 'pastoral' evokes images not only of rural tranquillity, but also of an idealized community in which can be found security, refuge and belonging. Allusions to community are particularly powerful. It is, as Williams points out:

> the warmly persuasive word to describe an existing set of relationships, or the warmly persuasive word to describe an alternative set of relationships. What is most important, perhaps, is that unlike all other terms of social organisation ... it seems never to be used unfavourably, and never to be given any positive opposing or distinguishing term. (Williams, 1983, p. 76)

Whether 'community' is seen to describe either the existing or the alternative relationships of schooling is not important here. What matters is that the concept refers to a specific set of relationships. That this set of relationships should be, or is, embodied within the school is significant in terms of the perceived lack of community to be found outside the school.

Adolescence

The 'discovery' of adolescence as a distinct phase between childhood and adulthood has been the subject of a variety of analyses (Musgrove, 1964; Stone and Church, 1975). Indeed, Aries (1975) has nominated this 'the century of adolescence'.

While 'adolescence' became significant for the organization of education in the early years of the century,[1] it was not until the middle years that the concept became associated with 'danger', 'uncertainty' and 'crisis'.[2] From the late 1940s there appears to be a growing concern with the 'difficulties' of the adolescent. A considerable number of psychological publications on the 'adolescent' appear, typically titled: 'Character synthesis: the psychotherapeutic problem of adolescence' (Gitelson, 1948), 'Ego reintegration observed in analysis of late adolescence' (Adatto, 1958), and *Adolescence and the Conflict of Generations* (Pearson, 1958). Child-rearing practices and sociometric scales were used to compare and contrast 'normal' and 'abnormal' development, e.g. *Adolescent Aggression: A Study of the Influences of Child-training Practice and Family Interrelationships* (Bandura and Walters, 1959).

There can be little doubt that this upsurge of research stemmed in part from increasing concern about the apparently 'anti-social' tendencies of post-war youth who were seen to be 'teetering on the brink' (Wall, 1968, p. 9). The press and literature of the time reflect moral panic over teenage subcultures, fuelled by alarm at civil disturbances in the USA:

> A new floating generation of adolescent discontent seems likely to emerge. Although the situation in England is not directly comparable with that in the United States, we would ... emphasize the seriousness of the problem and join the many others who are calling for urgent action, through the educational system and otherwise, before it is too late. (Schools Council, 1970, p. 17)

The perceived need to do something 'before it is too late' was embodied within the now much-maligned concept of 'compensatory education'. Although compensatory education is usually perceived in terms of the need to diminish inequality of opportunity, it was also considered to be important for social stability: 'The pressures on many children are such that the alternative to a policy of compensatory education is acquiescence in despair – or revolt' (Schools Council, 1970, p. 8). The concepts of adolescence and community become interwoven in the pastoral discourse, mutually reinforcing each other. We have the turbulence of growing up as opposed to the tranquillity of communal security, instability as opposed to stability. There are also stronger connections, where it is argued that the turmoil of adolescence is causally related to loss of community.

The loss of community, and lost rural community in particular, is a constant theme in many literary and social-scientific studies. The concept of 'lost communities' provides both the focus and the explanation for social discontent. Although it may have emerged particularly strongly during Victorian times, when the 'countryside of the mind was everything industrial society was not – ancient, slow-moving, stable, cosy, and "spiritual" ' (Wiener, 1981, p. 6), the opposition between rural community and urban centre is still powerful.

In terms of educational discourses generally, the opposition between rural and urban has been a recurring theme around which theories of learning and childhood have been structured and images of progress and tradition, corruption and innocence, and spiritualism and materialism evoked. The influence, for instance, of romanticized primitivism and the belief in 'natural' childhood which underlies the child-centred ideologies of primary schooling has been well documented (e.g. Bantock, 1980; Walkerdine, 1984). For older children, a rural environment is also perceived in terms of its therapeutic effect. May, for instance, on the location of schools for the juvenile delinquent in the mid-nineteenth century, wrote:

> The best situation was the countryside, the 'rural antidote to town poisoning'. Exemplary substitutes for defective parents and neighbourhood influences should be provided by a devoted staff who organised the school on the family system. The guidance of the upper classes missing in the slum areas was supplied by voluntary managers. (May, 1981, p. 281)

Walkerdine also illustrates the faith in the reforming powers of the countryside on juvenile delinquents, stressing the idealized nature of the rural imagery:

> The use of the country as a natural environment is important, but it is equally important to remember that this natural countryside, holder of all that is good and beautiful, is the country of the 'country house' of the aristocracy or the idealized rurality of natural life (swains and shepherdesses) and not the poverty-stricken farmland of peasants and farmworkers. (Walkerdine, 1984, p. 179)

The concept of the 'lost community' provides a key explanation in the discourse of the adolescent discussed earlier. The increasing perception of adolescence as a time of crisis is often couched in terms of the destruction of traditional identity. Post-war youth no longer knows where it stands or what it is. The spirit of adventure which the 'natural' child may have satisfied harmlessly finds its outlet in the more dangerous antics of the adolescent:

> the well fed, the well housed, physically well cared for modern child may lack a number of psychological essentials. The environment of the town or suburb ... has been rendered unsafe for play by the motor car and rarely provides a natural challenge to physical adventure ... Many boys and girls arrive at puberty with a thirst for danger and exploration unassuaged in its primitive early forms, with no basic felt understanding of community ... It does not seem fanciful ... to suggest that some adolescent escapades which result in crime are child's play conducted with adult means, that the exaggerated need to identify with a group is a reaction to a depersonalized and incomplete experience of a human community. (Wall, 1968, p. 70)

There is a perceived disintegration of values: 'Population migrations tend to cut traditional roots and disrupt the mores inherent in stable neighbourhood communities' (Schools Council, 1970, p. 8). The city is a scene of dislocation and moral danger, where 'adventure means sexual intercourse or daring younger children to endanger their lives among rotting timbers' (Schools Council, 1970, p. 27). In contrast, the country provides purity and security. The perceived therapeutic effect of the countryside remains evident in the many publications that stress the benefits of taking children out of towns into the countryside. There are numerous case studies of children who 'found themselves', 'opened up' and 'let off steam' while out in the country. The popularity of Outward Bound courses, usually undertaken by pastoral carers, can be interpreted as attempts to provide a more 'natural' environment for 'self-expression' and 'self-realization'. It is also uncommon to find schools for those with 'emotional behaviour difficulty' situated anywhere but in the countryside.[3]

Where physical presence in the countryside is impractical for any length of time, however, pastoral care offers a substitute community. Tutors can provide that intimate security within the larger community of the school. The school can be seen as a refuge from the deprivation and impersonality of the urban environment, though as Haigh points out: '[t]he trouble with pastoral care is that it is suspended for several weeks of each school year while the children are on holiday' (Haigh, 1975, p. 141).

It is the concept of adolescence as a universal period of danger rather than a distinctive phase of learning which has been significant for the developing pastoral discourse. Early pastoral publications draw on psychological 'truths' in a similar manner to that outlined by Walkerdine (1984) in her analysis of the insertion of Piaget into the primary school. For the adolescent there is 'weathering the passing "storms" of growing up to become increasingly the master of his own destiny' (Baldwin and Wells, 1979, Introduction). Hamblin (1978) refers to the problems of 'the pre-pubertal growth spurt which makes them feel clumsy and very visible. Some may be already experiencing a change in body chemistry which can lead to an upsurge of emotionality and a sense of uncertainty' (Hamblin, 1978, p. 5). However, as the discourse has developed, there has been a noticeable shift away from deterministic and fixed perspectives of adolescence to those that concentrate on the development of a fluid and flexible 'self'.

Self

The pastoral discourse of the 1980s and 1990s does not draw on biologically based developmental psychology, but from what could be loosely described as interpretative sociology and socio-psychology. Examination of the references of pastoral publications reveals frequent use of a number of key sources. Instead of Piaget we have Mead, Laing and Rogers. Adolescent crisis and deviance are not interpreted directly in terms of biological drives or deficient child-rearing practices. Becker, Goffman and Garfinkel are seen to provide more relevant terms of reference. Personality is not fixed, but changing and actively constructed; Kelly has supplanted Cattell.

A useful comparison, which will be explored further, can be made between this collection of theories and those that underpin the 'invisible pedagogy' (Bernstein, 1977, pp. 116–56; 1990). In the 'invisible pedagogy', diverse theories have been recontextualized on the basis of particular characteristics, such as an emphasis on the universals of development, the invisibility of learning that makes overt control problematic, and the abstraction of personal biography from cultural and institutional context.

The theories drawn on by the pastoral discourse are similarly diverse. They too have been selectively relocated to provide a cluster of concepts such as 'self', 'wholeness', 'individuality' and 'identity'. 'Real' learning is seen to be experientially based, unamenable to control or coercion. The 'self' is the key to identity and the adolescent is active in its construction and presentation. Rather than focusing on external determinants, pastoral discourse stresses the need to recognize personal responsibility for actions. Rotter's (1966) and Phares's (1976) work on the correlation between success and realization that the 'locus of control' rests with oneself, not others, are common themes in the literature.

Quite why these theories should have become more significant for the pastoral discourse than the psycho-biological research of the 1950s and 1960s is hard to ascertain. It could reflect the crisis within social science that brought about a rejection of positivistic approaches generally. The 1970s witnessed a reaction against 'overdetermined' explanations. Behaviour became action, and subjectivity gained ascendance. The reasons why such changes occur are highly complex, though it is hard to doubt that the rise of the 'individual' in all spheres of social life is a key factor.

What is more relevant here is not so much why these theories prevailed, but what their recontextualization offered pastoral care. The move towards discourses based on the importance of a social 'self' has enabled pastoral carers to claim greater applicability for their practices, not only through extending the population for whom pastoral care is suitable, but also through increasing the perceived likelihood of successful interventions.

If adolescence is a universally experienced time of crisis, of 'coming to know oneself', then all pupils will need professional guidance through it – not just the 'pathologically deviant'. As writers on the pastoral discourse frequently remind us, the concern is not for 'problem children', but for 'children with problems' – and who does not have problems at some time or other? The number of possible clients is therefore vastly increased. The concept of 'self' as actively constructed and subject to change also justifies intervention. The psycho-biological theories of the 1950s and 1960s emphasized external determinants, often in early childhood. With the adolescent, 'behaviour modification' would therefore be exceedingly difficult. The ideas expounded by Wall (1968) hardly hold out much hope for the success of pastoral care: 'the years up to the age of eight are most critical and that, if things have gone wrong, the effort required to set them right at the secondary school must be disproportionately great' (p. 107). The less deterministic concepts of self-realization and personal responsibility for outcomes offer far more optimistic tenets for the pastoral carer.

PASTORAL DISCOURSE AND THE COMPREHENSIVE

What then are the features of the discourse that gave it significance for the comprehensive school, enabling it, as argued in the last chapter, to reconcile some of the contradictions of comprehensive schooling?

Firstly, as argued by Williams (1983), the idea of the community evokes a particular set of social relationships that provide powerful symbolic persuasion. The comprehensive offered, like the ideal community from which it was modelled, a place for everyone. Everyone is to be of equal value, even if not of equal ability: 'It is the foundation stone of pastoral care, as well as a matter of basic ethics, that no child is worthless' (Haigh, 1975, p. 14). This inclusiveness does not necessarily mean equal provision or expectations. Like the community, it merely asserts the importance of 'belonging' in an environment of mutual interdependence without specifying the nature of the internal relations. Indeed, appeals to 'lost communities' as both the cause of adolescent alienation and the rationale for comprehensive schooling have often been made (e.g. Hargreaves, 1982).

The emphasis on individuality as expressed through the 'self' is also an important persuader. It indicates an added dimension to the meaning of 'comprehensive', where it is 'all of the person' that is catered for, rather than just 'all-comers'. It is the role of pastoral carers to look at their charges as 'persons':

> He [the tutor] will look after the pupils as whole persons. (Blackburn, 1975, p. 5)

> The Rogerian idea of 'whole person' learning involves the integrated functioning of the total organism... This holistic conception is embodied in the experiential model of learning. (Bowes, 1987, p. 185)

The pastoral emphasis on educating the 'whole person' was another important facet of the continuing credibility of the comprehensive school, replacing both the 'narrowness' of the grammar school and the 'relevance' of the secondary modern. The comprehensive school not only rejected compartmentalization of its students, but also distanced itself from the ties between education and occupation that were implicated in tripartitism. It could thus claim to offer 'true' education, rather than merely serving the needs of the economy.

PASTORAL DISCOURSE AND PASTORAL PEDAGOGY

The dissolution of the importance of hierarchy, and the expressed need to embrace the 'whole' child in positive, experiential and rewarding ways, is important for understanding the nature of pastoral pedagogy and its relationship to the academic.

As mentioned in Chapter 1, it is often held, either implicitly or explicitly, that pastoral care is a liberating discourse; that, in its advocacy for the restructuring of social relations within the school, it has the potential for freeing pupils from the stigmatizing effects of the academic. This section considers the basis for these claims.

It was noted earlier that there are strong similarities between the principles of pastoral discourse and the 'invisible pedagogy' of child-centred education (Bernstein, 1977, pp. 116–56). There is also a clear connection to be made between the components of the academic side of the curriculum and Bernstein's 'visible pedagogy'. The obvious benefits of such neat categorization must of course be tempered by the dangers of caricature. It should be remembered that both the academic and the pastoral are internally differentiated. Nevertheless, Bernstein's typification of these pedagogies provides a useful framework within which to analyse the discourse of pastoral care and how it compares with that which prevails in the academic domain. Using this framework, the visible and invisible pedagogies, and, for us, the academic and the pastoral respectively, can be further understood and explored in terms of the identification of the relationship between their fundamental rules of hierarchy, sequence and criteria.

Hierarchical rules

In Britain we have a welfare state, of which the education system is a part. Within that system teachers are professionally, morally and legally responsible for the welfare of the children in their charge, which means, in broad terms, that they are responsible for their personal and social development. Teachers also stand in loco parentis while the child is in school. (Tattum, 1985, p. 43)

Caring is a professional concern. To care about what happens to your client is integral to the traditional model of the professional person. (Tattum, 1985, p. 46)

Students' negative feelings about themselves may be a contributory factor in student disruption... Despite the evidence supporting the advantages of enhancing pupils' self-concepts many teachers argue that their role is to teach subject matter and not to change personalities, ignoring the fact that they work in a person-changing institution. (Tattum, 1985, p. 55)

The school as a caring community only has meaning through the quality of the relationships that exist ... Children need to feel that they belong and that adults care about them, and this is as true of school life as it is of family life. (Tattum, 1985, p. 56)

These extracts provide a typical sample of pastoral discourse. They show the prominence that is given to the 'welfare' dimension of schooling. Education is presented as part of the welfare state, and schools as person-changing institutions. The emphasis on welfare not only denies the primacy of the school subject, but also suggests a different ordering of social relations within the school. The academic dimension is structured around the social relations of 'teacher' and 'pupil'. With reference to welfare concerns, however, Tattum invokes two contrasting relational categories that stand in opposition to teacher–pupil; those of professional–client and adult–child.

Such different categorizations give clues as to the underlying principles of the structure of a discourse, as they inevitably highlight some inherent properties while at the same time marginalizing or concealing other properties (Lakoff and Johnson, 1980). In particular, relational categories stress or hide dimensions of inequality between groups. In terms of pedagogies, these hierarchies can be either more or less explicit, more or less visible (Bernstein, 1990).

Within the subject-centred academic domain, the rules of hierarchy tend to be explicit and unambiguous. Relations between teacher and pupil, teacher and teacher, and pupil and pupil are based on an authority constituted through the possession of various kinds and degrees of academic knowledge. Although differences in seniority are usually implied, these are marginal relative to the significance of 'specialist' knowledge.

The relations proposed within the pastoral discourse, however, emphasize different properties. The relational category of professional–client elevates both parties to different, but parallel, positions. Although the possession of expertise is implied (though it is important to note that this is to be practised rather than imparted), it is to be set against the increased status of the client as 'consumer' as against the professional as mere 'service provider'. Age difference is irrelevant. Within the context of schools, the relation of professional to client hides power differences and legal constraints between teacher and pupil. Although the relational category of adult–child embodies a sense of hierarchy and the filial and communal duties of the tutor community, there is more ambiguity of status of the various members. Within the discourse of pastoral care, therefore, power relations are less explicit. And in common with other invisible pedagogies:

> The more implicit the hierarchy, the more difficult it is to distinguish the transmitter. We can define an implicit hierarchy as a relationship where power is masked or hidden by devices of communication. In the case of an implicit hierarchy the teacher acts directly on the context of acquisition but indirectly on the acquirer. (Bernstein, 1990, p. 67)

Unlike the teacher, the tutor is no longer the source of authority. Tutorial programmes stress the need to share power with tutees. Ultimately, 'the tutor's role is to feed their own self-discovery and not to pre-empt it' (Button, 1981, p. 16). The development of individual uniqueness and subjectivity of the self renders didactic, 'authoritarian' modes of teaching inadequate. The hierarchy on which they are based is untenable. Teachers take on the role of 'facilitators', 'sharing' rather than 'imposing': 'The creation of a facilitative climate entails risk for the teacher, investment of responsibility in the learner implying a less directive stance and a sharing of power' (Bowes, 1987, p. 183). Indeed, Sadler feels that even the word 'role' is too restrictive to describe the position that a tutor holds in relation to her tutees. She claims that it emphasizes institutional imperatives which lead to endless pretence and 'bad' pastoral care, as 'there can be but limited regard for dignity or respect for others in the school if one is subjugating dignity within oneself' (Sadler, 1989, p. 28).

Control no longer rests with the teacher, but must be given back to the pupil:

> My role ... was to be a promoter of awareness in the pupils, awareness about the basis of their actions and behaviour ... the aim of this scheme was to shift the locus of control from the teacher, or external source, to the pupil i.e. to enable the pupil to take responsibility for his/her own learning. (Bond, 1984, p. 183)

This is a task that is sometimes hard in the prevailing conventions, as Bond (1984) acknowledges: 'I would get caught up over and over again in repressing the pupils' (p. 182).

Efforts are also made to dissolve hierarchy between pupils. As discussed in the last chapter, tutor groups, unlike subject classes, are constructed to be heterogeneous social units: 'The one place where the dignity of the pupil can be upheld through respect for her personness is in the social group of the school, the tutor group' (Sadler, 1989, p. 28). The tutor must strive to overcome divisive influences within the group and weld it into a 'community' through 'mutual trust' exercises, such as 'blind trust', 'supporting someone' and 'hand-taking', where 'part of the symbolism represented by hand-taking is that we are making contracts with one another for mutual support in the pastoral group' (Button, 1981, p. 5). These are activities, of course, in which the tutor must always be an active and equal participant, for, as English warns us, emphasizing differences will lead to 'an unwholesome fragmentation where divisions grow up between those who give care and those who receive care' (English, 1991, p. 19). Emphasis is also placed on the value of pupil-led activities in tutorial work, such as brainstorming and discussion. Teacher-led directives are replaced by group negotiations. Elkin gives advice on how to reorganize the classroom space to create 'a democratic ring' and talks of the benefits of 'the conferred status which comes from all of us, including me, sitting as equals' (Elkin, 1992, p. 40).

The invisibility of the tutor as the controlling agent does not mean, however, that there is an equal distribution of power within the group. The transmitter, as Bernstein (1990) says, may not act directly on the acquirer, but acts directly on the context. For the tutor this involves not just moving the furniture or organizing groups, but regulating the nature and direction of transmissions. Indeed, it might even involve careful presentation of self. McNamara (1992), for instance, outlines the attention which tutors should pay to eye contact, voice tone and facial expression. Neill (1988) points out the many negative consequences of not paying sufficient attention to body language.

In pastoral care, the significance attached to 'self', and the concomitant belief in learning through experience, inevitably leads to a rejection of anything that smacks of didactic methods. Pastoral care strives to be pupil-directed. It could, therefore, be argued that the lack of structured content renders the tutor without authority. There is certainly less explicit content than in school subjects. In the academic domain, the content of the subject can be represented by the textbook. The writer is, literally, the authority. Of course, the teacher may add to and mediate the text, but it remains a highly visible source of authority for both pupil and teacher. In the pastoral side there is no such source of authority. There are, of course, pastoral texts containing tutorial programmes, such as *Active Tutorial Work* (Baldwin and Wells, 1979, 1980, 1981), but these are not of the same order as academic texts.

However, lack of content does not mean that the tutor has no authority. It is less visible, but it is not absent. Indeed, it could be argued that the lack of explicit content actually enhances the power of the pastoral carer. In the academic dimension, for instance, both teacher and pupil have texts. In fact the pupil may work on his or her own from the text without the teacher mediating at all. In pastoral care, the text always remains in the hands of the teacher. It is not intended that pupils should see it; its contents are designed to be mediated and controlled by the tutor alone. Pastoral texts may advise that pupils be given sheets or illustrations, but the overall plan, method and objectives remain invisible to them. It is in many ways all pedagogy. It could be argued that pastoral care is, in itself, a recontextualizing discourse (Bernstein, 1986). The rules by which other materials are recontextualized are, however, known only to the tutor:

> In the case of an invisible pedagogy the discursive rules (the rules of order of an instruction) are known only to the transmitter, and in this sense a pedagogic practice of this type is (at least initially) invisible to the acquirer, essentially because the acquirer appears to fill the pedagogic space rather than the transmitter. The concrete present of the acquirer is manifest rather than the abstract/abstracted past of the controlling discourse. (Bernstein, 1986, p. 71)

The methods of transmission are always indirect and include analogy, metaphor and parable, all of which occur again and again in tutorial programmes. Figures 3.1 and 3.2 show typical examples of such work from the still widely used *Active Tutorial Work* scheme. In Figure 3.1 tutees are invited to use the analogy of a river to draw out the important features of their lives so that they might be prepared 'for dealing with family relationships in the Fifth Year'. Note also how the tutor is encouraged to 'reveal' his or her own personal background, playing down the difference between tutor and tutee. Figure 3.2 is similarly concerned with enabling the pupil to understand family relationships and offers the metaphor of 'family as tapestry'. (It is also worth noting that only 'normal' families, i.e. two parents, more than one child, are to be used as illustration through role play.)

As in the assembly, analogy, metaphor and parable are key learning methods which help pupils 'see' aspects that would be unacceptable if

Summer term

FOURTH YEAR: This unit follows on from WHAT'S GOING ON HERE in the Third year, and prepares for dealing with family relationships in the Fifth year.

Pupil Objectives	Activities	Organisation and Method
	THE RIVER OF LIFE Imagine a river as your life, starting as a tiny stream and growing into a fully grown-up river. The river will have danger points, fast-flowing parts, and slow-moving stretches. It will have eddies and, perhaps, whirlpools, as well as waterfalls. *Example* 5: Started school but became seriously ill. Off school for one year 7: Moved house, changed schools – very happy at this school. 10: Had a good friend. 11: Went to secondary school. Didn't really work – not much to aim for. 14: Got a girl friend. 15: Present . . . underground waterfall narrow gorge bridge	Using the analogy of a river, the teacher introduces the idea of critical incidents in one's life. These may not have been seen as critical at the time but, looking back, they may have been turning points. The pupils are in pairs and are asked to draw their own 'river', marking in events, people or places which were turning points or were important in some way. The pairs are encouraged to help one another to remember. 'Didn't anything happen between seven years and ten years? It seems a long gap!' It may be helpful if the teacher prepares a 'river' of his own, perhaps showing how he became a teacher, what influenced him, etc, so that the pupils understand what to do.

63

Figure 3.1 'The River of Life', from J. Baldwin and H. Wells, *Active Tutorial Work Book 4*, p. 63 (Basil Blackwell, Oxford, 1980)

Pupil Objectives	Activities	Organisation and Method
To interpret for himself the roles which people take in marriage, home and family, by examining the role expectations which each sex has of the other.	3 *Role play – Weaving the Tapestry* a) Enact the family scene as directed by selected pupil and teacher. After-tea scene. b) Look back about eight years. Re-enact the same scene as you think it was then. c) Look forward about eight years and again act out events as you think they will be. How does the role of the mother change? Does the father's role change? What differences are made by the children at different ages? d) Discuss the child's expectations of family life when he is a parent. Act out an ideal scene. Allow all the children to suggest their own ideas of the parents' roles.	3a) Before the lesson the teacher will need to select a child from a two-parent family with more than one child and prepare the after-tea scene as it is on a working day in the child's house. The pupil will choose members of the class to take the parts of members of his family. He will describe the scene for them and then ask them to carry on with the action as they think it might have been, with the pupil/director stopping, prompting, guiding them as necessary. In order to help to set the scene the teacher might ask questions such as: What is mother doing? What is father doing? What do the children do? b) Then move the time backwards and forwards as suggested opposite. d) Organise two other scenes as suggested. Lead to discussion of and perhaps the acting of what the child himself expects to happen when he is a parent. (See the introductory notes on role play, p. xxi, and on deepening role play, p. xxii.)

67

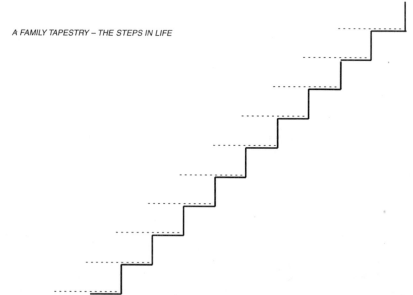

A FAMILY TAPESTRY – THE STEPS IN LIFE

Figure 3.2 'A Family Tapestry – The Steps in Life', from J. Baldwin and H. Wells, *Active Tutorial Work Book 4*, pp. 67 and 96 (Basil Blackwell, Oxford, 1980)

directly proselytized. The control of the tutor may be less explicit, but it is nevertheless there:

> The teacher's role is to encourage contributions from one group after another, to move in close to groups from time to time, to intervene, to suggest points missed, add emphasis, crystallize, support and draw out the timid and soft-spoken... His sense of pace is important – more often moving things forward in a lively way, yet allowing pauses for introspection or a greater depth of contemplation. He must be sensitive to feelings and be able to convey warmth and encouragement. (Baldwin and Wells, 1979, p. xvii)

Although the explicit hierarchy embodied in the teacher–pupil relationship is rejected in the pastoral discourse, it does not mean that there are no hierarchical rules. As we saw earlier, the relational category of adult–child also has a power dimension, although it is more ambiguous. So has that of professional–client, even when not legally enforced. In the context of the school, and in conjunction with the relational category of adult–child which is embodied through 'in loco parentis' (Shaw, 1981a), this power could be even more pervasive. In addition, the notion of a school community, particularly when it emphasizes the respective positions of adult and child, is also an expression of unequal social relations. Those elements of the pastoral discourse which 'liberate' the pupil from passive recipient to 'client' with rights and responsibilities are thus counterbalanced by other aspects of the discourse which 'shelter' and 'constrain' the pupil as child member of the school community.

The relation of professional and client elevates the individual in terms of independence and autonomy, dissolving hierarchy and replacing it with a vision of pluralism. However, the notions of community in general, and pastoral community in particular, elevate the dependency and obligation of belonging. They represent a reformulation rather than radical reworking of staff and student positions.

Sequencing rules

> Something must come before and something must come after. (Bernstein, 1990, p. 66)

As with hierarchical rules, these can be more or less implicit or explicit. The school subjects of the academic domain can be characterized as having explicit sequencing rules, visible to both staff and pupils. Not only is the career of the pupil temporally punctuated, but the terminology of academic development is shot through with sequential references; pupils can be 'advanced' or 'forward', they may be 'lagging behind' and they may be in need of help to 'catch up'.

The pastoral lacks such visible temporal definition. As with the invisible pedagogy, it emphasizes flexibility. Its lack of formal content and willingness to take hold of issues as they crop up indicate this flexibility. Another indicator is the use of resources. For the tutee, these are at most worksheets, lacking the permanency of the text. The principle of flexibility elevates spontaneity over planning:

> Role play should arise spontaneously in response to a need to communicate 'what it was really like' or 'might have been like' ... as an essential part of active tutorial work, flowing in and out of events as they occur, e.g. 'Don't tell us – show us'. (Baldwin and Wells, 1979, p. xxi)

Such spontaneity is, however, carefully managed. Figure 3.3, again taken from *Active Tutorial Work*, outlines directions for the tutor to follow when 'facilitating' an exercise in role play. These instructions on how and when the tutor should speak, what to say, and when to pause, are more tightly framed than even the most rigid lesson plan: 'The important skill for the teacher lies in being able to forecast a series of questions, each of which represents a small step forward' (Baldwin and Wells, 1979, p. xvi). Rather than 'doing' subjects, topics are returned to again and again. The 'River of Life' activity featured earlier is designed to 'follow on' from a previous exercise in Year 9. Although the sequencing may not be comprehensible to the pupil, it does in fact have an order that only the tutor understands: 'There is sequence and continuity in these programmes, which facilitates the steady build-up of personal growth. The programmes are therefore offered as a coherent whole: they are not a series of exercises that can be picked out at will' (Button, 1981, p. 1). Rather than progression being linear and dictated to by external subject requirements, development is seen to be cyclical and based on pupil maturity. As with invisible pedagogies, pastoral discourse is underlain by recognition of the biological basis of maturation and 'readiness'.

Individual pupil misdemeanours may be similarly 'read off' and interpreted according to tacit notions of what constitutes 'normal' adolescence, with some kinds of deviant behaviour being classified as 'natural' adolescence, while others could be perceived of as indicators of serious pathological disturbance.

The hidden rules of sequencing mean that pupils may neither understand where they should be, nor know what stage they are at. They are not aware of the criteria by which their behaviour is evaluated.

Criterial rules

The criteria for evaluating the successful transmission and acquisition of the academic again tend towards the explicit, though, of course, internal variations between, say, the sciences and humanities should not be forgotten. Pupils are usually aware of whether they are considered 'able' in a subject, even if, as for example in art, these criteria might be seen as open to contestation:

> A visible pedagogy (and there are many modalities) will always place emphasis on the *performance* of the child, upon the text the child is creating and the extent to which that text is meeting the criteria. A visible pedagogy puts the emphasis on the external product of the child. (Bernstein, 1990, p. 70, his emphasis)

This is not the case with the pastoral. There is no visible, gradable standard against which pupils can measure themselves. As Bernstein claims of invisible pedagogies, difference reveals uniqueness. It is the central tenet of pastoral care that every child is unique, that 'we are all individuals'. This emphasis on uniqueness and lack of standardization means that 'Where transmission realizes implicit criteria, it is as if the acquirer is the source of the criteria' (Bernstein, 1986, p. 71).

Throughout tutorial programmes, tutees are invited to set their own objectives, to appraise their own efforts: 'The young person tells himself where he stands ... and could well be our best informant... It is desirable that the young people should be involved in their own evaluation as an important addition to their experience' (Button, 1981, p. 27). While pupils may set their own attainment targets and officially assess their own behaviour, it would be a mistake to assume that these are the only criterial rules of pastoral care. As with all invisible pedagogies, the tutor learns to 'read' the child: to look for key indicators of difference, and to assess what stage they are at. How significant these evaluations are to the career of the child can only be assessed in relation to other evaluations and may depend on the facility with which some pupils learn how important it is to be good tutees as well as good pupils, itself dependent on the extent to which they are capable of penetrating the rules of the pedagogy. What does seem likely is that these kinds of evaluation will become more important. The continuing growth of profiling and Records of Achievement, for example, assigns a central role to tutorial evaluation and oversight. Such schemes will evoke all kinds of tensions between the academic and the pastoral given the contrasting definitions of the nature and pace of successful learning.

PASTORAL DISCOURSE AND THE ACADEMIC CURRICULUM

Analysis of the discourse of pastoral care not only indicates the kind of practices, and interpretations of those practices, which are likely to be forthcoming, but also reveals one possible source of the tension that resides between the academic and pastoral dimensions. Through dissection of the discourse of pastoral care, it is clear that it is underlain by pedagogic principles which are different from and oppositional to those which prevail in the teaching of school subjects.

Thus, while the emergence of pastoral care may have provided one means by which the hierarchical and segregative academic curriculum could survive and flourish within the newly established comprehensive school, the increasing sophistication and expansion of pastoral discourse now challenges academic dominance. This challenge stems from pastoral rejection of the academic as 'real' education. In addition, pastoral care has an inherent tendency to 'encroach' into other pedagogic areas.

The discourse of pastoral care is constructed on a rejection of the validity of any form of person compartmentalization. The notion of the importance of the 'whole child' that is stressed so often within the pastoral discourse restates the original connection of the words 'indivisible' and 'individual' (Williams, 1983). A curriculum that attempts to cater for only part of this 'whole' – to divide what is essentially a unity – is, by these

Autumn term

PREJUDICE, STAND-POINT TAKING, AND PERSPECTIVE
This exercise is concerned only with stand-point taking and perspective and not with any 'moral' which the story may be perceived to contain.

Pupil Objectives	Activities	Organisation and Method
To develop the ability to take on the role, the feelings, the perspective of another person and to allow for different feelings and stand-points in discussion and in social situations.	*AS I SEE IT – FROM WHERE I STAND* This is a ring game activity: it is about taking a particular stand-point and arguing a case from that point of view. *Outline of the activity* The pupils listen to a story or narrative and are given a stand-point from which to argue a persuasive case. After arguing 'their' case twice to two different people, they reverse their stand-point and argue the opposite case with a third person. One of the main objects of the exercise is to discover how difficult it can be for some people to see an opposite point of view when they have previously invested themselves, their time and their effort in reaching conclusions about an issue.	You will need: APPENDIX 6: *A Story* 1 This activity may be carried out in one large or two or more small rings. Seat six or more pupils in a circle facing outwards. Round them arrange another circle of the same size with each person facing inwards, opposite a partner. 2 Then say something like: 'In a moment I'm going to tell you a story. I want you to listen closely. I'm not going to tell you anything more about this activity at the moment, except that – as you will see – it obviously concerns listening, which is a very important skill.' 'Think for a moment about how difficult we find it really to listen to what someone else is saying.' 'Now for the story…' 3 The story (APPENDIX 6) can be read out, if necessary, but it is better done from memory, adding one's own *ad libs* in order to make it sound easy and natural.
To develop the ability to take on the role, the feelings, the perspective of another person, and to allow for different feelings and stand-points in discussion, and in social situations.	*Agenda* i) Who would you like to be? ii) How would *you* feel if you were Paul? iii) How would you feel if you were father?	4 *After the reading* a) Use the Agenda opposite to encourage the pupils to consider the characters and circumstances in the story. b) After a pause with discussion just beginning, say: 'Stop! Don't bother! I'm going to ask you to be one of the characters. The inside ring people are the father who wishes to retire and to persuade David to return to the business. People in the outside ring are David at the height of his success, who does not wish to do so. Try to make each other understand your point of view.'

Figure 3.3 Extract from 'As I See It – From Where I Stand', from J. Baldwin and H. Wells, *Active Tutorial Work Book 5*, pp. 55–7 (Basil Blackwell, Oxford, 1981)

Pupil Objectives	Activities	Organisation and Method
		c) Give about five minutes for each to persuade the other to his point of view. After five minutes move the outer ring two places to the right, and tell the pupils that, now they have organised and rehearsed their arguments, they have three or four minutes to persuade their new partner to their point of view. Say something like: 'Now … you have just been thinking back to the story and putting together your argument. You should be quite good at it now – so I'm going to give you less time. I want you to take the same stand-point with your new partner and make your argument really crisp this time.'
		d) After three or four minutes, move the inner circle one place to the left. Then say: 'Now that you've got to grips with your case, I want you to be the other person. Now you have three or four minutes to convince your new partner of the 'right-ness' of your new point of view.'
To develop the ability to take on the role, the feelings, the perspective of another person, and to allow for different feelings and stand-points in discussions and in social situations.	*Follow-up discussion* This is the crux of the exercise. How easy is it to listen, when you have a point of your own which you want to put? How easy is it to change roles? What makes it difficult? How much of the other person's argument had you taken in? Was it as easy to be one person as the other? Which one did you prefer to be? Were you more successful with one of your partners than the others? Why was this?	5 After three or four minutes, halt the discussion. You may find that many pairs have not really got started, and that some pupils have invested too much of themselves in their previous 'arguments' to be able to come round to or frame arguments for the opposite point of view. This will be a good lead into the important follow-up discussion (see opposite). This story can be replaced or supplemented by others of your own choice or composition. Suitable stand-points would then have to be ascribed to the inner and outer circles.

Figure 3.3 *(continued)*

terms of reference, inevitably partial and, therefore, deficient.

However, not only is the academic side of schooling inevitably partial and deficient, but it is also damaging. The need to embrace the 'whole' child in positive, experiential and rewarding ways is set up in opposition to the negative and ultimately alienating experiences made available through the academic dimension. Its system of labelling, differentiating and grading pupils thwarts pastoral objectives of the promotion of self-esteem. As Tattum (1985) points out, 'the academic impetus of schools has an inbuilt potential for rejecting and hence alienating a significant number of pupils' (p. 46). He goes on to refer to 'the battered self-images of the system's rejects' (p. 46). Pupils' problems are *created* by academic differentiation.

Also embedded within the discourse of pastoral care is the momentum for all other aspects of schooling to be increasingly brought under its gaze. Pastoral carers must not only protect the child, but, as professionals, represent their interests even if these are apparently at odds with those of the subject teachers. This might involve surveillance not just of students, but also of staff: 'The tutor needs to discover something about the members of staff who teach his group' (Blackburn, 1975, p. 15). Sometimes it might be necessary to intervene: 'From time to time the voice of protest has to be heard in the right place for the sake of the pupil' (Blackburn, 1975, pp. 217–18).

Deviance is not just unwillingness to learn, it is a rational response to the situation in which pupils find themselves – a situation for which the academic side of schooling is responsible. Truancy and trouble-making represent a form of political resistance. As Mosely puts it:

> If we accept that most prevalent curricula in current school systems reflect a traditional, didactic approach, that secondary schools still package knowledge into subject areas and that teachers are then required to pass on the relevant information to their pupils – then we must accept that implicit in this current process is a view of the child as passive and *untrustworthy* ... the only way she can challenge this view is to adopt actively disruptive strategies, slip into bored apathy, or merely absent herself from school altogether. (Mosely, 1988, p. 10, her emphasis)

Resistance is normalized and naturalized as the sign of clients' inevitable dissatisfaction: 'youngsters seek to protect their self-images as they return the verbal, physical and organization assaults on their perceptions of self with similar abuse. To be passive is a denial of self and a loss of self-respect' (Tattum, 1985, pp. 55–6). In the advocacy of their clients' interests, the discourse of pastoral care, far from simply accommodating the academic, challenges it.

At the start of this chapter I argued that because pastoral care may have arisen as a means of reconciling the exclusivity of the grammar school tradition and the inclusivity of the comprehensive spirit, it should not be assumed that this resolution would be unproblematic. And indeed, in a clear example of how discourses can extend beyond authorial control (Donzelot, 1979), we can see that far from accommodating and servicing the academic, the discourse of pastoral care now poses a challenge. We have seen how the discourse of pastoral care has undergone expansion, sophistication and professionalization. Drawing from alternative ideologies of schooling as 'welfare', it embodies a pedagogy that stands in opposition to that which prevails within the academic dimension of the curriculum. Using Bernstein's characterization of 'visible' and 'invisible' pedagogies, I have attempted to illustrate that not only does the pastoral differ from the academic, but it is fundamentally oppositional. It might be that this opposition provides one reason for the tension between the two areas and the maintenance of the boundary. Again, though, just as it is not possible to interpret the effects of the pastoral–academic boundary from the reasons why it emerged, neither is it desirable to read off its significance from discursive features alone. The next chapters undertake an empirical exploration of this tension and some of its possible consequences.

NOTES

1. The discovery of 'adolescence' as a distinct phase between childhood and adulthood was officially encapsulated in the Hadow Report of 1927 on the nature of secondary, as opposed to primary, education.

   > There is a tide which begins to rise in the veins of youth at the age of eleven and twelve. It is called by the name of adolescence. If that tide can be taken at the flood ... we think it will 'move on to fortune'. (Board of Education, 1927, p. xix)

   Its 'discovery' not only made possible the segregation of children on the criterion of age, resulting in the apparent discontinuity between primary and secondary education, but also resulted in the system of age grading which is dominant in most but the very early and late years of education. In the nineteenth century, it was not uncommon to find classes containing pupils of varying ages. Bamford (1967) has shown from statistical analysis of class composition in public schools in 1861 that an average age difference between pupils of three years was common, while in some classes age differences could exceed six years.

2. Although Walkerdine (1984) argues that the creation of 'adolescence' must be understood in relation to the discourse of juvenile delinquency and concern over increasing crime during the Victorian era, there is little evidence to support this connection. As May (1981) illustrates, during the mid-nineteenth century, the 'juvenile delinquent' was a pathologically deviant 'child'. Its deviance was that it 'violated images of childhood' (May, 1981, p. 274). There does not appear at this stage to be widespread recognition of 'normal' adolescent behaviour differentiated from both childhood and adulthood. It is not until the 1950s and 1960s that the idea of a 'normalized' adolescent crisis becomes, as Walkerdine would put it, 'scientific truth'.

3. The reasons why these schools are situated in the countryside can, of course, be explained in terms of segregation and fear of 'pollution' of 'normal' children as much as in terms of the benefits of a rural location.

CHAPTER 4

Elmfield School: a case study of the pastoral and the academic

The last two chapters explored the emergence and development of pastoral care. Chapter 2 focused on the educational context surrounding its appearance. It argued that pastoral care provided one means by which some of the contradictions embodied within the establishment of a comprehensive system of secondary education could be reconciled. Specifically, pastoral care helped to resolve the problem of retaining the exclusive tradition of the grammar school within the inclusive ethos of the comprehensive movement. Chapter 3 looked at the development and increasing sophistication of the professional discourse of pastoral care. Analysis of its underlying principles shows that, in many ways, pastoral care, far from accommodating the academic tradition, is increasingly opposed to the subject-centred side of the curriculum. While the academic is organized in terms of clear hierarchies, linear sequencing of content and explicit criteria of evaluation, the pastoral attempts to level hierarchies, provide flexible learning structures and reject explicit assessment criteria.

This chapter looks at the implications of this opposition for the institutional organization of pastoral and academic provision through an ethnographic investigation of Elmfield School.[1] It begins with a brief introduction to the school and then explores the relationship between the pastoral and the academic in terms of its significance for teacher allegiances and identities.

ELMFIELD SCHOOL: A CASE STUDY

Elmfield is an LEA-maintained co-educational comprehensive school on the edge of the city. It draws pupils, predominantly white, from a variety of areas – both rural and suburban, and middle and working class. It has about 800 pupils on its register, of whom 80 are in the sixth form.

It was selected as a case study school because it has a 'specialized', rather than a 'whole school', curriculum (Marland, 1980) in which the pastoral and the academic are explicitly demarcated. This should not, of course, be taken to indicate that the situation at Elmfield will be representative of all such schools, for each school has inherited peculiarities. Without delving too deeply into the history of Elmfield, it is necessary to mention at this stage two significant features of the school which bear on the data gathered; firstly, a relatively recent amalgamation, and secondly, the resulting inheritance of a split site.

The two sites are located over a mile apart. The site that is now the lower school (Years 7 and 8) was formerly the Grant School for Girls, while the upper school site (Years 9 to 13) was previously Overton Comprehensive. Eight years after the amalgamation, 39 of Elmfield's full-time staff of 52 are ex-teachers from Grant and Overton (a staff list is shown in Appendix 1). The headteacher from Grant, Miss Howard, took over the management of the new combined school.

Although Elmfield's history will contribute to the perceptions and allegiances of staff, these peculiarities should not be seen as mere 'interference', for the way in which particular histories are worked through can be as revealing of underlying tendencies as more general patterns. At Elmfield, for instance, the amalgamation and consequent redistribution of teachers has resulted in retrenched allegiances which reinforce curricular divisions – and particularly that of the pastoral and the academic.

THE PASTORAL AND THE ACADEMIC: A DIVIDED CURRICULUM

As mentioned earlier, Elmfield operates a specialized curriculum. Its pastoral care provision is administered through a year-based system. The academic dimension operates through faculties and departments. Each side has its own organizational structure, holds its own meetings and outlines its own agenda. Although nearly all staff have both academic and pastoral roles, inasmuch as departmental heads are usually assigned tutor groups and heads of year also teach subject lessons, they have divided allegiances. This division is both reflected and reinforced by the fact that, at Elmfield, it is generally not possible to hold both academic and pastoral positions of responsibility.

At the level of official school policy, the dual structure is presented in terms of a rational division of labour; enabling subject specialists to concentrate on pupils' academic development while pastoral carers look after their social and emotional needs. Underneath such rhetoric, however, the picture is far more complex. While the separate pastoral and academic dimensions work alongside each other, it would be a mistake to presume a happy and equivalent co-existence. At Elmfield, the relationship between the pastoral and the academic is fraught with tension. The next sections explore this tension through looking at the contrasting way in which both areas are organized, the relative strength of each dimension and how the boundary between the pastoral and the academic is constantly maintained and defended.

THE PASTORAL AND THE ACADEMIC AT ELMFIELD

Bernstein (1977, pp. 79–115) argues that the curriculum can be usefully explored through examining the way in which its components are interrelated: the strength of insulation between the various elements, the structure of their progression and the means by which students and staff are assigned particular educational identities. He presents two contrasting models of curricular organization: that based on the 'collection code' and that structured through an 'integrated code'. These two models provide a valuable framework within which to compare and contrast the organizational features of the pastoral and the academic at Elmfield.

The organization of the academic

The academic dimension of Elmfield appears to be structured along the principles of Bernstein's collection code with 'strong boundary maintenance creating control from within through the formation of specific identities' (Bernstein, 1977, p. 96). Its key features – the emphasis placed on academic specialization, the hierarchical ordering of subjects and early selection processes – are all clearly recognizable.

The compartmentalized structure of Elmfield's academic provision is visible in the way in which subject knowledge is organized into a series of discrete units, each clearly bounded and sequential in character. The academic career of the secondary school pupil is divided into prearranged stages, from the single unit of 35 minutes that comprises the 'lesson', to the term and then the school year. The timetable graphically illustrates such boundaries; it shows the clear-cut demarcations and the lack of ambiguity over where, when and what each pupil or teacher is doing at any given time.

The temporal segregation of the timetable is endorsed by spatial separation. Subjects have 'homes', whether on the scale of the science block or the single geography room. The subject identity of these rooms is clearly visible through the material displayed and/or specialist equipment. Where the subject department is large enough, these areas take on the significance of 'territory'. Workrooms can become the exclusive meeting place of subject members, where entry of non-members is perceived as intrusion. These areas not only strengthen subject allegiance, but also diminish interaction with other staff, thus perpetuating subject insulation.

At Elmfield, for instance, members of the science department in particular are rarely to be seen in the staffroom. Indeed, subject loyalty is so strong that it impinges on staff social occasions. Wendy Tozer, who organizes social functions, usually has to take departmental membership into account, for instance:

> 'Some departments want to sit together for Basil's leaving meal: science, maths and modern languages.'

At Elmfield, as with all curricula structured through the collection code, 'it is the subject which becomes the linch-pin of one's identity' (Bernstein, 1977, p. 96). Although there are faculties at Elmfield, these are not particularly significant in terms of teacher identity. Many teachers were unable even to recall the names of the faculties or their subject components, let alone identify their co-ordinators. No such problems existed in the identification of departmental heads.

The subject specialism of the teacher provided the primary source of reference for both staff and students. Even when pupil involvement with a teacher was of a pastoral nature, it was the teacher's subject identity which was the dominant means of identification:

SP: What about your tutor?

P1: Well, Mrs Kemp.

SP: And are you all in the same group?

All: No.

P2: I'm in Mrs Wade's. She's in charge of RS.

SP: Tell me about your tutors then. What do you think your tutors are for?

P2: RS.

P1: No, they ain't.

P2: Mine is.

P1: Mine is maths.

With the exception of heads of year, staff were rarely, if ever, referred to in terms of their pastoral identity, even by other predominantly pastoral staff. Subject identification was significant even where, as with the headteacher, there were no teaching duties. As one teacher said of Miss Howard:

'She's only a needlework teacher.'

Being 'only a needlework teacher', of course, reflects not only the importance of subject identity, but other ways in which school knowledge is compartmentalized, specifically in terms of 'manual' and 'mental' attributes, and 'male' and 'female' subjects.

It is a key feature of the collection code not only that subject specialism is the dominant form of identity, but also that subjects are differently valued. As Bernstein (1977, pp. 85–115) suggests, the hierarchical ordering of subjects does not depend upon the intrinsic merits of the subject matter, but on the purity of categorization and degree of insulation from less 'specialized' subjects. The importance of maintaining subject boundaries as the basis for one's academic status is clearly apparent within the science faculty at Elmfield. Being a 'general' science teacher is to be somehow 'less' than a specialist chemist, biologist or physicist. The Head of Physics and science faculty co-ordinator, Gareth Evans, makes the following claim:

'In this department we have a number who'll teach more than their own specialism. I don't. I only do physics. I can't do anything else.'

The mutually exclusive nature of specialization means that claims of inability in one area naturally imply ability in alternative areas. Thus art teachers who are 'hopeless with numbers' endorse their artistic prowess, and the geography teacher who 'can't even draw a straight line' emphasizes his scientific ability. The importance of these implications is outlined in Bourdieu's critique of the 'naturalness' of aptitudes, in which teachers'

> charismatic ideology encourages them to regard intellectual careers as personal vocations based upon 'gifts' so mutually exclusive that possession of one rules out possession of the other: to proclaim that you are no good at science is one of the easiest ways of assuring others and yourself that you are gifted on the literary side. (Bourdieu, 1971, p. 206n)

Weakening of subject purity threatens not only the status of specializations but also the means by which differentiation is achieved: 'Any attempt to weaken or *change* classification strength (or even frame strength) may be felt as a threat to one's identity and may be experienced as a pollution endangering the sacred' (Bernstein, 1977, p. 96, his emphasis). The resistance to any weakening of subject specialism is evident in Gareth Evans' comments on the prospect of introducing an integrated science course for all pupils at Elmfield, rather than just the lower-ability groups:

> 'Integration means dabbling in all three. The trouble is that at A-level you need the basis to be able to cope with it … it means a drop in standards. Because of the large syllabus they're deliberately making it easier. That makes it more difficult later on – but they're changing A-levels too… The standard of GCSE is disappointing. It's the questions. I mean the one on acid rain – you didn't have to have studied chemistry. Any member of the public could have answered that.'

It is important to note that it is not just the dilution of specialist science in itself that troubles Mr Evans, but a weakening of the procedures that differentiate scientists from non-scientists, 'chemists' from 'any member of the public'. A key aspect of the collection code is that 'as you get older, you become increasingly *different* from others … specialization very soon reveals *difference from* rather than commonality with' (Bernstein, 1977, p. 95, his emphases). The importance of subject boundaries to educational identity is such that, at Elmfield, even the limited integration of the sciences up to GCSE level is seen to make vulnerable these differences and render educational status ambiguous.

A key feature of the collection code is the creation of a hierarchy not just *between* subjects but also *within* subjects. At Elmfield, academic position, whether that of departmental head or Year 7 pupil, is explicitly and unambiguously structured along clear vertical lines of authority. These positions have been ascribed through 'careful screening procedures to see who belongs and who does not belong' (Bernstein, 1977, p. 96).

As we saw earlier, among staff, subject purists can be distinguished from those with more 'generalized' identities. This demarcation became particularly pronounced after the amalgamation of Grant and Overton. The redistribution of posts shows a re-emphasis of specialized academic priorities. Staff often couched the redistribution in terms of the headteacher's favouritism for teachers from Grant:

> 'All it [the interview] was, was about putting Overton down and saying what a wonderful school Grant was.' (Basil Hunt)

'You see, everyone's taking early retirement from Overton. There have been no promotions, they've all been from Grant.' (Wendy Tozer)

While it is the case that several teachers from Overton were redeployed elsewhere or relocated to less prestigious positions within the new school, this redistribution is not simply the result of personal favouritism. It can be more adequately explained in terms of the priorities of the newly amalgamated school and, in particular, with an emerging emphasis on the academic dimension as structured through the collection code.

Overton, prior to amalgamation, can be characterized as operating in the secondary modern tradition despite its 'comprehensive' designation. On amalgamation and reformulation into 'Elmfield', however, academic priorities were emphasized through the appointment of more highly specialized staff, the introduction of a sixth form, and provision of additional resources, such as a new science block. Not only does the incorporation of a sixth form require the appointment of academic specialists, but it also has ideological significance through symbolizing a traditional mode of schooling based on stratification, specialization and the promise of higher education. Overton staff, who often lacked strong subject identities, were therefore more likely to be displaced than those from Grant, where traditional academic priorities were already well established.

There are significant parallels here with Riseborough's (1984) study of how secondary modern teachers perceived their careers after incorporation in a comprehensive school. Alternative priorities gave these teachers 'spoiled' identities, a significant aspect of which was the translation of academic responsibilities into pastoral positions. Such dislocations are also apparent at Elmfield. Basil Hunt, for instance, who had been head of maths at Overton, was given a head of year post in the new school:

'I didn't have a degree. They wouldn't have a non-degree person to run a sixth form, would they? I mean you couldn't have a non-graduate in a sixth form. Not that I couldn't have done it ... but that wasn't viewed – especially by a head that's very degree-conscious. So I had to be moved.'

Valerie Goddard was moved from a position of Scale 4 status at Overton to a Scale 1 post at Elmfield:

'There was nothing else for me, I didn't expect to get on in languages, I didn't have a degree – though that wouldn't have mattered in some schools.'

The ex-deputy head at Overton, Henry Perrett, now head of Year 11, reflects on his current value at Elmfield:

'I'm the lowest of the low – I've only got a two-year teaching certificate.'

This lack of academic identity not only debars non-specialists from prestigious academic positions but also renders them liable to lose identity even further through being forced to mix categories – in terms of both subjects and pupils;

'I get put into funny subjects. They've given me art – I said "I can't draw".' (Steve Woods)

'I teach across seven subjects. I get no support. I can't go to all the meetings. I don't know what I'm supposed to be doing – no books, no help, no feedback. I'm an odd job man ... I only take the bottom bands; they leave the top bands for the specialists. I'm just filling the timetable. I'm being used. I can keep them quiet, do something, but that's all.' (Tony Haskins)

Just as the academic dimension at Elmfield positions teachers according to the degree of subject purity, it also grades and sorts pupils.

The screening of pupils starts from analysis of primary school records, where pupils begin to be divided into two basic types – the 'normal' and the 'remedial'. From the beginning of the first year at secondary school, the remedial group is excluded from the rest of its age cohort for all lessons, with the significant exception of those which are 'practically' oriented – CDT, art and home economics, where the lower status of the subjects might make mixed pupil categories less important. Throughout the rest of their academic career, pupils are regularly tested and differentiated on the basis of a variety of factors. Broad banding takes place at the end of Year 8 on the criterion of linguistic ability. Setting within bands is established on the basis of tests in science, maths, humanities and English.

The process of pupil sorting not only indicates the significance of selection within the academic dimension, but again reflects and reinforces the hierarchical ordering of subjects themselves. Academic priorities are established at all levels of organization. For example, here Mr Easterbrook explains how he constructs the timetable:

'I block out the main requirements and then music, geography and RS are left to fill in the places – then other subjects such as careers are left behind that.'

Of course, he claims this is only in the interests of expediency:

'It's not because they're less important, but because it's easier to do the timetable that way.'

These priorities are visible in the pecking order through which pupils are selectively screened. As previously mentioned, ability in French is the baseline indicator of banding. This can cause resentment:

'It's the tail that wags the dog. I mean, is German any harder than French?'

However, it is conceded that:

'You usually find that those who are good in French are also good in science.'

Those pupils 'who are good in French' are also expected to take German. This prioritizing means that other subjects have to be found to fill in the timetable. Citizenship, for instance, is taught to all Year 8 and 9 students who are not considered capable of taking German:

'There's a subject that some poor people have to teach – a waste of time.'

When pupils take their GCSE options at the end of Year 9, the subject hierarchy is also visible, with some subjects being more capable than others of resisting the allocation of 'unwanted' pupils:

'David Green has been put into drama – the excuse is they think he'll be uncontrollable. I don't see why I should have him on those grounds. He wants to do motor vehicle maintenance. He's in the travelling fraternity; perhaps he'll need it. I've had kids before like this.' (Dorothy Parfitt, Drama)

'I get that in computing ... They say, "the riff-raff can do that".' (Shirley Skinner, Computer Studies)

Although, as Ball (1981) indicates, tutors can be influential in the academic realms through directing and 'helping' pupils with subject options, at Elmfield it is the subject teachers who are the 'decision-makers'. The role of the counsellor in channelling pupils into academic and non-academic tracks (Cicourel and Kitsuse, 1963) does not appear to be as established here as it is in the USA.

In summary, then, the academic dimension at Elmfield is structured along the lines of Bernstein's collection code. School knowledge is divided into clearly demarcated subjects which are strongly bounded from each other and which provide the basis of teacher identity. Each subject is insulated from others and tends to have a linear structure. The academic dimension is also characterized by hierarchies: hierarchies between different subjects, hierarchies within departments and hierarchies between staff and students, and between student groups.[2]

The organization of the pastoral

Just as the academic at Elmfield can be represented in terms of the specialized collection code, it is also possible to find parallels between Bernstein's model of the integrated code and Elmfield's provision of pastoral care. While the collection code is characterized in terms of strong boundary maintenance, hierarchical ordering of subjects and progressive screening of students, the integrated code signifies weak insulation between areas, lack of hierarchy and no formal student screening. Indeed, the very invisibility of its organization and lack of formal structure renders its analysis more difficult.

Although there is a formally demarcated slot of pastoral time at Elmfield, a daily 25-minute tutorial (incorporating two assemblies each week) and 5-minute registration period, this time is not displayed on the school timetable. In addition, it is classified as 'non-teaching' time in official accounts of the school day. For the main part, pastoral care is administered on an *ad hoc* basis throughout the day. The lack of insulation means there are no formal divisions into periods, nor even any formal separation of 'contact' time from 'non-contact' time for those with pastoral responsibilities. Neither is the spatial demarcation of pastoral provision at Elmfield as clear-cut as that of the academic. Although tutor periods are located in tutor rooms, these rooms do not have the status of 'territory'. While notice-boards may display administrative notices of the tutor groups, these are marginal when compared to the dominant subject identity of the room. Pastoral staff areas are likewise not as exclusive as the subject workroom. Staff and pupils may, and often do, enter unaccompanied and uninvited.

The lack of official demarcation of pastoral time and space is also reflected in a lack of clear identity for pastoral staff. As the data on pupil perceptions reveal, pastoral identity is subsumed by academic identity. The low organizational visibility of pastoral care endorses Lang's conclusion from interviews of pupils that 'few ... had any developed concept of a system or network designed to help them' (Lang, 1985, p. 80).

This does not mean, however, that pastoral staff have *no* identity, but rather that it is established along different lines. Lacking the hierarchical and clear-cut criteria of formal academic differentiation underlain by possession of specialist subject knowledge, pastoral identity is usually couched in terms of personal attributes:

'Steve's [head of year 8] got a lot of charisma... They're lucky. Steve's very good, one of the very few people who are teachers by vocation. There aren't many of them about.'

Pastoral staff are not identified through 'cleverness', but through personal attributes of patience, sensitivity or kindness. This means that, inevitably, it is deemed preferable for them to take the 'difficult' classes. As Gareth Evans explains to Reg Hawker (head of year 9) on his taking the 'less able' students:

'That's the advantage with you. You've got the patience to deal with them.'

There are, of course, significant gender dimensions to this opposition between personal virtues of patience and caring and cognitive attributes of cleverness. As mentioned in Chapter 1, the extent to which this division has implications for reflecting and reinforcing gender divisions is commented on by Richardson in her analysis of the appointment of a senior mistress at Nailsea Comprehensive, where the sex-linked nature of the roles

can be understood only if they are examined in relation to each other. In terms of the curricular/pastoral split, these two people felt themselves to be equally trapped in strait jackets – the one as 'the administrator', the other as 'the carer'. This division of strengths with its implied distribution of weakness, was also a reflection of ancient assumptions about masculinity and femininity. (Richardson, 1973, p. 218)

At Elmfield, the larger departments (science, English, maths, French, geography and history) are all headed by men. The curricular deputy is male. While it is the case that most heads of year are also male (four of six in the first year of the research) they are seen to need female counterparts as deputies. The new introduction of the post of deputy year head was explained as follows:

'It's needed because if the girls are playing football in the gym and one of them has an accident, I can't go in.' (Henry Perrett)

That a female head of year might need a male deputy was never expressed. It is perhaps significant, in the light of the fact that these posts were created primarily for women, that they carried no allowance of time or money for the work involved. It is also worth noting that Mr Alcock, the pastoral deputy, was often criticized in terms that seemed to question the nature of his sexuality: his smart 'designer' haircut, excessive concern over his appearance and 'fussy' attention to detail.

Because the pastoral aims at inclusiveness rather than exclusiveness, there is no need for the formal screening and differentiation of pupils into graded categories which prevail within the academic dimension. Although pupils are divided by age within the year system that operates at Elmfield,[3] there is no subdivision on the basis of 'ability'. In line with the spirit of the comprehensive school movement discussed in Chapter 2, Elmfield tutor groups are deliberately constructed to contain a cross-section of ability. And again, although there is a pastoral syllabus, this is not formally assessed or selectively distributed on the basis of any pupil attributes other than age.

The principles underlying pastoral care also result in authority relations between staff which differ from those found within the academic dimension. Relations between pastoral staff are not expressed in terms of a hierarchical and linear nature. Although there is a pastoral deputy, emphasis is placed on the importance of working as a 'team', a term which denotes collective responsibility rather than simple linear delegation. Unlike in subject departments, membership of the pastoral team is not tightly defined or fixed. While the pastoral deputy and year heads could be said to form the nucleus, on some occasions the 'team' also includes the Head of EPR, the school nurse, and the educational welfare officer.

Not only are relations between staff on the pastoral side different from those within the academic dimension, but there are also significant contrasts in the way in which teacher–pupil and tutor–tutee relations are formulated. These contrasts, however, will be more fully explored in the next chapter.

In summary, it would appear that the specialized curriculum at Elmfield has resulted in a dual structure of provision where the academic and pastoral are clearly demarcated and segregated. The boundary between the two areas is visible in the contrasting modes of organization which contribute to the divided allegiances between members of staff.

STRADDLING THE BOUNDARY: AREAS OF AMBIGUITY

The above comparison rests on highlighting the differences between the pastoral and the academic dimensions. Where the academic is visible, the pastoral is invisible. Where the academic has strong insulation, the pastoral has weak insulation. It is perhaps worth questioning whether these are substantive differences or merely analytical caricatures. Are they real contrasts, or are they simply contrived, as Pring (1975) argues, 'on the interesting logical device of dividing things into two types which ... depends upon making one category simply the negative of the other' (p. 71)?

At first sight it does appear as if pastoral care is always defined in the negative – fewer boundaries, less identity, less screening. Is this because, as Pring suggests, the nature of the categories is essentially flawed? Is the use of Bernstein's framework helpful in understanding the relationship between the two areas, or is it simply making a point of difference through unhelpful contrast?

It is certainly the case that the division of the school curriculum into mutually exclusive areas is an analytical convenience which glosses over a degree of messiness within and between each dimension. There are some areas of the curriculum which it is hard to identify unambiguously as either academic or pastoral. However, the ambivalence of these elements, rather than disproving the fundamental nature of the opposition, can be used to further illustrate the tension that exists between the pastoral and the academic.

Some subjects, for instance, that appear on the timetable at Elmfield are not 'proper' subjects at all in the eyes of academic specialists. These 'pseudo-subjects' appear to exist simply by virtue of their use for those perceived unable 'to do a subject' (Keddie, 1971). Although they may have all the trappings of a subject – a demarcated slot on the timetable, syllabuses, textbooks and even some kind of formal assessment – they are often considered to be 'artificial'.

The orientation and principles of these elements often appear to be closer to those of the pastoral rather than the academic. Citizenship, for instance, is a subject that those deemed unable to take a second foreign language follow. Indeed, as mentioned earlier, it is seen as a 'timetable filler'. However, its objectives bear strong resemblance to pastoral prescriptions: 'Citizenship is about increasing awareness of one's relation to others in society' (Elmfield Options Booklet). Then there is community studies:

'The aim is to produce certain skills, for instance guiding a blind person, communicating with the deaf... It's geared for pupils who go into the caring options... It tends to attract more of the pupils who are less, well, academic.' (Jean Taylor)

The perceived affinity between this kind of subject and pastoral care is evident in the fact that Jean Taylor, who is also Head of Religious Education, is the only member of staff with a departmental headship to be offered pastoral responsibility as well. Most other academic posts render one ineligible for pastoral work. It would appear that a subject identity founded upon religious education and community studies increases eligibility for pastoral responsibility.

Local studies, the non-examination 'history' option, again seems to have few academic objectives:

'It's really just to try and teach them some social graces – to stop them shouting at each other by the time they leave school. It attempts to civilize them – half way through the 5th year we see if we can take them out without trouble.' (Graham Anstey)

A history field trip for local studies pupils is therefore not the same thing as that for the GCSE History class. Sometimes subjects can take on different status on an *ad hoc* basis. Here, Tim Cornish, a geography teacher, finds a solution to the problem of litter on the playing fields:

TC: I'm going to take them out and pick up litter... I mean it's a better use of a geography lesson at this time of year.

SW: Yes, well, it's environmental studies.

It is significant that picking up litter could not be 'geography' – although it could be 'environmental studies'. The lack of precision and insulation within the word 'studies' distinguishes it from the specialization of 'discipline' and is a common feature of other 'low-status' academic subjects such as rural studies and European studies (Goodson, 1983, 1988). It has significant associations for community studies at Elmfield:

'It's the word "studies". It puts them off. They think it's well, you know, less.' (Jean Taylor)

If some subjects do not fall neatly within the academic side, others that are ostensibly 'proper' subjects take on pastoral significance because of the lack of academic status of their pupils. Official timetable designation may not necessarily describe content. Remedial lessons, for instance, can have subject titles such as 'French' or 'Maths' but actually contain quite different contents from subjects of the same name which the non-remedial pupils are following. Here the history teacher and head of Year 10, Maureen McColl, discusses lessons for the remedial group with the Head of Remedial Education, Ian Loveless:

MM: As a group, I'd like to abandon teaching with them, and teach them how to relate to each other as normal human beings.

IL: Yes, I think that's a good idea. I think I've got some stuff about that.

MM: I'd like to do something like that with them.

Ian Loveless, through his association with special needs pupils, also tends to be characterized in terms of personal attributes rather than academic aspects. Although he is an English 'specialist', his identity is often defined along the same lines as that of pastoral carers, e.g.

'Ian Loveless. Now, he's very caring.'

Out of all these areas, it is 'education in personal relationships' (EPR, Elmfield's version of personal and social education) which has the strongest pastoral associations. Although it is formally timetabled as a 'subject', and Simon Reed, its head of department, claims to have 'never thought of it as pastoral', he clearly rejects the dominance of the academic subject-centred curriculum:

'You tend to forget that the school is a mass of individuals. You tend to forget individual needs. It's very subject-oriented. I'm trying to get away from content and back to individuals. There's a poor individual stuck in there. The content may not be relevant.'

EPR, like pastoral care, has a 'team' that includes mainly pastoral staff. Again, the inclusive ethos of the team enables the school nurse to take her own sessions:

'She'll learn a lot. She's part of the team. She isn't teaching, you know.' (Simon Reed)

These comments reflect many of the key principles of pastoral care. For instance, they too challenge the academic assertion that knowledge resides only with subject-specialist teachers and suggest that both staff and pupils engage in the learning process simultaneously. Again, like tutor work, EPR is unassessed. All pupils take EPR. There is no internal stratification on the basis of ability. Attempts to erode hierarchy are also apparent in the use of teachers' first names by pupils within the EPR lessons.

The problematic status of these 'pseudo-subjects', their affinity with the pastoral dimension and their concomitant lack of explicit progression of content can cause demarcation problems. Quite what belongs within which boundary is often difficult to determine. There are, of course, issues of ownership within the academic dimension. At Elmfield, for instance, physicists, biologists and geographers sometimes contest the proper location of particular topics. However, the absence of formal boundaries within the pastorally oriented areas renders them particularly vulnerable to 'poaching':

'I don't want it [tutor work] to be too organized. I don't want people coming up to me saying you can't do that because we're doing that.' (Jean Taylor)

The lack of insulation, hierarchy and explicit content makes such contests more difficult to resolve. And the underlying rejection of curricular compartmentalization makes ownership claims even more awkward:

'Oh, this is a problem. She keeps doing stuff we do in EPR. It's awkward. What do you do?' (Simon Reed on Jean Taylor's syllabus)

The ambiguous nature of these subjects can also cause problems with teachers' identities. Some promote their academic pedigree through playing down their own involvement in such pseudo-subjects, e.g.

'I'm science trained. EPR is an aside.' (Simon Reed)

Others, however, choose to dismiss any pastoral connections and promote their area as unambiguously academic, e.g.

'It [community studies] is an academic subject, and they're preparing for exams in the subject.' (Jean Taylor)

However, at another moment, Jean Taylor uses a different tactic through rejecting the validity of the distinction:

'I suppose it's largely of a pastoral nature. But then I mean every teacher is a teacher of pastoral care. They're so interwoven.'

On the other hand, some teachers choose to identify with the pastoral side, at least temporarily, rejecting academic associations, e.g.

'I used to run a media studies course for the less able, but it began to attract the kids it wasn't intended for. We had some smashing kids. I got fed up – sort of gave it up.' (Ian Loveless)

In the sixth form, a possible confusion between the more pastorally laden vocational education course (CPVE) and the academically orientated A-level student appears to have caused Simon Reed some difficulties:

'My CPVE group is great. About the same size as last year – but this is a better group in some ways. You know last year some were all over the place – it was hard to know whether they were doing A-levels or CPVE. This year we've got a well-defined group.'

For those who identify with the academic side, but, especially since amalgamation, have been unable to match identity with position, moves into the pastoral side can cause similar confusion over status:

'When I was given head of careers, it was a lonely position. You did so little teaching that I didn't really feel I was teaching. I was part of a team – it was very awkward. You haven't got any real authority.' (Tony Haskins)

For those brought in to cover these pastorally orientated subjects to supplement their teaching hours, the nature of the work can seem amorphous:

'Third year careers has been a disaster area – no structure. If a subject's important it must be in the timetable, but people who do careers aren't trained. Careers hasn't got a work scheme, no structure, no linking. It's been an absolute and utter disaster... It's just a period with nothing to do ... I said to Irene Platt [Head of Careers] unless you can come up with something for me to do, I'll do science, that's what I teach.' (Andrew Diamond, Head of Biology)

Such examples illustrate the opposition between the pastoral and the academic at Elmfield School. The ambiguous status of certain areas, such as EPR, community studies and citizenship, highlights the tension between the pastoral and the academic. Whether the pastoral or the academic dimension of these areas is emphasized, the force of the tension is such that dual identity appears uncomfortable and undesirable.

There can be little doubt, then, that specialized curricula, such as that at Elmfield, contribute to divided staff allegiances. Teacher loyalties, however, reflect more than personal biographies, priority and preferences. The casting of one's identity to one side of the divide rather than the other is inextricably linked to the struggle for status and power.

PASTORAL OR ACADEMIC SUPREMACY?

Although pastoral care operates as a distinct curricular area running parallel to the subject-centred side in schools such as Elmfield with a specialized curriculum, it is nevertheless perceived as a threat to the academic. This threat is reflected in studies which suggest that pastoral care specialists have achieved a position of dominance over academic staff.

AMMA (1988), for instance, is concerned by 'the increasing tendency for the pastoral tail to wag the academic dog' (p. 1) and 'the unfortunate and unfair implication ... that in earlier years pastoral care did not exist' (p. 2).

The 'pastoral bandwagon on its inexorable path' has not only 'hi-jacked' traditional teachers' responsibilities, but has, in so doing, reduced their status:

> All manner of everyday problems, many of a social rather than educational nature, are referred too easily to year heads and other 'pastoral specialists', rather than be dealt with by the ordinary classroom practitioner, who thus becomes a mere trainer, if not just a dispenser of knowledge. (AMMA, 1988, p. 2)

Redican (1985) reports on the increasing power of pastoral staff and the subsequent erosion of the subject-centred academic curriculum. Pastoral care is seen to represent an intrusion into the 'real job of teaching' and the 'sanctity of the lesson'. He argues that the supervisory and guidance aspects of welfare have been extended by pastoral staff to exert control over subject teachers. Using interviews and observation, Redican constructs a variety of indicators to determine the relative status of subject teachers and pastoral staff: access to confidential information, office space and negotiation procedures. He concludes that pastoral staff are 'selectively promoted' despite 'inferior qualifications'. Through the delegation of authority outside their areas of competence, they have employed strategies to erode the base of the subject teacher. It is a further illustration of the strength of the pastoral–academic boundary, and the way in which it demands allegiance to either side, that Redican himself can only refer to those on the 'pastoral side' with thinly disguised hostility. Those on the pastoral side are, in his own words, 'petty administrators', 'managers' and 'supervisory' staff. Subject teachers, on the other hand, are the 'doers', the 'real' teachers of 'proper' subjects displaying the qualities of 'academic leadership' over 'administrative management'.

It is worth considering whether such accounts accurately portray a change in the balance of power or merely signal a potential threat to academic dominance. To what extent has pastoral care gained ascendancy over the academic dimension at Elmfield?

As we have seen, the demarcation and distribution of time and space can be used to analyse contrasts in modes of organization. It can also be used to indicate the relative strength of each area. The allocation of such resources is not an unambiguous representation of 'truths' about the relative merits of types of knowledge, but a reflection of the success with which competing interests have been able to legitimize their validity and command resources.

At Elmfield, the academic is administered largely in purpose-built areas, whether classrooms or playing fields, which comprise almost the entire area of the school. Each department has its own space, which may be only a single room for a small department, to a whole specialized block with lecture theatres for large departments such as science. 'Private' space is provided by resource rooms and workrooms located next to the teaching areas to which all members of the department have access. As already mentioned, in those departments with particularly strong subject loyalty, these areas take on the significance of 'territory'.

Pastoral care is also administered in both public and private areas, although the flexibility of its boundaries and the many *ad hoc* pastoral encounters make such a distinction less visible. Registration and tutor work are carried out in the teaching classrooms. Although it could be argued that these rooms are therefore shared between the pastoral and the academic, these areas exhibit their academic identity far more strongly. Furniture and equipment are arranged for academic lessons, and do not appear to be altered for tutorial work. Tutor work is rarely, if ever, displayed on the wall. The blackboard is often covered with academic classwork and there may be instructions for this to be left alone. When a particular room is required for other purposes, usually academic, the tutor group moves. It appears, therefore, that although these rooms could be designated as both pastoral and academic, the pastoral is very much the 'guest', and at times of conflicts of interest it is academic needs which prevail. The hall can also be categorized as public pastoral space, inasmuch as assemblies are conducted here each day. Even here, though, it is more likely that pastoral interests will make way for academic concerns, such as examinations and drama productions.

Private pastoral space is provided by the 'year' rooms. Although it could be argued, as Redican (1985) does, that heads of year are favoured through being the only staff, apart from senior management, to have their own offices, the extent to which they can be categorized as 'private' is questionable. At Elmfield, other staff also use these rooms for phone calls or looking through records. And while pupils are almost always excluded from subject workrooms, they may often be seen in a head of year's office. Analysis of the allocation of space at Elmfield would not appear to support the assertion that the pastoral has usurped academic territory.

As with the distribution of space, the academic curriculum dominates the timetable. Contact time within subject categories far outweighs that of pastoral care. Its claims for time also extend into pupils' out-of-school time through homework. At Elmfield, pastoral contact time (assemblies and tutor periods) is located at the margins of the school day. For some subjects, such contact time may exceed lesson time:

> 'I mean pastoral time is more than subject time. It's one hour forty minutes.' (Una Roberts, PE)

But for many subjects, academic contact is greater:

> 'I'm a much better tutor to the pupils in my classes than I am to these children. I see them for two to three hours a week.' (Paul Seymour, Maths)

As with the allocation of space, pastoral 'time' is often displaced. There is a tendency for tutor time to be interrupted if there are more 'important' things to be done – administrative tasks, academic errands, or general caretaking duties.

At Elmfield, pastoral interruption of academic time is rare, although not unknown. Pastoral staff may be invited into a lesson to remove a particular pupil at the direction of the subject teacher. This can be categorized as 'servicing' the academic, however, rather than 'intrusion'. Pastoral 'intrusion' does occur occasionally, and can then become the focus of general staffroom disapproval, for instance:

'I'd settled them quite well when Basil Hunt came in with those envelopes – you can imagine the chaos that caused. I was so cross. All that for a PTA thing.'

Private staff time can be assessed through the allocation of 'free' periods and again used as an indicator of the relative importance attributed to academic and pastoral responsibilities. Analysis of the timetable shows that senior pastoral staff tend to have fewer free periods than their academic equivalents. In part this is due to deliberate timetabling, where their tasks are not seen as commensurate, but it is also because pastoral staff seem more flexible in what they will teach. Because they do not have high subject status, they appear to be less able to resist having to teach outside their own areas. High-status subject specialists, particularly departmental heads, do not teach outside their subject areas.

Although year heads are given 'free' periods in which to undertake specifically pastoral work, their deputies, as already mentioned, are not. The benefits of being a deputy head of year are couched in terms of career opportunities rather than extra time or salary:

'It's a chance for them to gain experience. There's no money or time allocation. We won't write the timetable around it.' (Martin Alcock, Pastoral Deputy)

For those pastoral staff who are allocated free periods, this private time must also be assessed in terms of quality. Free periods may mean different things for different staff. Observation of staff during these periods seems to indicate that academic 'frees', especially for senior academic staff such as heads of department, are often used exclusively for their subject preparation in their private areas – undisturbed. It is possible to hide away. The different principles which underlie pastoral provision, with its lack of clear boundaries between free time and work time, between public and private, mean that their free periods are not as sacred as those of their academic counterparts. Pastoral staff are expected to be always contactable and are frequently interrupted with pastoral matters during time set aside for their academic obligations. It is possible to argue, therefore, that their 'frees' are of inferior quality, in terms of privacy and interruption, to those of their academic colleagues.

The distribution of space and time is particularly important in schools where a split site operates. The resolution of issues concerning who is to move, when and for what, can be used to indicate underlying priorities. At Elmfield, the pastoral side tries to achieve continuity for tutor groups through encouraging tutors to stay with them as they progress through the school. However, this would involve staff being based largely on the lower school site for two years. Such an arrangement is not acceptable for those staff with a high academic profile who derive much of their prestige from teaching the top-set examination classes. Because these specialists wish to be located mainly at the upper school site, the system of tutor group progression is made unworkable.

The dominance of academic concerns not only disrupts tutor–tutee progression from year to year, but also wreaks havoc on attempts to

Year 7	Mon. a.m.	p.m.	Tues. a.m.	p.m.	Wed. a.m.	p.m.	Thurs. a.m.	p.m.	Fri. a.m.	p.m.	% contact
Group 7A	X	✓	X	✓	✓	✓	X	X	✓	✓	60
Group 7B	X	X	✓	X	✓	X	✓	✓	✓	X	50
Group 7C	X	✓	X	✓	✓	X	X	✓	X	✓	50
Group 7D	X	✓	✓	X	✓	X	✓	X	X	X	40
Group 7E	✓	X	✓	X	X	X	X	X	X	X	20
Group 7F	✓	X	X	X	X	✓	✓	✓	X	✓	50

achieve regular pastoral contact on a day-to-day basis. While attempts are made to ensure continuity of lessons, particularly for 'top-band' groups, this is not the case for tutor time. Indeed, tutorial requirements do not appear to feature on the list of timetable priorities at all. This means that tutor groups are taken by whoever happens to be on site at the time. Few tutor groups, 3 out of 36, get to see their tutor at every tutor time. In some cases they may hardly see them at all. For instance, one tutor group sees its tutor once during the ten available contact times. Figure 4.1 shows the proportion of times that tutors are 'officially' available to take their Year 7 tutees at the lower school site for morning and afternoon tutorials. The 'unofficial' availability is likely to be even lower.

Although prioritization of time and space also occurs within the academic, where some subjects/classes/staff are able to achieve less disruption and greater continuity,[4] it would appear that the academic side of the curriculum as a whole dominates the allocation of time and space. There is certainly little evidence from Elmfield to support the assertion that the pastoral dimension has significantly encroached on academic territory or time.

MAINTAINING THE BOUNDARY

While the academic has not been undermined as some commentators have suggested, this does not mean that pastoral care does not pose a threat. As we have seen, school subjects tend to stand in closed relation to each other, organized and separated into discrete units of time and space. But pastoral care attempts to locate a multitude of schooling practices within its domain.

Pastoral care not only challenges academic versions of schooling; the principles which underpin it have the potential for increasing surveillance and evaluation of the academic. As discussed in Chapter 3, pastoral care attempts to remove curricular differentiation and stratification, whether this refers to properties of one pupil (e.g. scientific skills, linguistic capability) or those of groups of pupils (e.g. the A stream, the remedial class). It therefore threatens the cornerstone upon which the academic dimension traditionally constructs educational identity. Furthermore, the relation between 'professional' and 'client' also entails the pastoral carer in representing the students' interests, and this may involve surveillance of other teachers.

At Elmfield, two incidents demonstrate the nature of the pastoral challenge and the ways in which academic specialists sought to preserve their territory from what they perceived as pastoral intrusion. One concerns the attempt by the pastoral team to ensure that all tutors follow the pastoral syllabus in tutor time. The other involves a questionnaire survey about the extent to which issues relating to health and social education were being addressed across the curriculum.

The first incident arose from the suggestion by senior pastoral staff that tutor periods be relocated. Gareth Evans, Head of Physics, comments on this to his science department over their regular Friday pub lunch:

'Have you heard of their latest ploy? They're trying to make us move out of our rooms for tutor periods.'

The comment, or 'warning', is interesting for several reasons. Firstly, the language is clearly adversarial. There is 'them', the pastoral, and 'us', the academic. The term 'ploy' is significant in terms of its subversive and tactical connotations, and the reference to 'our rooms' is clearly territorial.

The reason why the pastoral side should adopt such 'ploys' has to be understood in terms of the nature and obligation of tutor work. Although, as already mentioned, nearly all staff have tutorial responsibility, this does not mean they have pastoral allegiance. On the pastoral side, heads of year frequently complain that tutor time is not taken seriously. As we have seen, it is a principle of pastoral care that such work should be flexible and not formally assessed. This makes it difficult for pastoral staff to supervise or evaluate the extent to which it is carried out, giving those without allegiance to the pastoral side scope to ignore or modify their tutorial responsibilities. For many staff, the tutor period does not signify time set aside for mutual exploration or experiential learning. It means time to get ready for the academic day. A stroll through the corridors during tutor periods regularly reveals a significant number of classes where pupils are engaged in conversation or finishing off homework, while their teachers are preparing for lessons. It was mooted by pastoral staff that the dislocation of subject specialists from their teaching rooms would reduce this 'misuse' of pastoral time. This issue of pastoral surveillance of tutor work is also brought up in tutor meetings. Here the head of Year 8, Steve Woods, explains to his tutors that he intends to 'help' them next term:

'I'd like to come in. How do you feel about that? Can I just say that I won't be coming in to check up on you, but to join in. To find out if the sheet is helpful or not. I'm just coming in to observe and join in.'

Whether this is intended as a 'genuine' gesture of support or a roundabout way of 'checking up' on other staff is not important here. What matters is that the lessening of hierarchy and the flexible nature of the pedagogy makes such 'help' or 'interference' possible. Staff with allegiance to the academic dimension are aware of this, and, as we have seen, resent such interference. The proposed move never took place.

The second incident concerns the defensiveness which subject specialists exhibit when pastoral staff go even further than checking on their pastoral duties and start to ask questions about what goes on in their subject lessons.

The year heads, together with Simon Reed, teacher in charge of EPR, were undertaking a survey on the extent to which aspects of social and personal education were covered throughout the curriculum. Although there are several interesting aspects to this survey, for instance what is seen to constitute an adequate 'social' curriculum and the substantive survey findings, the various responses to the survey illustrate the ways in which some teachers attempt to maintain curricular boundaries and resist intrusion.

The survey elicited a variety of reactions from teachers, including a significant amount of hostility, particularly from those with primary allegiance to the academic. This hostility suggests that the survey was seen to somehow constitute a threat. There might be several reasons why this should be the case. Firstly, the survey located the academic dimension as only a narrow part of the educational process, subsumed within the pastoral. Secondly, through locating the academic within the boundaries of the pastoral, it empowered pastoral specialists to intervene in the academic domain. Thirdly, it implicitly held up a model of 'good practice' where these 'social' objectives should be taken on board.

The survey stressed that the academic development of the pupil was only one aspect of education, thereby refuting its primacy. As the introduction to the resulting report states:

> Social Education embraces a range of knowledge and skills. In the same way that academic qualifications will give students greater autonomy to choose and follow careers of their choice, so Social Education will impart autonomy and the ability to achieve greater independence in personal lives and matters of everyday living. (Health/Social Education Survey Report, Elmfield)

The academic curriculum is presented within the survey only in terms of its instrumentality. Cognitive development is restrictively presented as 'academic qualifications', and the benefit of such qualifications is couched in terms of their utilitarian value only. It is social education that is seen to contribute to personal, rather than professional, growth. Inasmuch as all education, as opposed to 'training', is about personal development, the 'social' must subsume the academic. It is therefore logical that those with the broader conception of education should survey the narrower aspects.

Not only does the survey state that social issues are of equal, if not greater, significance than subject-based knowledge, but it also implicitly suggests that academic teachers broaden their horizons. Note, for instance, the survey's approval of the maths department:

> It is encouraging to note that, unofficially, mathematics teachers are prepared to tackle other SE issues than money management. (Health/Social Education Report, Elmfield)

Through monitoring the activities of subject teachers, the survey not only challenges the autonomy of the subject teacher and the sanctity of the lesson, but also holds up a model of 'good practice' derived from terms of reference outside, and possibly at odds with, those of the subject specialists. The difference between the underlying principles of the academic and the pastoral, and the extent to which the pastoral strives to encompass the academic, can be illustrated through trying to imagine the situation reversed. It is inconceivable that heads of departments would conduct a survey to find out whether pastoral staff were covering academic matters in their tutor time.

The survey consisted of a questionnaire to be completed at year tutor meetings. Staff comments at these meetings and questionnaire responses reveal a variety of reactions which indicate attempts to undermine the importance of the survey and minimize any possible consequences stemming from it. These reactions can be broadly categorized as 'status scepticism', 'mock deference', 'denial of authority' and 'distancing'.

Scepticism of the status of the survey is revealed through the way in which the title of PSE (personal and social education) is questioned and ridiculed:

SW: Simon Reed asked about PSE...

T: What's that? [General laughter]

While the question 'what's that?' may have been a straightforward enquiry, the laughter that followed implies an element of derision. As we have seen, EPR (Elmfield's equivalent of PSE) can be classed as a 'pseudo-subject'. Its perceived affinity with pastoral care makes it suspect. Incorrect or deliberately 'confused' allusions can be used to confirm dubious standing – as can mispronunciation:

'I don't hold with all this *pastorial* nonsense.' (Gareth Evans)

Status scepticism is often seen in areas where academic equivalence is sought, and some subjects are particularly prone to it. Sociology, for instance, is often presented as 'pseudo-knowledge'.[5]

The intrusion by the pastoral into the academic through enquiring about subject lessons is diffused and rendered trivial through mock deference. Even though the purpose of the questionnaire is explained by Steve Woods in terms of the need to avoid excess duplication, the respondents appear to interpret it differently. Far from being concerned with excess duplication they are mainly worried about finding enough things to enter – about whether they have missed out things they should have done:

MW: I've got trouble to think of things. Oh, I've done smoking – that's all right.

VG: When should I have done that?

BH: It's on the syllabus.

VG: I haven't done it – it must have been when I was away.

UR: If you spend your tutor time preparing for assembly – you miss out on the syllabus.

GA: It's all right if you're doing RE. You're covering these things all the time.

The last comment, in particular, implies that not entering enough responses will be seen in a negative light. However, such concerns do not appear to last long and are deflected through trivialization:

GA: I think I've finished mine – have I passed?

UR: Sir, will you check that for me?

The mock deference of comments such as these reveals both a suspicion that the questionnaire is a pretext for surveillance and a refutation of the appropriateness of such intrusion.

Scepticism over the significance and value of this 'pastorial [*sic*] nonsense', coupled with suspicion of the purpose and appropriateness of the survey, is also reflected in the denial of the authority of pastoral staff. Resentment was caused by the inability of the year heads to give subjects their 'proper names'. Alistair Silcox was particularly upset about CDT (craft, design and technology) being referred to as metalwork and woodwork, commenting on his questionnaire 'No woodwork or metalwork is taught in school as a specific subject.' Other teachers pointed out omitted subjects, which included music, drama, community studies and sociology. These omissions and incorrect titles were seen as an indication of year heads' ignorance of the academic side of the curriculum: 'It just shows how much he knows about the subject.' By far the most prevalent strategy for resisting pastoral intrusion and maintaining the pastoral–academic boundary is 'distancing', where the issues are simply not seen as relevant to the academic. This distancing can take several forms. In one case, questionnaire sabotage illustrates the degree of hostility to such interference. Non-response can also be seen as an indicator of distancing. This had been anticipated by the pastoral team, which had asked for it to be undertaken in directed time. It is significant that there was a very poor response rate from those staff unable to attend the year meetings when it was distributed.

The most interesting examples of distancing can be seen from the completed questionnaires. Certain teachers, who undoubtedly cover concerns relevant to the questionnaire, failed to make any response in these areas. Some English teachers, for instance, claimed that there was no connection between their subject and issues concerning personal relations and prejudice or attitudes. The most striking example of this kind of distancing, however, comes from the sociology teacher. The questionnaire asked whether in their subject lessons, issues relating to the family, marriage and social relations were touched upon, whether formally through the syllabus, or informally arising out of class discussion. The sociology course actually contains a module on 'the family'. Citizenship, which this teacher also takes, is classified as essentially about 'social and personal relations', and yet none of these areas was registered on the questionnaire. Not one of the aforementioned categories was ticked. This lack of response could be interpreted as incompetence in answering the questions. However, this teacher had no difficulty in identifying areas of social education she had covered in her tutor work. It is more probable that the apparent lack of any relationship between sociology and social education is explained by different conceptions of 'social' and academic knowledge. This also reflects the path that 'new' subjects have been obliged to take in order to gain academic credibility: sociology as an academic subject that is not in any way to be confused with anything that could be loosely characterized as having 'behavioural', rather than 'intellectual' objectives (e.g. Whitty, 1985).

The above examples reveal ways in which the boundary between the academic and the pastoral is defended on a daily basis. Through a variety of strategies the academic resists and denies the pastoral significance. It does this through problematizing the status of the pastoral, and, consequently, the status of pastoral staff. But, most significantly, the boundary resists the suggestion that there is any relation between the two areas. By containing the pastoral and maintaining the opposition between the pastoral and the academic, the subject specialists preserve their territory. Indeed, in the comprehensive school, it may well be that the existence of the boundary provides an oppositional basis from which the academic can generate even more of the exclusivity from which it partly derives its authority. This issue will be pursued in the following chapters.

In summary, from the data presented in this chapter, it is possible to demonstrate that at Elmfield the boundary between the pastoral and the academic signalled by separate and alternative demarcations of responsibility is more than just administrative convenience. The opposing principles of the pastoral and the academic are reflected in a 'divided' curriculum, where each dimension differentiates staff, staff and pupils, and pupils in contrasting ways.

That this division is an area of tension is illustrated by the boundary which is actively constructed and maintained by the academic. The strength of the pastoral–academic boundary reflects the extent to which the academic has been able to resist pastoral surveillance and incursion. Through containing the pastoral, the academic preserves its dominance of the secondary school curriculum.

While it is clear that the boundary contributes to the oppositional and differentiated construction of teachers' identities, hindering and enhancing ability to control the allocation of school resources of time and space, it must also have consequences for pupils. These will be addressed in the next three chapters.

NOTES

1. Throughout the book, pseudonyms have been used for schools, teachers and pupils. Other aspects of identity, such as gender and subject specialism, are unchanged.
2. It perhaps indicates the degree of insularity within the academic dimension of Elmfield School that contemporary debates on school and curricular policy initiatives were rarely mentioned. It is hard to believe that the fieldwork was being conducted at a time when the 1988 Education Reform Act was causing major upheaval in the education system.
3. Where the pastoral system operates through houses, even stratification and segregation based on age is minimized.
4. Year 7 pupils in the remedial class are able to command hardly any continuity. At the time of my fieldwork they had 17 different subject teachers each week.
5. Examples of this scepticism can be found in *Punch*'s spoof 'Sociology A Level' paper (reproduced in Meighan, 1986) or Maureen Lipman's British Telecom advertisement where she is delighted that her grandson has an '-ology'.

CHAPTER 5

Pastoral care as radical practice?

The last chapter explored the relationship between the pastoral and the academic in terms of staff demarcations and curricular divisions. It examined how a specialized curriculum, such as that at Elmfield, contributes to divided loyalties and dichotomous educational identities. The tension between the two dimensions is reflected in the extent to which a boundary between the academic and the pastoral is actively constructed and maintained. The containment and marginalization of the pastoral by the academic also serves to privilege subject teachers' claims over curricular resources.

However, the opposition between the pastoral and the academic represents not simply a battle over resources, but an ideological struggle over the nature of schooling. As we saw in Chapter 3, both areas are underlain by contrasting principles which embody different perceptions of what constitutes 'real' learning. Where school subjects are narrow, pastoral care claims to be broad. Where the academic domain tends towards closure and specialization, the pastoral side aims for openness and permeation. Where subject specialists emphasize differentiation and stratification, the pastoral side promotes individual worth over hierarchy. Still drawing on Elmfield as illustration, the next chapters move beyond considering the institutional significance of these tensions for staff allegiance and resource allocation and consider their implications for the central function of schooling itself – the nature of its educational transmissions.

As discussed at the beginning of the book, the merits of pastoral care are much contested. Critics from both left and right present pastoral care as either ineffectual or even damaging. As is evident from the preceding chapter, even at school level academic specialists are less than enthusiastic about it. On the other hand, advocates and practitioners of pastoral care claim that it is currently, or potentially, capable of generating alternative and less repressive educational experiences than those made available through the subject-centred side of the curriculum.

This chapter evaluates the case *for* pastoral care. It starts by considering whether there is in reality a distinctive 'pastoral' pedagogy which reflects the tenets of the discourse as analysed in Chapter 3. It then discusses the significance of these practices in terms of their radical or reproductive potential.

PASTORAL PEDAGOGY: RHETORIC OR REALITY?

Before the possible significance of pastoral practices can be explored, it is necessary to consider the 'reality' of pastoral care. This is particularly important in the light of existing research (see Chapter 1) which suggests that pastoral processes bear little relation to pastoral policies. Indeed, it has been claimed that the reality of pastoral care runs counter to its official rhetoric.

It is always difficult to unravel underlying pedagogic principles from the constant flux of schooling. However, in relation to pastoral care, this task is especially complex. Three factors, in particular, make its exposition problematic: switching between discourses; variation within the discourse; and the diversity of pastoral encounters.

Firstly, as in all social settings, people switch between frames of reference. As Walkerdine points out, albeit for different referents:

> [They] are not unitary subjects uniquely positioned, but produced as a nexus of subjectivities, in relations of power which are constantly shifting, rendering them at one moment powerful and at another powerless... Particular individuals are produced as subjects *differently* within a variety of discursive practices. A particular individual has the potential to be 'read' within a variety of discourses. (Walkerdine, 1987, pp. 166–7, her emphasis)

As already discussed, most teachers officially operate in both the pastoral and the academic realms, even if they have a dominant professional identity and allegiance. They can, though, within limits, change their orientation as the context demands. Occasionally they may articulate this switch, for instance: 'I'm putting my pastoral hat on now' (Steve Woods). But in most cases these shifts are unnoticed or unannounced.

A second factor which contributes to the difficulty of recognizing a clearly identifiable pastoral pedagogy stems from tensions within it. In parallel with educational welfare officers (Shaw, 1981b), pastoral care has inherited both control and welfare ideologies. There is, as mentioned in Chapter 3, the 'firm but fair' school of pastoral care exemplified by Haigh's (1975) writing. This approach tends to dismiss attempts to theorize as 'jargon', decrying pastoral certification as merely 'bits of paper'. Basil Hunt provides a good example of this in his reminiscences of how 'difficult' pupils were dealt with in the past:

> 'In those days you could dap kids if you wanted to. Dap them on the backside. And also on the hand with the ruler, bang! You could administer your own punishment. It was much more acceptable, to the kids as well. I favour using the dap still ... Girls, that's where you've got a difficulty. They've got to be treated differently. I don't think you would dap them. You would perhaps use a ruler on the hand. I don't see why not. I

think it's more effective because I catch you stealing something, and I go "Come here", bang! You go away, and think about it. If I catch you now, I write to your parents, I get your parents in. I tell you off. I give you a detention. By the time all that's done, it's taken a long time. The effect, I don't think is as great. And quite often, a week later, when you get parents in, you're onto something else then.'

This pastoral equivalent of the 'short sharp shock' treatment would, however, be anathema to the properly 'professionalized' pastoral carer, for whom true learning is always self-motivated and never imposed. Despite this divide, it seems likely that the more sophisticated 'client-orientated' welfare version of pastoral care will supersede the 'firm but fair' school. Although all pastoral carers may draw on the latter from time to time, it is most often articulated by long-serving, ex-secondary modern teachers, such as Mr Hunt, who have missed out on, and are antagonistic towards, the subsequent professionalization of their area.

A third difficulty in attempting to distinguish unambiguously 'pastoral' practices relates to the diversity of contexts in which they occur. Unlike school subjects, which are disseminated almost entirely in a designated space and time to a prearranged group of pupils, pastoral encounters take place with individual pupils on an *ad hoc* basis throughout the day, as well as collectively through tutor periods and assemblies. Although it is easier to observe and analyse the collective encounters, this does not mean that the one-to-one interactions are not rule-bound, only that the rules are less easy to observe and extract.

Despite these difficulties, it is possible to identify a distinctive pastoral pedagogy at Elmfield which is structured along the lines of Bernstein's (1990) invisible pedagogy with distinctive rules of hierarchy, sequence and criteria (see Chapter 3).

Hierarchical rules

The key feature of the power relations embodied within the discourse of pastoral care is that teachers as 'tutors' cease to be visible controlling agents. They are no longer the source of all knowledge, but facilitators.

This shift in the balance of power is evident at Elmfield, in both tutor periods and *ad hoc* encounters. In one case, the change in relationship is signalled by the tutor using his, and my (as observer), first names with the class. Tutees are rarely compelled to join in the tutorial sessions. Those who wish to talk among themselves, or finish off the previous night's homework, are usually allowed to do so, even if reluctantly. In one session, a planned piece of tutorial work was abandoned because of lack of pupil interest. And while tutor periods are often tutor-directed rather than student-led, tutees do have influence. The following comments are typical of many pupils' perceptions of their involvement in determining the content and direction of tutorial sessions:

SP: What do you do in your tutor times?

P1: Anything we like.

SP: What, anything?

P1:   Yes. Well, sometimes we talk about things.

SP: Who decides what you discuss?

P2:   Miss tells us what to talk about.

P1:   No she doesn't. Only if she can't get us to think of anything.

Although tutees may do written work in tutorial sessions, it is not marked or graded. There are no facts to be learned. The purpose of the pastoral encounter is not the acquisition and reproduction of knowledge, for, as we have seen, pastoral care has no content in the usual sense of the term. As pastoral carers often emphasize, it is the *process* rather than the *product* of learning which counts. Pupil ownership is therefore more important than teacher scrutiny or inspection, as the following Year 10 tutor illustrates when talking about tutor work:

'I don't usually look at it. It's for them. Sometimes I'll ask for it if it looks really interesting, but not usually. It's really just for them. They hang on to it; I don't know what they do with it. I suppose most of it ends up in the bin. But then it's doing it that counts.'

In the individual *ad hoc* encounters, the role of the tutor continues to be different from that of the teacher. In many instances these encounters are initiated by the pupils. Even when they are instigated by the pastoral carer as a result of concerns from other members of staff, the tutee is not simply a passive recipient but someone whose version of events is solicited. There are some occasions when the tutor as listener or confidant will take the tutee's side. In these encounters it is possible to see a shift in relations from teacher–taught to professional–client. Here a Year 8 tutor, Eileen Chandler, talks to a pupil:

EC: This isn't like you. What are you doing getting these detentions?

P: It's Miss, she's always picking on me for nothing.

EC: And why should she do that?

P: I don't know.

EC: Do you do anything to upset her?

P: No. Some of the others are always messing about. But she picks on me.

EC: Well, I'll have a word with her for you.

Although 'having a word' would often constitute little more than a tutor's request for a teacher to recognize particular difficulties a pupil may be going through, there are frequent occasions on which a tutor would consider and complain (even if only to other staff) that one of their charges is being unfairly victimized by partisan or incompetent subject specialists.

In summary, the rules which underpin relations between tutor and tutee tend to be more flexible and person-orientated than those which typify the hierarchical relationship of pupil and teacher. As discussed in Chapter 3 this does not, of course, mean that both are equal players, but rather that the principles which govern the encounters are less visible.

Sequencing rules

The apparently greater tutee control over encounters means that programmes cannot be rigidly structured. Spontaneity is of high value. Nevertheless, as discussed in Chapter 3, this flexibility is structured by psychological and biologically based theories of development that recognize stages of cognition and awareness. Linear progression is replaced by cyclical programmes. Pastoral care 'spirals' (Martin Alcock). However, as with hierarchy, it is not the presence or absence of rules which distinguishes pastoral pedagogy from that of the subject side of the curriculum, but the degree of visibility.

At Elmfield, the invisibility of the sequencing rules is illustrated by the tutees' lack of awareness of any organization in their tutorial sessions. The following comments come from members of a tutor group of Year 8 pupils which closely follows the recommended pastoral syllabus:

SP: And what do you do in tutor time?

P1: Well, Miss takes the register to make sure everyone's here and then we just talk.

P2: We discuss things.

SP: What sorts of things?

P1: Nothing.

P2: We do. We discuss things like jobs.

The blurring of the distinction between 'just talking' and 'discussing' parallels a similar process in models of child-centred education in which 'play' becomes 'work' (Bernstein, 1977, pp. 116–56; Walkerdine, 1984). As I shall indicate in the next chapter, this blurring is an important factor in the tutor's ability to 'read' the child.

Flexibility is apparent in the frequency with which scheduled tutorial sessions are abandoned to take up either suggestions from the pupils or issues in the news. It is also illustrated in the way in which work is stored, if at all. As mentioned in Chapter 3, there are no pastoral textbooks, only suggested programmes, such as *Active Tutorial Work*. Likewise, tutees' work is not recorded in a linear fashion. In the lower years, they use exercise books that are significantly referred to as 'notebooks', reflecting their casual, disposable nature. They are for the tutees' own use inasmuch as staff rarely look at them. In the upper years, tutees use files, associated with models of further/higher education and indicative of looser structure and greater tutee control over learning. In the exercise book that comprises the principal means of setting down and displaying academic lessons, the order of work is unalterable. Missing or spoilt work remains visible. With files, pages can be added or removed.

Rather than progression being linear and dictated to by external subject requirements, development is cyclical. From the following comments on the content of tutor work, it is clear that some topics make frequent appearances:

P2: Smoking.

P1: Yes, loads of that.

P2:   And drinking.

P1:   Loads of that.

These areas are covered at least once a year as the student is considered able to deal with them in ever more meaningful and complex ways. As with other invisible pedagogies, pastoral discourse is underlain by biological theories of maturation and 'readiness'. For some sensitive areas, such as sex education, this concept of 'readiness' is the primary consideration. 'Careful timing' is seen to be vital. Wolpe's ethnography (1988), for instance, shows that while it is acceptable for younger pupils to learn the 'facts' of reproduction in biology, they are not considered ready to deal with aspects of 'relationships' until much later. Teachers at Elmfield frequently express concern over the delicacy with which such timing should be managed – weighing up the danger of 'corrupting innocence' against that of 'compounding ignorance'.

Criterial rules

Unlike the academic dimension, pastoral care does not match pupils against explicit gradable standards. While it does recognize differences between students, it tends to celebrate these as indications of the uniqueness of individuality. In particular, pastoral care rejects any superficial differentiation and fragmentation, preferring instead to delve deep into the 'whole person'. In the following transcript of part of an assembly, the head of year, Steve Woods, has just narrated a parable where a scruffy man turns out to be the popular hero Bob Geldof, and a nun turns out to be a bankrobber:

> 'It just goes to show you cannot judge people by appearances. We tend to put people into brackets, to stereotype people you could say. But everyone is an individual. You're all individuals. It's the same with teachers. They're all individuals. You look at them. They're each different. They have individual ways; they are individual in the ways they teach.'

As the parable also illustrates, pastoral carers, particularly those who undertook their training during the last twenty years, are cautious of 'giving a dog a bad name'. Familiar with the concepts of labelling theory and deviancy amplification, they talk to each other of the dangers of 'pigeon holing' and the damaging effect their categorizations may have on their tutees. Here, prospective Year 7 tutors, Valerie Goddard and Kevin Smart, discuss the problems created through the transferral of primary school records:

VG: I'm not wishing to appear critical, but I like to make my own mind up. I don't want to prejudge them. I mean if it's a separated home then I think I should know. But things like 'careless'? I don't want to have a preconceived idea of this child now.

KS: Yes, I'm in danger of reading, for example, 'troublemaker', and treating them as such. I'm not disputing what the junior school has said, I respect that, but I don't want to be biased.

Parallel with the need to prevent early stigmatization is the pastoral imperative of always giving positive encouragement. Not only is everyone an individual, but everyone is also a *worthwhile* individual:

> 'Every single one of you, I could tell you something about every single one of you. Some good things and some bad things. But there are far more good things in you than bad. Never let anyone tell you you're bad. OK, so you've done some things wrong. But on the whole this year is really good.' (Steve Woods, Year 8 assembly)

And if pupils have some 'bad things', then so do their teachers. It is as much a tenet of pastoral care that 'nobody's perfect' as it is that 'everyone's an individual':

> 'I'm here to help any one of you that's got problems within the school or at home to overcome your problems in anyway I can... Help you to develop yourselves. Help you to look at yourselves. We've all got problems. I've got things I can improve; we can all improve. There's a lot you can do for yourselves. You can be aware of the others in the group, aware of other people's problems.' (Kevin Smart to Year 8 tutees)

The assertion of individuality together with the universality of strengths and weaknesses mean that rather than be assessed and ranked against externally imposed grades, pupils are invited to evaluate themselves. Such evaluation should not be based on fixed attributes, but on personal recognition of positive points to be further developed and negative aspects to be overcome. Pupils are encouraged to set their own targets and reflect upon the success with which they have reached them in a variety of ways, but increasingly as a negotiated Record of Achievement.

Through the above extracts and observations it is reasonable to suggest that, at Elmfield at least, pastoral care is not just rhetoric. While recognizing that there is variation within the pastoral dimension, just as there is within the academic side, it is possible to identify a distinctive pastoral pedagogy which is structured along lines alternative to those which tend to underpin school subjects. In the light of these differences, the next section asks whether pastoral care offers an alternative educational experience. It briefly considers whether those 'hidden' processes of the curriculum which are seen to contribute to educational inequalities are equally applicable to pastoral care. Finally, it discusses the possibilities which pastoral care might hold for pupil empowerment.

PASTORAL CARE AND THEORIES OF THE HIDDEN CURRICULUM

As discussed in Chapter 1, the school curriculum can no longer be considered 'innocent'. Although there is no consensus about precisely where guilt lies, it has been frequently implicated in the perpetuation of educational and social inequalities. Such accusations, however, are usually levelled at school subjects. This section considers whether they can be adequately translated to pastoral practices and transmissions.

Such translation is difficult in the case of the correspondence theory of the curriculum (Bowles and Gintis, 1976), which claims that the social relations of the school reflect and reproduce the various skills and dispositions essential for the capitalist economy. Not only has this theory been roundly criticized (e.g. Apple, 1979b; Hogan, 1981), but it is also hard to see how it can be straightforwardly applied to pastoral care. Pastoral care is not selectively distributed. Nor are its social relations overtly hierarchical. The relationship between tutor and tutee is not one of simple domination and subordination. Tutees are not 'producers' in any direct sense. They do not have to engage in the production of fragmented pieces of work.

Other explanations of ways in which the curriculum reinforces educational inequality centre upon the disjuncture between school knowledge and pupil knowledge. In these accounts, students are unable to access the curriculum because it is removed from their own experience – a distance that is particularly insuperable for working-class children (e.g. Vulliamy, 1976). Again, however, it is hard to see how such a charge can be laid at the door of pastoral care, for it attempts to break down boundaries between pupil experience and school knowledge. Indeed, it aims to take as its subject matter the world of the pupil.

Finally, school knowledge is seen to perpetuate inequalities through the messages it transmits. School knowledge, it is argued, presents distorted and biased images of the world as objective fact (e.g. Gleeson and Whitty, 1976) and/or stereotype-affirming messages which impact upon pupils' self-images and limit future horizons (e.g. Steedman, 1982).

This last charge is perhaps easier to uphold than the previous accusations. Despite the fact that pastoral care has no formal subject matter to be transmitted and reproduced, this does not mean it is free of bias or distortion, whether in pastoral materials or tutorial interactions.

The tutorial worksheet 'Life and Choice' (Figure 5.1) provides a clear illustration. Although dated now, such schemes are still widely used. They are drawn from heavily at Elmfield. Stereotype-affirming messages are evident in the assumed naturalness and inevitability of 'normal' family life encapsulated within the option 'Whom shall I marry?', rather than 'Shall I marry?'; 'How many children shall we have?' rather than 'Shall I/we have children?' Girls are presented with the possibility of choosing between working as a waitress or as a nurse. Boys' alternatives comprise decorator, mechanic, plasterer or carpenter. It could be argued that these messages present the existing sexual divisions and inequalities of work and home as natural, inevitable and therefore 'right', thus artificially limiting pupils' occupational and social horizons.

This same worksheet also presents tutees with visions of choices that are likely to be false. The question 'Where shall we live?' offers them a choice between a country bungalow and an urban tower block. 'Shall we move house?' offers the possibility of a half-timbered detached property which looks as though it belongs in the stockbroker belt. In terms of occupation, the tutee is asked to consider 'Where do I want to work?', never 'Will I be able to find work?' The lack of recognition of the social context in which such 'choices' are made could, arguably, reproduce social relations through promising fictional opportunities, presenting personal biographies

APPENDIX 9

DECISIONS! DECISIONS!
LIFE AND CHOICE

Excerpts from the average life and the choices to be made.

1 Which rattle shall I play with?

2 Which primary school should I go to?
3 Which secondary school should I go to?

4 Which subjects should I choose to study?

5 Which career or job do I want to follow?

6 Where do I want to work?

7 Whom shall I marry?

8 Where shall we live?

10 What names shall we call them?

12 Shall I change my job?

9 How many children shall we have?

13 Shall we move house?

11 How shall we bring up our children?

14 Shall I be buried or cremated?

Which period of your life seems to contain most choice? Why?
Which period of your life seems to contain least choice? Why?

Which do you think will be the hardest choices?
Which do you think will be the easiest choices?
Why should there be choice in life, whether we like it or not?

Figure 5.1 'Decisions! Decisions! Life and Choice', from J. Baldwin and H. Wells, *Active Tutorial Work Book 3*, p. 71 (Basil Blackwell, Oxford, 1980)

as the result of individual decision-making, thereby drawing attention away from structurally embedded inequalities.

There are, however, difficulties with these accusations, in relation to both pastoral care and the curriculum in general. For instance, there is the thorny problem of the potency of such messages. As Hurn (1978) claims, there is a tendency 'to assume that students do in fact learn what schools intend to teach them. More specifically, most of us assume that schools are effective at teaching the things we dislike and ineffective at teaching the things we like' (p. 189). As Whitty (1985) points out, we are also faced with a contradiction. In explanations which focus on the gulf between school and student knowledge, inequalities are reproduced through what pupils *don't* learn. In other accounts, it is what pupils *do* learn that counts. Furthermore, there is some inconsistency in arguing that both *accurate* and *distorted* portrayals of social relations lead to the same conclusion.

Thus, while it is certainly the case that there are stereotype-affirming messages in pastoral transmissions, the potency of these messages and the mechanisms through which they are deemed to be effective are by no means clear. It may be the case that powerful voices speak through the pastoral discourse, and, indeed, it would be surprising if they were absent. But given that pastoral care is not underlain by principles which uphold the impregnability of school knowledge, it could be argued that it also provides a channel for these same distorted messages to be revealed and confronted. Indeed, the principles of the pedagogy invite challenges to stereotyping. It is easy to imagine a tutorial session in which the worksheet 'Life and Choice' is used to expose rather than transmit hidden assumptions. Moreover, subsequent publications reveal the extent to which pastoral carers are likely to be sensitive to 'bias' in published materials. Pepper *et al.* (1984), for instance, provide a range of tutorial activities which are designed to promote awareness of sexism both without and within school walls. The exercise 'Marcia' (Figure 5.2) aims to alert pupils to the pressures of gender-stereotyping at option time. Through studying three hypothetical conversations, pupils are asked to consider varying sources of discouragement. The finger of blame is clearly pointed at the subject teacher inasmuch as the pupils are asked to discuss whether 'the teacher would have said the same to a boy who had done as well as Marcia' (Pepper *et al.*, 1984, p. 49). The fact that so little critical analysis went on at Elmfield may be a reflection of the school ethos and the lack of awareness of the pastoral staff as much as an indictment of pastoral care itself.

The above discussion would seem to indicate that, at the very least, pastoral care is innocent of many of the charges which have been levelled at school subjects. Does this mean, as Thewlis (1988) suggests, that pastoral care has radical possibilities which progressive and radical teachers can exploit? The next section considers the transformative potential of pastoral care through analysing sections of a Year 8 tutorial session. At one level, it provides an, albeit poor, example of the way in which pastoral care attempts to explore, and presumably diminish, prejudice in society. At another level, it illustrates the limits of such an

Tutor Notes

YEAR 9 CHOICES
3. MARCIA

Purpose of exercise

To alert pupils to pressures of stereotyping at option time. This exercise is not about becoming an architect; the job was chosen because the field can be entered at a variety of levels (e.g. CSE/ Technician to qualified architect or draughtsperson). The emphasis should be on keeping all options open.

Requirements

Time   20 mins +

Materials   copies of sheets

Age range   Year 9

Method of use

The purpose of the exercise need not be explained beforehand.
Allocate parts and read through.
Discussing the following points may be useful:

Scene I

Do you think that graphics is a boys' 'subject'?
Why do you think that some people feel that it is?
How much do you feel that your friends influence your subject choices?
Would it matter to you if they felt that you were choosing different subjects?

Scene II

Do you think that Marcia's teacher wants her to do graphics?
Now try to explain your answer.
Do you think that the teacher would have said the same to a boy who had done as well as Marcia?

Scene III

How is Marcia's tutor encouraging her to choose the subject?

General discussion points

1. Why did Marcia decide to choose graphics in the end?
2. What else can be done to encourage more girls to choose graphics?
3. What other subjects might girls feel unsure about picking?
4. What subjects might boys feel unsure about picking?
5. If you are the only girl/boy in a particular subject, what problems do you think you may face?

Further Reading

E.C. leaflet (free) *A parents' guide to option choice*

Figure 5.2 'Marcia', from B. Pepper, K. Myers and R. Coyle/Dawkins (eds), *Sex Equality and the Pastoral Curriculum*, pp. 49–50 (ILEA, London, 1984)

approach in general. As we shall see, there are many difficulties with the content of the lesson. However, I shall argue that, even if these were overcome, it is unlikely that the pastoral pedagogy would afford more radical possibilities.

OPTIONS

Marcia likes designing things and drawing plans. She likes looking at buildings and rooms and thinking about how exciting it would be to see one built which she had designed herself. She has studied design and technology in a mixed class at school. She is now in her third year and has to make her choices. She would like to do graphics.

Scene I – tutor time in her classroom

Susan:	I don't know what subjects to pick. What are you going to do, Marcia?
Marcia:	I'd like to do graphics 'cos I want to design buildings.
Mary:	Ugh! You'll be with all the boys.
Marcia:	Oh, don't girls choose graphics?
Susan:	Nah, stupid – it's a boys' subject.
Marcia:	I don't want to be the only girl – why don't you lot pick it as well? It's really good.
Michael and boys:	We don't want you lot with us, you're silly.
Marcia:	Not as silly as you. I got a better assessment than you.

Scene II – the end of a design and technology lesson

Marcia:	Can I do graphics, Sir, next year?
Sir:	Why do *you* want to do graphics?
Marcia:	Well I like it, Sir, and I want to do architecture!
Sir:	You know you might be the only girl in the class. You wouldn't want to be with all the boys. Not many girls become architects.
Marcia:	But I'm good at it, aren't I, Sir?
Sir:	Yes, but it gets much harder later and you probably won't like it then.
Marcia:	OK, thank you, Sir.

Scene III – tutor time again

Tutor:	Have you thought about your choices yet, Marcia?
Marcia:	Well, I thought about graphics but I've changed my mind 'cos I don't want to be with all the boys, Sir.
Tutor:	But you've had a good assessment in it, haven't you?
Marcia:	Yeh, but my teacher thinks that it'll get too hard for me later on.
Tutor:	Well it'll get harder for everyone, but I'm sure you'll manage.
Marcia:	What about all of the boys though? They'll laugh at me.
Tutor:	They might laugh at you for a bit, but so what? If you want to do it, do it. You'll probably do really well.

Marcia decides to pick graphics after all. As a result, three or four of her girl friends decide to do it too.

Figure 5.2 *(continued)*

A lesson in tackling prejudice

The tutor, Valerie Goddard, starts by indicating that one of her tutees has something to tell the group, something of a 'personal' nature that relates to what they have been discussing:

> VG: You remember back on Tuesday we talked a bit about people who felt a little bit left out – isolated. Well, at lunchtime, Susan came

and told me a story. I asked her if she would like to tell you that story. She did a little think about it and said 'I will'. She's very brave and you must listen. It's very hard sometimes to say about things that really happen to us. Susan, will you tell us in a nice loud voice?

Then the tutee, Susan, with the help of Miss Goddard, explains how she has a Chinese brother. She tells the class about when they came to live back in this city and were treated as 'outsiders'. Her brother, she recounts, was 'made fun of'. Miss Goddard places a lot of emphasis on the kind of suburb they moved to:

S: When we came back from Hong Kong, we came to live in Oak Dell.

VG: Do you know where Oak Dell is? Put your hands up all of you who don't know where Oak Dell is.
[Pupils put hands up]

VG: Would you say that it was an expensive area, Susan? Would you say the houses are cheaper or dearer than here?
[Susan nods]

VG: Yes, they are dearer. It costs a lot of money – it's rather an expensive area to live in and that's rather important.

Miss Goddard then asks the class about why Susan's brother might have been 'made fun of'. Having elicited that it was because he 'looked different', she then points out what a ridiculous reason this is:

VG: I don't know why people say some people look different because I don't think David looks like Steve – they've got different noses. And I certainly don't think Craig looks like Charlotte [class laughs]. Isn't it funny that they picked on Susan's brother because he looked different?

She then asks the only two black boys in the group if this has ever happened to them:

VG: [To Justin] Have you ever had that experience?
[Justin shakes his head]

VG: No.
[To Gary] Have you ever had that experience?

G: Yes.

VG: At school or outside?

G: At school.

VG: Oh. Has it been done as a joke – or has it been done nastily?

G: To cause offence.

On this, the tutor turns to the group and asks them if they ever think of the colour of people's skin. She then recounts about how she was thinking of what she was going to do before the session:

VG: I thought on my way to school about Susan's story. And I thought to myself, 'Isn't it a shame we haven't got anyone who's a different colour we can ask?' Then I thought, 'Oh, but we have, we've got Justin and Gary – I'll ask them.' You see I just forgot. We don't even notice any more. [To class] Do you notice?

Miss Goddard then goes on to summarize what they've achieved as a group:

VG: Perhaps in our own group we've shown that the colour of skin is no reason for leaving people out.

The limits of this session are clearly apparent. However, as with the work-sheet discussed earlier, it is necessary to consider to what extent the weaknesses stem from the nature of pastoral care in general, and how much from the individual tutor.

There are certainly many criticisms which can be levelled at the content of the lesson and the tutor's handling of the subject. Some may argue that her condescension, her tight control and the closed nature of her questions make it 'bad' pastoral care – she is being too directive, not letting pupils take enough control. There are also, of course, problems with the way she deals with the area of 'prejudice'; the inference that such things only go on in 'expensive areas', the claim to her own colour blindness, her attempts to 'pass off' and deflect what Gary is telling her. However, the next section suggests that even with more awareness of and sensitivity to the issues, it is unlikely that the overall message of the lesson would have been significantly altered. I shall argue that pastoral care, as currently constructed, is unlikely to provide much scope for pupil empowerment through critical enlighten-ment because of its concentration on individual attitudes and identities.

PASTORAL CARE: LIMITS TO PUPIL EMPOWERMENT

As we have seen, one of the key characteristics of pastoral care is the emphasis placed on recognizing individualism and acknowledging the validity of personal experience. Although this may offer an inviting alterna-tive to the hierarchical standardization of the academic domain, it too has limitations. The concentration on personal experience and the removal of that experience from its cultural and social context, together with the cele-bration of unique differences, construct a particular orientation to issues such as 'prejudice'. It is, in fact, highly unusual for them to be tackled as directly as they are in the tutorial just cited. Other tutorial programmes from Elmfield deal with these issues through analogies and metaphor. For instance, in one session pupils are asked to consider whether it is sensible to hold negative characterizations of musicians and athletes. Through inference, pupils are then meant to deduce that if it is silly to be prejudiced against these categories of people, it is silly to have any prejudice at all. After all, it is a central tenet of pastoral care that we are all unique anyway. All categorizations are therefore inaccurate, being distortions of our indi-viduality.

Pastoral care tackles issues, such as racism or sexuality, from the perspective of 'liberal humanism' (Kitzinger, 1989). From this standpoint, prejudices are presented as divorced from the economic, political and social basis of their construction. For example, while a gender-sensitized worksheet such as 'Marcia' (Figure 5.2) clearly confronts stereotyping head on, it ignores the material basis of power. The problem is always limited to subjective perception, without rooting this in the social context.

It is important to understand that these limits are structured within the pedagogy itself. Analogy, metaphor and parable are key learning devices. Even where the more direct transmission of knowledge might be more appropriate, the construction of pastoral discourse as a 'fact-free' zone makes information-led approaches unacceptable. This is likely to lead to quite limited understandings of the historical, political and material contexts of students' perceptions and attitudes. Pastoral care identifies attitudes as private property, located *inside* individuals. Moreover, how we 'feel' about things seems to be more important than how things 'are'. This position carries the implicit assumption that if we can only sort these problems out in our heads, then we will have solved them.

In summary, a pedagogy such as pastoral care which intends to enlighten through subjectivity has trouble encompassing structural relations, not only because subjectivity is itself structured by them, but also because it denies the primacy of an overriding objective reality. The lack of acknowledgement of the setting outside the school and the emphasis on students' individuality makes it hard to see how pastoral care can provide critical and alternative educational experiences.

However, some critics go further and argue that pastoral care is not just ineffective, but even more regulatory than the academic domain. Take the emphasis placed on self-knowledge as the path to personal autonomy. As Jeanette Raymond states:

> Stress should be laid on the personality characteristics, as these are the factors that are probably most under the control of the individual. By becoming aware of their own nature, adolescents are more likely to attribute cause to themselves and so begin to take appropriate action rather than see themselves as victims of fate or external circumstance beyond their control. (Raymond, 1985, p. 184)

Yet this pastorally desirable end might have undesirable consequences. Hamilton (1988), for instance, claims that courses which emphasize 'self-realization' can serve a functional capacity of shifting responsibility away from structural deficiencies and onto individual deficit. From this perspective, students are being misled into attributing cause to themselves. They *are* victims of fate and external circumstance beyond their control. Viewed in this light, pastoral care may not be simply ineffective, but more capable and more culpable of 'social control' than the academic dimension.

This chapter began by illustrating that pastoral care is not just rhetoric, but that it generates distinctive and alternative practices which can be represented in terms of their difference from those which commonly underpin academic pedagogy. It argued, however, that while pastoral care is not as 'culpable' as school subjects in some directions, it is equally unlikely to be very effective as a source of critical enlightenment leading to pupil empowerment. Indeed, some have suggested that it is more damaging than the academic dimension. The next chapter considers the case *against* pastoral care.

CHAPTER 6

Pastoral care as social control?

Several writers, drawing on the work of Michel Foucault, claim that pastoral care represents an extension of disciplinary power and control (e.g. Follett, 1986) through which the 'gaze' of the professional facilitates the internal regulation of the 'self'. Wolpe argues that the, albeit unintended, consequence of the pastoral system is to 'augment disciplinary control over pupils through the detailed knowledge of them obtained by surveillance which includes home visits and the personal file system' (Wolpe, 1988, p. 23). Far from providing a channel through which pupils can be heard and empowered, she locates pastoral care as part of the institution's system of control 'whereby an ever present but subtle coercion over them is maintained' (Wolpe, 1988, p. 22).

From this perspective, it could be argued that it is those very features which others identify as having liberating potential which serve to make pastoral care more intrusive and regulatory than the discipline imposed by the subject-centred side of the curriculum.

READING THE CHILD

There are several facets of pastoral care which render it vulnerable to such a charge. In particular, the inclusiveness of its 'gaze', and its invisible rules of hierarchy, sequence and criteria all make pastoral care a powerful tool for surveillance and control.

The inclusiveness of the pastoral gaze stems from the concern to cater for the 'whole' child rather than just those aspects of its identity which comprise the 'pupil'. Boundaries between home and school become less distinct, and the opposition of inside and outside, private and public less marked. The emphasis on personal rather than positional relationships means that the anonymity of 'pupil' is replaced with intimacy. Bernstein maintains of invisible pedagogies in general that 'the socialization encourages more of the child to become visible, his uniqueness to be made manifest. Such socialization is deeply penetrating, more total as the surveillance becomes more invisible' (Bernstein, 1977, p. 126). The invisibility of the rules which underlie the pastoral discourse means that pupils are left unaware of and, therefore, unable to resist this intrusion. For instance, the processes of pastoral assessment remain hidden. What is perceived by the tutee to be 'just talking' or 'chatting', innocent of significance, may hold great weight for the tutor. It is through such informal talk that the tutor begins to evaluate the student, a process of which the tutee may be unaware. The following comments come from Joyce Cox, a Year 10 tutor:

'They'll hopefully chat for ten minutes and get through last night before the lessons start... It's what I like to do, it's how I get to know them a lot better.'

Her strategies, however, are not visible to her tutees, e.g.

P: And then she comes round to all the tables and she talks to all the groups about them and everything.

SP: Is that to get to know you or something?

P: No, she never does that. This is my second year in her class and she's never done that to me before.

Through observation and listening the teacher learns to 'read' the child, compiling a record of any details that may be considered relevant to interpreting their visible behaviour:

'Steve gives us each a notebook with the name of each child that we know something about. Observations, IQ levels, parental details, general background, physical deficiencies. We make a note about size. Miriam is a large girl ... Tina is conscious of being little.' (Kevin Smart, Year 8 tutor)

The documentation of student careers has been expanding greatly with the growth of Records of Achievement, an area which has increasingly been seen as a pastoral responsibility. And while many claim that such profiles offer students the opportunity to be both more involved in the process of assessment and offer up a wider range of themselves for appraisal, some commentators have expressed concern about their invasiveness. Hargreaves (1989) claims that they have the potential to increase selection and conformity through this increasing surveillance. Indeed, he goes so far as to claim that they constitute 'a threat to individual liberty, personal privacy and human diversity, no less' (Hargreaves, 1989, p. 138). On the other hand, it might be the pastoral endorsement, rather than denial, of individuality which makes it invasive. As Rose claims:

Rather than basing a critique upon the need to rescue individual responsibility and subjective fulfilment from social repression, we need to recognize that the extent to which our existence as selves, our awareness of our individuality, our search of our own identity, is itself constituted by the forms of identification and practices of individualization by which we are governed, and which provide us with the categories and goals which we govern ourselves. (Rose, 1989, pp. 130–1)

The heightened emphasis on individuality becomes yet another form of control – intrinsically no better than others and maybe worse. It certainly does not represent freedom from external constraint, merely a different mode of regulation.

Pastoral concentration on subjectivity leads to an ongoing process of 'reading' the child. This process is intrusive not only because the criteria by which tutees are evaluated are invisible, but because pastoral care itself has no 'content'. Unlike the academic, there is no 'product' that can be considered distinct from the producer. The child and its work are inseparable. So when pastoral carers look for evidence of learning outcomes, they can do so only by looking at the acquirer. Furthermore, evaluation cannot be explicit, for that would destroy the process of acquisition. The art of the tutor lies in deciding which aspects are significant, which behaviour indicates a deeper malaise. These indicators are then either registered on pupil records or passed on informally to heads of years and others in tutor meetings, staffrooms and corridors. These comments form the basis of pastoral interpretation of the internal state of the child.

This emphasis on observation, interpretation and explanation of 'unique individuals' contrasts with the mode of evaluation which prevails within school subjects. Here, there are externally gradable standards to be met – whether these cover work or classroom conduct. Although empirical evidence suggests that pupils' classroom behaviour is also subject to different interpretations (e.g. Keddie, 1971), there is a notion of 'offence' and concomitant 'punishment'. These punishments may take the form of detentions, extra homework or lines, but they are unlikely to have any value other than deterrence. The pupil lines pinned to the staffroom notice-board indicate a simple conception of misbehaviour and punishment:

I must pay attention every lesson without fail.
I must be silent when asked to.
I must work harder in lesson.

On the one hand, such punishments may be seen as coercive and repressive. On the other, they also offer the culprit the possibility of atonement. When the punishment is done, the transgression is past. The offence is separated from the offender. Because pastoral care is about subjectivity, individuality and uniqueness, behaviour cannot be separated from the person. With pastoral care there is no such thing as transgression, for behaviour is merely symptomatic of different unique subjectivities. Behaviour cannot be 'punished', but can only be 'treated'. What other, less 'aware', teachers may see as a simple misdemeanour can be understood only as a part of the whole. The significance of the act lies in its symptomal value. In this sense, there are many parallels between the processes of pastoral interpretation and those of the juvenile court analysed by Donzelot:

Juvenile court does not really pronounce judgment on crimes; it examines individuals. There is a 'dematerialization' of the offence which places the minor in a mechanism of interminable investigation, of perpetual judgment ... The spirit of the laws ... requires that more consideration be given to the symptomal value of the actions of which the minor is accused, to what they reveal concerning his temperament and the value of his native milieu, than to their materiality. The investigation is meant to serve more as a means of access to the minor's personality than of a means of establishing the facts. (Donzelot, 1979, pp. 110–11)

Just as the social worker may compile dossiers of information on young juveniles, so the pastoral carer constructs an 'internal' picture of their tutees, and in particular those who are deemed to be in difficulty. This transformation of transgressions into symptoms initiates further surveillance – a process which might be seen to act as a mechanism through which pupils are 'normalized' into conformity.

The operation of such processes is hard to trace because of the pastoral emphasis on individuality. Because all tutees are unique, so too will be the symptoms. What may be indicative of internal disorder in one pupil may be seen as irrelevant for others. In the following examples, pupil behaviours which would often be interpreted as indicating deep-rooted problems are dismissed as only minor 'blips'. Dave Bonds, for instance, has been reported for breaking a window and cutting another pupil's coat:

'The trouble with Bonds is that he's a nice kid. He just gets bubbly sometimes and gets carried away.' (Steve Woods)

Even more alarmingly, Gary Kendall set fire to a pile of aerosol sprays in a hotel while on a skiing trip. Although this might augur criminal proceedings elsewhere, for the tutor it seems to be nothing really to worry about:

'He's a silly lad, a nice lad who got involved. It's his first and last time. It's unlikely to happen again.' (Year 8 tutor)

While little is made of these apparently serious incidents, great significance can be attributed to what might otherwise be seen as trivial matters:

'What about Gary Page? ... There's something wrong there ... His handwriting's gone weird.' (Year 9 tutor)

'I think we should look at Martin. He's always forgetting his dinner money.' (Year 7 tutor)

Similar discrepancies are apparent in relation to the ways in which absence from school is interpreted. Irregular attendance can be seen as symptomatic of other problems:

'Here's Melanie. She's been away for three weeks now. Mum rang in to say she had tonsillitis, but I'm not convinced. I think there may be something wrong. We'd better look at this one.' (Steve Woods)

In other cases, though, even prolonged or frequent absence is not seen to be cause for concern, e.g.

'This girl, Ann. She'll catch everything, but she's a good girl, she just gets every illness going.'

In some cases, despite 'genuine' symptoms, illness is seen to be faked, e.g.

UR: Alistair, he's thrown up on the floor with the sink next door. It's all show, isn't it?

BH: He wouldn't come to school. He told his grandma, he forgets to do the work and he gets worried. I said, 'Now where were you yesterday?' 'At home,' he said. I said, 'Why?' Well he said, 'Oh.' He ends up crying in the end.

UR: Well he went off. He was sick on the floor, making a lot of noise.

What we see here are the different ways in which pastoral carers construct absence as 'genuine', 'suspicious' or blatantly 'bogus'. It shows the way in which they imply different degrees of trustworthiness – whose explanations are to be believed and whose are to be discounted.

It is these differences which arguably provide one of the mechanisms through which pastoral care contributes to the reproduction of educational inequalities. Not only does pastoral care lead to increasing surveillance and regulation, but it might also, through the production of normalizing judgements, construct 'failure' along pre-ordained dimensions. It is possible to show that teachers' readings of the child are selective, and that particular kinds of tutees are more likely to be favourably read than others.

And while such differential evaluations are undoubtedly also a feature of the academic domain, the potential for discretionary judgements is vastly increased within pastoral care. There is so much scope for 'other voices' to speak. And despite the apparent 'uniqueness' of these diagnoses, pastoral carers inevitably draw on socially constructed definitions of 'normal' behaviour. And, of course, what constitutes normal behaviour for one group of pupils is not the same as for another. It is, therefore, possible to argue that stereotyped perceptions of normality form the yardstick by which pupil behaviour is differently interpreted.

SELECTIVE READING OF THE CHILD

There will, of course, be unlimited dimensions to the ways in which teachers evaluate and respond to each student. Nevertheless, despite the uniqueness of responses, there are clear indications that behaviour is interpreted differently according to criteria of ethnicity, gender and class.

In terms of ethnicity, as Valerie Goddard claimed in the last chapter, Elmfield is 'colour blind'. Black students' experiences certainly remain invisible to staff. Travellers, however, are frequently the subject of general staffroom discussion and the stereotyped nature of pastoral pronouncements becomes apparent. The behaviour of these children is explicitly differentiated from that of non-travellers. Absences in particular are seen to be just a normal part of their heritage, e.g.

'Marie, she's from a settled gypsy family. Mum can't write. There's illness in the family – they're regularly away. But it's part of their culture – you have to accept that absence.' (Steve Woods)

Similarly, 'violent' and 'unsocial' behaviour is also seen as inevitable, e.g.

'Patrick's got himself into trouble again. The gypsies, they fight, you know, they're built like brick shithouses. They're always feuding.'

Issues of ethnicity are also interwoven with social class. In particular, the connection between being working class, incompetent and ignorant is rarely directly stated, but often implied:

'She's only a council-house type. Here's another, Steve Simms. Mum and dad split up. She couldn't keep up the mortgage. They were homeless. They live in a council house now. I mean I'm not class-conscious. I mean I come from a solid working-class background, but really, I've got to say, she's the real old dumb-blonde type. [He mimics how she talks] You can see where the problem is.' (Steve Woods)

As can be seen from Steve Woods' comments, perceptions of pupils and their parents are also highly gendered. Stereotypically, girls are devious, and boys rebellious. Here, Steve Woods talks to Brenda Champion, the educational welfare officer who liaises closely with the pastoral team and is also responsible for certain school-related benefits:

SW: She lies, twists, cheats and gets away with it.

BC: I can work with boys super. Boys respond. The weak point is the boy's mother. You can play on the relationship. You ask a boy if he loves his mother. If there's something good in a boy, he'll say 'yes'. You can manipulate boys. They're so frank. They open up and you can get to the root of the problem – not like girls. Boys are more appealing.

Although sentiments such as these provide clear indicators of gendered perspectives, less blatant references are likely to be just as prejudicial. Indeed, the fact that assumptions are hidden can render them more intractable. In the following conversation, the criteria by which students are evaluated are so tacitly understood by teachers that they do not need to be articulated:

T1: She's gone off a bit.

T2: She has gone off a bit.

T3: I think she's going off a bit.

T4: I thought she had gone off a few weeks ago. But I thought she was coming back a bit.

It would be surprising if 'going off' and 'coming back' were not related to norms of female sexuality. Female sexuality presents a constant problem for pastoral staff. Girls not only have a devious and untrustworthy nature, but they can also signify danger for male staff. Although the nature and cause of this danger is never specified, male staff often comment on how they have to be 'careful', e.g.

KS: Amanda was crying.

SW: You know it's that thing with her sister always doing better than her. [To me] And you can't put your arm round them now.

KS: I do.

SW: Yes, so do I.

KS: You've got to do it.

Indeed, the head of Year 11, Henry Perrett, claims, 'If I have a girl in my room, I always leave the door open.'

The complex properties of sexuality and gender are also clearly apparent in the differentiated constructs of disability. It is part of the pastoral carer's role to monitor, record and, where necessary, publish relevant details of 'disabilities'. At Elmfield, this information is compiled annually into a 'disabilities list' and placed on the staff notice-board above the statements of special needs and suspension stages. These lists cover a wide variety of disabilities, from 'small stature', 'hearing problems', 'asthma' and 'eczema', to 'heart condition' and 'leukaemia'.

In some cases the implications of these disabilities are specified. The disability might be followed by direct instructions: 'should sit at front'; 'seek immediate medical help if injured'. However, in many other cases, the point of publishing and recording disabilities is apparently not to pass on directions but to make academic teachers 'aware'. Staff can then make the link between particular behaviour patterns and personal problems. Being short, for instance, can be seen to constitute an abnormality for boys, 'explaining' deviant behaviour and poor academic performance:

> Peter goes to judo and tends to compensate for his small stature by using martial arts at school with overmuch determination. (Elmfield record)

> Peter is a very intense boy. He is physically small and possibly over-reacts, especially in disputes with his peers, to compensate. Left alone, Peter will 'come round'. (Elmfield record)

In making these connections it could be argued that teachers construct definitions of inadequacy which are self-fulfilling. The gender dimension of health is certainly reflected in the fact that girls feature twice as often as boys in the 'disability list'. Girls' disabilities are also accounted for differently. They are more likely to be suffixed with comments referring to psychological condition. While a boy may simply have asthma, a girl 'can become wheezy if anxious'. Some girls' disabilities are simply that they are 'nervous' or 'anxious'.

For the most part, however, it is impossible to extricate the individual facets which determine the nature of pastoral pronouncements. They result from a complex interlinkage of identities through which the nature, problems and appropriate 'treatment' of the child is diagnosed. Despite this complexity, there is one clear and overriding consideration – a concern, almost an obsession, with the provenance of the child. It is in the area of pronouncements on the family that pastoral care really comes into its own.

READING THE FAMILY

One of the main roles of the pastoral carer is the interpretation and explanation of pupil behaviour. These explanations almost inevitably make reference to the 'family', and are heavily underlain by both class and gender assumptions. Pastoral carers build up dossiers, both informally and formally, through talking to pupils, parents and, occasionally, social workers. Their interpretations show many parallels with professional evaluations made within the juvenile court. Donzelot (1979) identifies three types of families which are defined as problematic: 'unstructured', 'normally constituted but rejecting or overly protective' and 'deficient'. Like the social worker, the pastoral carer draws from these typical characterizations to interpret and explain pupils' problems.

'Unstructured' families are those 'whose domestic traits are professional instability, immorality or slovenliness' (Donzelot, 1979, p. 153). All kinds of pupil behaviour are seen to stem from this unstructured family background, from daydreaming:

> SW: I've cracked the Molton situation. Vanessa is the natural daughter, but the son isn't . . . same mother but by a different father.

> UR: I saw them at Parents' Evening. I thought they were, you know, all right.

> SW: Well she is, but he isn't. He's not the natural father.

> UR: No wonder he [the pupil] spends his time dreaming.

... to allegedly selling condoms behind the school kitchen:

> 'It sounds as if he might have been sexually abused ... father's in and out of prison, mother sleeps with loads of different men.' (Maureen McColl)

The allegation of promiscuity in the mother is a common theme running through these explanations:

> 'She's off the ropes again, drinking a lot, sleeping with any man she can.'

> 'He's one of three boys – each with a different father. Mother kicks him out in the holidays – poor kid, no wonder.'

The category of 'normally constituted but rejecting or overly protective' families covers a variety of situations, and seems to put parents in a 'no win' situation. Parents, and particularly mothers, who are seen to neglect their offspring can be the cause of pupil misbehaviour in class:

> 'Apparently mum said "I've never liked Matthew." That might be the source of the problem.'

> 'Mum said "I hate him." I can see why there are problems.'

> 'It's his mum; she hasn't got time for him.'

However, mothers are similarly blamed for overprotecting their children – 'mollycoddling', 'overdisciplining' or 'pushing' them too hard:

'Mum's too supportive; dad's not home much.'

'I remember in the first year she came along and thinking she seems to mollycoddle him.'

'Needs firm control; rather over-indulged by mother.'

'Mum's put the girl under a lot of pressure.'

As indicated earlier, the relationship between symptom and underlying problem might appear quite arbitrary to the untrained eye. In the following case, for instance, over-indulgence by the mother has contributed to problems with handwriting:

CB: He's not stupid.

MA: No, his mother is overprotective.

CB: His work is poor but mainly it's his writing.

MA: His mother has forced him to write with his left hand.

Parents, and of course mothers, contribute to all sorts of general 'anti-social' behaviour in their children while at school. They even contribute to problems with French:

'He's shy and nervous. He needs bringing out. Father is ultraprotective. He was an asthmatic. They're a large family, they all have their own places to sit in. They're well disciplined ... we should pull him out of it because he won't get that from home.' (Head of Year to French teacher's enquiry)

'Deficient' families are those that are considered abnormal simply through having only one parent, whether through death, divorce, or simply work commitments. One girl's decision not to go on the school trip can be explained through familial deficiency:

'Dad's a prison officer in Manchester; he's not home much. I don't think we've got to the bottom of this problem as far as the Everetts are concerned.'

Chatting in class stems from

'stepdad ... remarriage ... I'm not sure things are all they ought to be.'

Selling cigarettes at school can be another symptom of this 'deficiency':

Mrs Simpson [educational psychologist] and I realize that there are many relationship problems within the family. Parents are over-anxious about Lucy's work ... Lucy was given opportunity to talk about problems ... Lucy has a younger retarded sister who apparently has much attention from her mother and stepfather. Lucy feels she never has the opportunity to be with her mother. She needs much encouragement and needs to feel someone cares about her. (School records)

It is important to note that remarriage is not seen to reconstitute the family. Only biological parents count.

For one girl, too much make-up and sexually 'precocious' behaviour were attributable to her father's death and subsequent over-indulgence by her mother:

'Her father died a few months ago. It seems mum has come into a bit of money. I feel mum is being too supportive. I've had words with her about her make-up and behaviour. I think mum's trying to make it up to her.'

In many cases it is enough simply to mention: 'Single parent again.'

These readings of the family endorse a 'blame the victim' approach. It could therefore be argued that pastoral care contributes to social reproduction through 'explaining' pupils' problems in terms of family background. This could serve the ideological purpose of distracting attention away from the part schooling plays in reproducing inequalities as well as endorsing the assumption that pupils' difficulties are 'private problems' rather than 'public issues', the resolution of which only requires individual help rather than more structural social change.

Such processes can be seen to represent one part of a wider historical development where professional expertise rests upon the presumed inadequacy of the working class. The assumption of the educational incompetence of the working class in general, and the working-class mother in particular, stems from the extension of medical control over the rearing of working-class children:

The image was thus formed of the mother of the working-class family. She was more nurse than mother. Because of this nursing aspect, the link attaching her to her child would long remain questionable, arousing suspicions of laxity, abandonment, self-interestedness, or hopeless incompetence: the legacy of an encounter between the working-class woman and state assistance, in which the positive aspect in the eyes of her protectors would always be more the result of a conjunction and a forced dependence of the mother on the child than that of a desired procreation. (Donzelot, 1979, p. 31)

This extension of control is, of course, part of a larger history that relates to wider changes in the economic and social spheres of urban industrial development – aspects that are beyond the scope of this book. Nevertheless, the resultant social relationships, and class-based perceptions of 'mothering', are clearly discernible in the language of pastoral care. In ascertaining the reasons behind lateness and absence, for instance, the focus is on the deficiency of the working-class mother. Here the educational welfare officer, Brenda Champion, interviews a latecomer:

BC: Why are you late? What time does your mum get you up? What time does she go to work?

P1:   She doesn't call me till 8.45.

BC: Why can't she call you earlier? ... You had a tummy upset?

P2:   Yes.

BC: Did your mum give you any medicine?

P2: No.

BC: Did she take you to the doctor?

P2: No.

BC: No? Why not? Why didn't she take you to the doctor?

The relative social locations of pastoral carer and parent can be seen in pastoral carers' language. Working-class parents tend to be referred to chummily as 'mums' and 'dads'. The few occasions when pastoral carers use the term 'parents' are when referring to those who are quite clearly middle class and of higher socio-economic status than the teachers themselves, e.g. 'The parents teach at the university. There's some expectations there.' The uncomfortableness of 'mum and dad teach at the university' reveals the implicit class assumptions of pastoral carers' discourse.

PASTORAL CARE AS SOCIAL CONTROL?

As the above sections show, it is clear that pastoral pronouncements are underpinned by stereotypical assumptions of class, gender and ethnicity. It is, however, as hard to argue that pastoral care constitutes social control as it is to claim that it comprises radical educational practice.

Firstly, it is difficult to attribute these processes of surveillance and normalization to pastoral care alone. The academic domain is itself a powerful form of surveillance, capable of producing 'docile bodies' through hierarchical observation and normalizing judgement. In Willis' evocative words:

> Sitting in tight ranked desks in front of the larger teacher's desk; deprived of private space themselves but outside nervously knocking the forbidden staff room door or the headmaster's door with its foreign rolling country beyond; surrounded by locked up or out of bounds rooms, gyms and equipment cupboards; cleared out of school at break with no quarter given even in the unprivate toilets; told to walk at least two feet away from the staff cars in the drive – all of these things help to determine a certain orientation to the physical environment and behind that to a certain kind of social organization. They speak to the whole *position* of the student. (Willis, 1977, pp. 67–8, his emphasis)

Secondly, there are particular problems with identifying the mechanisms through which pastoral care might regulate. For pupils to internalize pastoral readings, they must be made aware of them. While such awareness may be easily acquired in relation to the academic domain, where evaluation is explicit and results in visible stratification, this is not the case with pastoral care. The rules of evaluation and subsequent pastoral assessment are not public, and are not easy to access. We are confronted again with the difficulty alluded to earlier. Is pastoral care effective because students have *successfully* learnt the rules by which it operates, or because some of them *fail* to appropriate them?

In indicating that we should be cautious over claims that pastoral care serves to normalize and differentiate, I do not mean to suggest that diagnoses made by pastoral carers are inconsequential. For individual pupils whose behaviour is seen to stem from seriously unsatisfactory family conditions, the intervention of pastoral staff can be far-reaching, irrespective of whether students have internalized the norms. In one case at Elmfield, the perceived deficiency of the family resulted in a pupil being sent to a residential school.

> 'With Craig Jones, well it's a case of ... he's got to get out of the house. I've spoken to dad about it, I've gone along to their home. Sometimes he's with mum, and sometimes with dad. I've talked to his dad for a long time on the phone expressing why I think he should go, giving my reasons; giving my personal point of view that I also agree with him that I would hate it, as a dad, sending my own son away. But I would if it were the best for him, and that's what I want. And I've done the same with his mum... All right, maybe you can say I'm interfering, maybe you're right. But I feel strongly enough that he's got to go.' (Head of Year 7)

For these children, pastoral care has a highly significant effect on their careers, and it seems possible that the ideological significance of these cases as a salutary effect on other families is greater than their numerical frequency. Again, though, it is hard to know what is distinctively pastoral about these processes. Such 'treatment' is by no means new. Exclusion and confinement have been a feature of the educational system for a long time. Whether such measures are couched in terms of the school's interest, as in Arnold's Rugby – 'ridding the school of polluting influences' (Bamford, 1970, p. 10) – or, as at Elmfield, in terms of the pupil's interest – being 'best for him' – is unlikely to make a significant difference to the career of the pupil concerned, or parental fear of its instigation.

In summary, there are a number of difficulties with arguments that pastoral care represents an extension of surveillance and normalization. Although it is the case that pastoral care directs its gaze to more of the pupil, the mechanisms through which it normalizes, regulates and differentiates are unclear.

While it is important to analyse dimensions of the curriculum, it is also important to look at the relations between these dimensions. As I have argued in Chapter 1, the curriculum is not a collection of discrete units whose form, structure and messages, whether implicit or explicit, can be considered in isolation.

CHAPTER 7

The pastoral and the academic: messages from the boundary

The last two chapters have considered whether pastoral care should be seen as a vehicle for pupil empowerment or an instrument of social control. Chapter 5 suggested that, while pastoral care may be innocent of some of the charges levelled at school subjects, it is, as currently constituted, unlikely to significantly alter students' experience of secondary schooling. Chapter 6 considered claims that, far from being innocent, pastoral care was more guilty than the academic side of the curriculum in that the inclusivity and invisibility of its pedagogy made it an intrusive form of pupil surveillance and regulation. However, while it acknowledged that pastoral diagnoses were likely to operate differentially along the lines of class, race and gender, it argued that it was hard to see what pastoral care added above and beyond existing processes. In short, neither of these accounts of pastoral care seems very convincing.

One reason why they fail to convince is that they suffer from the same weakness identified earlier in many accounts of the origins and significance of pastoral care. They too look at pastoral care in isolation. As Bernstein's work reminds us, any consideration of the curriculum should move beyond individual components and focus on the ways in which they are related to each other. In short, the curriculum is more than the sum of its parts.

In Chapter 2, I argued that one explanation for the rapid and widespread emergence of pastoral care lay in its potential to reconcile some of the tensions inherent within the comprehensivization of secondary schooling. The features and discourse of pastoral care enabled academic stratification to continue within the egalitarian and integrative ethos of the comprehensive school. However, as subsequent chapters have demonstrated, there is considerable opposition between the two dimensions. It is clear that the relationship between the pastoral and the academic is not one of mutual complementarity. Indeed, the boundary between the two areas is one manifestation of both the degree of tension and the strength of the academic domain. As Bernstein (1977) argues: 'Power is never more eloquent and penetrating than in the insulation it produces between categories' (pp.

198–9). Furthermore, the pastoral–academic boundary becomes more than a means of containment and marginalization of pastoral concerns. It takes on its own significance. As quoted in Chapter 1: 'The relationship between categories is itself a crucial message, perhaps the most crucial if these come to be considered inevitable and legitimate' (Bernstein, 1977, pp. 198–9). It is possible to identify at least three 'crucial messages' which emanate from the oppositional relationship between the pastoral and the academic. Firstly, the boundary between them sustains the 'objectivity' of the academic. Secondly, it contributes to the construction of 'ability' as natural aptitude. Thirdly, it conflates 'ability' with 'morality'. In these ways, the boundary which insulates the academic from pastoral intrusion not only preserves the dominance of the school subject, but actually strengthens it. This chapter argues that the pastoral–academic boundary reflects and reinforces the authority through which the academic dimension dominates the secondary school and determines educational identities.

SUSTAINING THE 'OBJECTIVITY' OF THE ACADEMIC

Most simply, and yet crucially, the pastoral–academic boundary perpetuates and regenerates the 'objectivity' of the academic dimension. It does this by just being there. To classify and isolate some issues as belonging within one category of the curriculum is to deny their presence in other areas. More specifically, the inclusion of social, moral and personal concerns within the category of pastoral care transmits the message that academic knowledge transcends this messy realm. The tacit implication is that the academic domain is rational and value-free.

The social purity of the academic is, of course, fictional. Not only has the status of facts become vulnerable, but their collection and organization within subject disciplines must be considered even more arbitrary. Even if we do not travel all the way down the relativist path (see Chapter 1), the narrow selection of what counts as *school* knowledge cannot be construed as anything other than socially and historically contingent (Whitty, 1985).

Reinforcing the fiction of academic purity and rationality is likely to have a number of implications. Some of these are evident in differentiated staff identities. As we have seen, Elmfield teachers have alternative allegiances. These are constructed not just on the basis of possession of expertise, but on contrasting personal qualities. You can be clever or caring, but not both. Pastoral staff are 'good with people'. Their identity is couched in terms of social attributes rather than cognitive faculties. However, social attributes do not have parity of esteem with cognitive faculties. Being 'good with people' means getting the most difficult classes to teach. It means you don't need expensive resources and specialist equipment, just a sympathetic ear.

And there are, of course, significant gender dimensions to the opposition between personal virtues of patience and caring and cognitive attributes of cleverness. As mentioned in Chapter 1, this is likely to have implications for reflecting and reinforcing the gendered division of labour in schools.

On a more general level, there are undoubtedly more nebulous but no less significant consequences. Through reinforcing the myth of school knowledge as value-free, the pastoral–academic boundary safeguards the academic right to be the arbiter and distributor of rationality, and, thus, educational identities.

ENDORSING THE 'NATURALNESS' OF COGNITIVE ABILITY

The pastoral–academic boundary not only sustains the objectivity of the academic, but also endorses the *naturalness* of academic ability. As we have seen, the pastoral side caters for the affective dimension of tutees – their social, emotional and moral side. The academic serves the cognitive dimension of pupils – fulfilling their intellectual and academic needs. The distinction and complementarity of the two dimensions can be most clearly seen in the way in which indicators of each are differently, and, most importantly, *alternatively* rewarded.

At Elmfield, there is an annual ceremony of prize-giving where pastoral 'credits' and academic 'commendations' are awarded. Steve Woods, head of Year 8, is reading out the list of pupils who have been given commendations for their achievements in school subjects:

'Now the subject awards. They go to the people who are top in their subject.'

Although there was some debate among subject teachers as to who should get commendations, there was relatively little disagreement. The only apparent pastoral concession is that teachers should nominate both a boy and a girl for each subject. Which sex this advantages is hard to establish. The only exception to this appeared to be citizenship, where there was no male candidate.

As the commendations are being announced, it becomes apparent that two girls in particular are being awarded prizes in several subjects. At one point the other pupils start to jeer and Mr Woods has to intervene:

'Now it's always awkward when some people are put up for lots of awards. It puts a lot of pressure on the girls; maybe some of you might be jealous. But we've talked openly about this and we said that if someone deserved it then we didn't see why they shouldn't have it. If they deserve it then they should get it. What you must be is pleased for them.'

Despite this statement, the monopoly which only a few people have on the commendations creates problems for the pastoral assertion that 'we're all good at something'. In the academic realm, some students are clearly good at many things. Steve Woods articulates this dilemma:

'This is the nicest day of the year, when you get awards. The only bad thing about these awards is that they're only for some of you. We should have something for everyone. Every one of you would have an award for something; we're all good at some things and not so good at others. However, life is competitive, and we've got to learn that.'

In order to soften this hard lesson and partially counteract the ceremonial statement of unequal worth, pastoral staff ensure that not only academic abilities are rewarded at prize-giving. Pupils may also receive 'credits'. As Steve Woods explains:

> 'Some of you will know that although you've tried very hard, you've still not achieved even the middle of the group. Life is like that sometimes; it doesn't seem fair. I can't draw a straight line for instance and I'm full of admiration for the things Mr Smart does. People make a lot of efforts, but maybe even then they're still not doing well. These are awarded for those people.'

There is a murmur of laughter when Mr Woods says this, indicative of the lower status which pupils attach to 'credits'. This is hardly surprising when to be awarded one is a public admission that despite your hardest efforts 'you've still not achieved the middle of the group'.

However, what is most important about credits and commendations is not just their different status but their alternative and mutually exclusive nature. For instance, one pupil is nominated for a credit award who has just been given a commendation. This causes Steve Woods some confusion as he reads out her name:

> 'Oh, well, Vicky Green is doing well anyway.'

Credits are not meant for those who are 'doing well'. They are designed by the pastoral team to be a recognition of motivation. It is also a recognition that the stratification of the academic is both partial and to some extent 'unkind'. What matter most to the pastoral staff are the 'internal' facets of the pupil rather than their 'external' performance. However, their attempts to upgrade effort only serve to further endorse the natural superiority of the academically able.

Moreover, the extent to which this alternative evaluation actually compounds the naturalness of academic ability provides a clear illustration of the inadequacy of explaining consequences in terms of intentions. The pastoral intention of providing an alternative evaluation is subverted by the oppositional relationship that exists between the pastoral and the academic.

So how does this alternative, and mutually exclusive, recognition of ability and effort strengthen the power of the academic domain? The alternative recognition divorces effort from achievement; it creates a mismatch between 'trying' and 'succeeding'. If, as Bourdieu claims, academic success is only the extent to which the dominant class celebrate what they already have, then this automatically disadvantages those who have to 'try' in order to achieve:

> Children from the lower middle classes, as they receive nothing of any use for them in their academic activities except a sort of undefined enthusiasm to acquire culture, are obliged to expect and receive everything from school, even if it means accepting the school's criticism of them as 'plodders'. (Bourdieu, 1976, p. 114)

If academic success is not just the extent to which one has access to cultural capital, but also the extent to which one can display the naturalness of this 'gift', then to 'plod' is to signify failure:

What the child receives from an educated milieu is not only a *culture* ... but also a certain *style* of relationship to that culture, which derives precisely from *the manner of acquiring it*. An individual's relationship with cultural works (and the mode of all his cultural experiences) is thus more or less easy, brilliant, natural, difficult, arduous, dramatic or tense according to the conditions in which he acquired his culture... It can be seen that by stressing the relationship with culture and setting great value on the most aristocratic style of relationship (ease, brilliance) school favours the most privileged children. (Bourdieu, 1976, p. 117fn, his emphases)

Through hiding its social basis and divorcing effort from achievement, the academic dimension obscures the extent to which children are differently privileged. Furthermore, it could be argued that this demand for an 'aristocratic' relationship to knowledge is sufficient in itself to deter working-class children from even trying. Turner's investigation of pupils' perceptions found that for many 'academic ability is a "natural trait" and that academic success *should not* be gained illegitimately through hard work' (Turner, 1984, p. 77, my emphasis). The extent to which performance must reflect 'natural' potential rather than simply 'hard work' may also have a gender dimension. Walkerdine argues in relation to girls' mathematical ability that

no matter how well girls were said to perform, their performance was always downgraded or dismissed in one way or another. These pejorative remarks usually related to the idea that girls' performance was based on hard work and rule-following rather than brains or brilliance (in other words what was supposed to underlie *real* mathematical performance). (Walkerdine, 1989, p. 268, my emphasis)

The separation of 'success' from 'effort' not only obscures the way that children are differently privileged, but also hides the extent to which academic achievement depends on two sites of acquisition: the home and the school. As Bernstein (1990) argues of visible pedagogies, by which we can characterize school subjects: 'Currently the visible pedagogy of the school is cheap to transmit because it is subsidized by the middle class family and paid for by the alienation and failure of children of the disadvantaged classes and groups' (p. 78). The fabrication of academic achievement without effort, through either privileging cultural capital (Bourdieu) or subsidy (Bernstein), also perpetuates the myth of 'intellect' as a scarce resource. This myth may have far-reaching consequences. It undoubtedly contributes to what Bisseret (1979) calls the 'ideology of aptitudes' in which ability is seen as personal attribute rather than socially bestowed. It also underpins the authority of the teacher:

It is the *idea* of the teacher, not the individual which is legitimized and commands obedience. This idea concerns teaching as a fair exchange – most basically of knowledge for respect, of guidance for control. Since knowledge is the rarer commodity this gives the teacher his moral superiority. (Willis, 1977, p. 64, his emphasis)

I am not suggesting that pastoral care is responsible for either the 'ideology of aptitudes' or the idea of knowledge as a 'rare commodity'. Indeed, pastoral care opposes such limiting concepts. However, the boundary between the pastoral and the academic, and the alternative celebration of effort and ability, far from challenging such ideology actually serves to strengthen it.

CONFLATING ACADEMIC ABILITY WITH MORALITY

The alternative evaluation of internal motivation and external performance also serves to conflate superior ability with superior moral and social attributes. At first sight this might seem contradictory. If, as I have just argued, social virtue and academic ability are separately rewarded, how can 'cleverness' and 'goodness' be conflated? Surely those who are pastorally rewarded must be more socially adjusted than those who achieve academically? That this is not the case, that teachers, both pastoral and academic, imbue the more able with more goodness, is evident in the way they often conflate the supposedly distinct realms:

'There's a lot of great kids, a lot of bright ones, nice ones.'

'Paul shouldn't go too far astray. He's in the top set. With the better boys, to be honest.'

Conversely, there is seen to be a correlation between 'low ability' and social incompetence and moral laxity:

'He's too stupid to know what consideration means.'

'As a group, I'd like to abandon teaching with them, teach them how to relate to each other as normal human beings.'

'It's really just to try and teach them some social graces – to stop them shouting at each other by the time they leave school.'

The relationship between 'goodness' and 'ability' can be summed up as:

'Some of them are thick and some of them are lovely.'

How can this apparent contradiction be explained? Firstly, I shall argue that this conflation of goodness and ability stems from the moral basis of the academic and, secondly, that despite challenges from the pastoral, it is reinforced by the academic bounding and marginalization of the pastoral.

The bestowal of academic appreciation and reward is as much a reflection of social orientation as of academic performance. It is about accepting the moral basis of academic authority. It is not enough just to be 'clever'; one has to be orientated to the academic in a particular way. The pupil has to endorse as legitimate and inevitable the basis of the stratification between teacher and pupil, and between pupil and pupil. Again, as Willis (1977) argues of the school conformists: 'It is not so much that they support teachers, but rather that they support the *idea* of teachers' (p. 13, his emphasis). Academic success is about subjecting oneself to academic discipline: 'The ability to "grasp a concept" in the context of the course and probably in a wider sense, refers to a pupil's *willingness* or ability to take over or accept the teacher's categories' (Keddie, 1971, p. 146, my emphasis). For example, it is possible for pupils to perform well in tests without exhibiting the necessary acceptance of the morality of the teacher and the subject discipline. However, teachers at Elmfield have a degree of leeway in which to make sure that such pupils do not get academic commendations and promotion into higher sets.

Craig, who was obviously the most 'able' in his French set, was not awarded a commendation because of his refusal, or inability, to submit himself correctly to the teacher's authority:

'Craig, he gets top marks, but he's so complacent. He goes, "Ugh, work's so boring." He's a lazy slob. I'm not giving him a commendation.'

Similarly, Gary is not promoted to top sets even though his test results might suggest otherwise:

'I don't think Gary should go up. It's not on to not really try hard throughout the year and then suddenly do well in the exam. There might also be children who deserved a place in a top set, but who just did badly in the exams. Lots of things have to be taken into account, practicals and all sorts of things.'

One of the problems with some forms of assessment is that they can elevate performance over submission to academic authority. It is possible, certainly in some subjects at secondary level, to do well in examinations without having the necessary style or orientation to authority. This discrepancy can cause problems. Indeed, it could have been the gap between test results and student submission to academic authority which caused many of the difficulties with the 11+ test and the tripartite system: difficulties that some would argue (e.g. Ford, 1969) led to the establishment of the comprehensive system. Grammar schools, the epitome of academic authority, contained a significant number of pupils who, although they had passed the 11+, were not correctly orientated to that authority (e.g. Jackson and Marsden, 1967; Lacey, 1970). At the same time those with the appropriate academic orientation, the many middle-class pupils who failed the 11+, were consigned to the non-academic secondary modern.

The extent to which academic success is really access to particular cultural categories, and, at the level of the secondary school especially, correct orientation to the discipline of the school subject, is visible in the definition of academic problems.

One might presume that an academic problem has something to do with cognitive development. While there may well be instances where this is the case, they are not frequently reported at Elmfield. For the most part, the 'learning difficulties' which seem to give subject specialists the most cause to reach for the record book stem from students' apparent reluctance to accept their authority. The files of pupils who consistently pose problems for subject teachers, those of Justin Moore for instance, reveal an inability or refusal to submit to the discipline of the school subject:

10/5 Detention [HE] 'Nuisance in class generally'

17/5   Detention [Music] 'Silly behaviour in class. He is to copy up missed work'

25/5   [French] '1. Repeated talking   2. Rude attitude when sent out of the room   3. Failure to do set homework'

20/6   Detention [Geography] 'Silly behaviour after repeated warnings'

22/6   Detention [Geography]

23/6   Detention 'Failure to complete detention for Geography'

5/7   Interview with head of year: 'A girl complained that J had tried to put his hand up her skirt. As far as I understand this happened during general larking about and was not really serious'

18/10   Detention [History] 'Persistent inability to bring book. I've no evidence of work being tackled'

27/11   Detention [HE] 'Failure to settle and do any work in the lesson'

2/12   Detention [English] 'Insufficient classwork and silly behaviour'

7/12   Detention [Maths] 'Homework late, unfinished and unacceptable'

16/1   Detention [CDT] 'Too much talking'

17/1   Detention [HE] 'Failure to do any work during lessons. Allowing paper to be defaced'

20/1   Detention [English] 'Gross insolence – refusal to do what asked'

22/2   Detention [English] 'Not doing homework'

27/2   Detention [head of year] 'Failure to be quiet when told several times'

22/3   Detention [Science] 'Unacceptable behaviour in class'

These record notes show the 'moral outrage' (Willis, 1977) that rejection of the authority basis of the academic causes: 'gross insolence', 'unacceptable behaviour', 'allowing paper to be defaced'.[1] Even where comment is made on the nature of pupils' work rather than their social behaviour in class, it refers not to the degree of ability or understanding displayed but to its subversive threat:

> 'In art he is aggressive. His art has a violent or coarsely rude look about it regarding subject matter... He is naturally clever with his hands... His language and manner are coarse on occasion and he sometimes brags about the fact that he steals. He is very streetwise and I think he watches unsuitable video material.' (Art teacher's notes)

It is quite probable that this same teacher who denounces the coarseness of her pupil's work might admire exactly the same quality in the work of professional artists. What makes the difference is not necessarily the artistic merit of the work, or even, in this case, the artistic skills, for this pupil is 'naturally clever with his hands'. What matters is the pupil's perceived orientation to the school subject of 'art' and whether he accepts the moral authority of the art teacher.

That the academic domain is morally underpinned is quite evident. That what matters is not cognitive development but submission to academic authority is also clear. However, here is a difficulty within the academic domain. How can it represent itself as neutral, value-free and objective, and at the same time lay claim to its moral superiority? Although the academic may derive some of its strength through constructing itself as objective, innate and value-free, it also needs to reappropriate its morality. Inasmuch as academic disciplines deny their moral basis, they offer a weakness which can be exploited. As we have seen, pastoral care is able to present the academic components of the curriculum as technicist, instrumental and narrow. The rationality of the academic provides pastoral care with the opportunity of exposing subject disciplines as oppressive and didactic rather than self-fulfilling and 'truly' educative.

The academic, however, diffuses this challenge through the bounding and subsequent marginalization of the pastoral. Pastoral care is, as are all invisible pedagogies (Bernstein, 1990), expensive. Its underlying principles which dictate that true learning must always be self-motivated, and that true evaluation must always be indirect, require greater resources of teachers, time and space. For pastoral care to undertake these tasks effectively and to transmit its alternative form of morality, it needs to restructure the school day. However, as we saw in Chapter 4, the academic dominates school time and space. Pastoral care tends to be pushed to the margins of the day. Pastoral carers are therefore severely restricted in their ability to 'read' the child. They must let the academic specialists do this for them.

As we have seen, pastoral surveillance of pupils can be invoked for a variety of reasons. The principal reason, though, is a perceived rejection or lack of respect for academic authority – from day-dreaming in class to gross insolence. The subsequent pastoral interpretation of these 'symptoms' in terms of individual and familial pathology endorses academic superiority through imputing social incompetence to those who are deemed to have 'learning difficulties'.

The reappropriation of the morality of the academic, with the unintentional collusion of pastoral care, does not necessarily derive its significance, as Willis (1977) argues, from reintegrating the disaffected. If it did, it would be remarkably inefficient in the light of his account of the lads' resistance. For our purposes, the importance of academically invoked pastoral attention for the less able and less willing is that it confers moral and social competence on those students who *are* academically able and willing.

In this chapter, I have sought to demonstrate that although the pastoral and the academic are distinct curricular dimensions, the oppositional relationship between them sends out its own messages. Most simply, the opposition perpetuates the fiction of the objectivity of the academic domain. It also contributes to the translation of 'achievement' into 'ability'.

The oppositional and alternative evaluation of effort and achievement divorces 'trying' from 'success'. It fabricates the myth of academic achievement without endeavour. This not only hides the extent to which classes differentially subsidize academic success, but also perpetuates the 'truth' of 'intellect' as a scarce resource. Finally, the academic invocation of pastoral attention for students who are deemed to have 'problems' conflates academic success with moral and social competence.

It is, therefore, in the nature of the oppositional relationship that the distinct significance of pastoral care can be located. Within a specialized curriculum, such as that of Elmfield, the bounding of the pastoral care turns a challenge to school subjects into a source of strength. Paradoxically, the pastoral–academic boundary reinforces the academic dominance of the curriculum.

If the boundary does all this, then what will be the consequences of pastoral–academic integration? Will erosion of the pastoral–academic boundary lead to diminution of academic hegemony? The next chapter addresses this question through looking at Kings Marsh, a comprehensive school where attempts have been made to integrate the pastoral and academic.

NOTE

1. Additionally, it reflects an interesting scale of priorities where the head of year dismisses what some might interpret as sexual harassment as 'not really serious' yet subsequently gives the boy a detention for 'failing to be quiet'.

CHAPTER 8

Kings Marsh School: integrating the pastoral and the academic

The last four chapters have used Elmfield School as a case study to show how a 'specialized' curriculum contributes to a dual structure of provision in which the academic and pastoral dimensions are clearly demarcated and segregated. Such demarcation is more than just administrative convenience. Each dimension has its own structure and organization which reflect contrasting underlying principles. While the academic is characterized by specialization, hierarchical ordering of subjects and progressive screening of students, the pastoral side of the curriculum attempts to flatten hierarchies and diminish student stratification. The 'collection code' of the academic rests on the segregation of subjects which remain insulated from each other, whereas pastoral care strives towards the integration of curricular elements.

That the relationship between the pastoral and the academic is fraught with tension is illustrated by the extent to which the boundary between the two areas is constructed and maintained. Through upholding the boundary, the academic dimension resists pastoral surveillance and encroachment, enabling it to retain its dominance of the secondary school curriculum. Furthermore, as we saw in the last chapter, the opposition between the pastoral and the academic not only preserves academic authority, but also reinforces it.

If the boundary provides the means by which pastoral care remains marginalized and school subjects ascendant, will its erosion mean that the academic dimension no longer dominates the curriculum? Will it be subsumed by the pastoral as only one aspect of a unified curriculum? The significance of the pastoral–academic boundary can be further assessed through exploring the effects of attempts to integrate the two dimensions.

This chapter uses another case study, Kings Marsh School, to examine the implications of pastoral–academic integration. It considers the nature of the strategies which have been adopted, and the degree of success and resistance encountered. It concludes by discussing the limits of integration.

BACKGROUND

Kings Marsh, like Elmfield, is an LEA-controlled co-educational comprehensive. It has 1100 pupils, 120 of whom are in the sixth form. As at Elmfield, the pupil intake is predominantly white. Although Kings Marsh is more rural in its location, it also serves two local towns as well as the surrounding countryside, drawing from both middle- and working-class housing areas. The list of staff, together with their official responsibilities, is shown in Appendix 2.

Although Kings Marsh has not experienced the upheaval of amalgamation, the arrival of David Hartnell, the headteacher, seven years ago marked the beginning of continuing attempts to integrate the pastoral and the academic; moves towards a 'whole school' curriculum (Marland, 1980).

These moves towards integration have been based on a clear recognition of the extent to which the academic side of the curriculum actively maintains the boundary and a consequent acknowledgement that the power of the subject department needs to be challenged if a 'whole school' curriculum is to be successfully implemented. The strategies have, therefore, been two-pronged; alongside those aimed at elevating and formally integrating the pastoral are those directed at the diminution of academic control. Each of these strategies will be considered in turn.

THE INTEGRATION AND ELEVATION OF THE PASTORAL DIMENSION

There have been two principal channels along which pastoral care has been officially integrated with the academic domain and its profile augmented. Firstly, attempts are being made to diminish the boundary by resisting demarcation within senior management levels. Secondly, there are moves to heighten the priority of the pastoral, reducing the marginalization that occurs while the pastoral–academic boundary remains.

Senior management at Kings Marsh has attempted to erode the boundary between the pastoral and the academic through avoiding formal demarcation. As we saw at Elmfield, deputy headteachers are assigned distinct responsibilities: curricular, administrative or pastoral. At Kings Marsh, such demarcation is explicitly rejected. The deputies have equal responsibility for all areas:

'It's a nonsense to have a dichotomy between one and the other, because it's one student we're dealing with.' (John Stephens, deputy headteacher)

Although it is difficult to determine the extent to which such duties are completely shared in practice, observation and interview data do seem to indicate that all deputies contribute to various tasks – from dealing with pupils' problems to constructing the timetable. Furthermore, they have moved out of their individual offices to a communal area:

'Offices are not territory.' (John Stephens)

Awareness of the problems of categorization is evident in a general refusal to identify areas even verbally:

> 'I don't like using the word "pastoral". We all share.' (Gwen Langfield, deputy headteacher)

This reluctance to demarcate teachers in terms of their pastoral or academic identities is also evident lower down the staff hierarchy. At Elmfield, it is not generally possible to carry positions of both pastoral and academic responsibility, the two areas being perceived as mutually incompatible. This is not the case at Kings Marsh, where academic and pastoral posts can coincide, and where more than one academic responsibility may be held. For instance, Christopher Lloyd, who is head of Years 9, 10 and 11 is also Head of Personal and Social Development (PSD). Mandy Price, head of Year 8, is Head of Drama and aesthetics co-ordinator. Gwen Langfield, deputy headteacher, is Head of Special Needs. Jack Ford, another deputy, is Head of BTEC.

The extent to which this constitutes 'real' integration is problematic. Integration is, of course, always relative. As Atkinson argues, in defence of Bernstein's use of 'integrated' as being relative rather than absolute:

> The prerequisite that knowledge contents are subject to some degree of selection and separation is clearly a prerequisite to anything recognizable as a curriculum. Without some such classification, the curriculum would be coterminous with the entire universe of possible knowledge and experience. (Atkinson, 1985, pp. 132–3)

Nevertheless, there is still an evident gap between the official rhetoric of integration and the day-to-day reality. Senior management may refuse to categorize their activities in terms of the pastoral and the academic, but the very existence of 'subject' and 'year duties' for staff lower down the hierarchy reflects continued demarcation. As at Elmfield, it is possible to distinguish an academic side to the curriculum, with its dominant allocation of time and space, and a pastoral side composed of tutorial responsibilities and year structures. Staff are allotted distinct tasks related to their teaching, as opposed to their tutorial duties.

Perhaps more crucially, it could also be argued that the coincidence of academic and pastoral responsibilities only takes place where subject identity is not prestigious. It is only in areas such as PSD, BTEC and drama that pastoral and academic posts have been combined. Even at Elmfield, despite the official policy of alternative academic or pastoral career routes, there was seen to be no opposition between being Head of RE and head of year. Although such shared responsibilities are more common at Kings Marsh than at Elmfield, it is significant that there are no science, language or maths specialists taking on board both academic and pastoral responsibilities.

However, despite these similarities, there are evident differences in the way the boundary has been addressed and challenged at Kings Marsh. For instance, at Elmfield, the formal syllabus of social education is administered primarily by pastoral staff. At Kings Marsh, attempts have been made to widen staff involvement and heighten its status. All tutors are expected to take their groups for PSD for one or two periods a week. Rather than presenting tutorial responsibility as an inevitable obligation that might become marginalized, attempts have been made to prioritize it:

'The tutor is the most important person. They take them for two lessons of PSD and also in the lower school for their main subjects.' (John Stephens)

Other attempts to elevate the status of tutoring have been made through restricting access, making perceived suitability to take PSD the principal criterion of selection, e.g.

'I'm not allowed to have a tutor group. I didn't go on the PSD training course... I'd like to be a tutor, and teach PSD... It used to be considered an honour to teach PSD.' (Vera Reynolds, RE)

As we saw in Chapter 4, at Elmfield the distribution and allocation of tutors is low, if not bottom, on the list of timetabling priorities. This marginalization, compounded by the split site, results in little tutor–tutee contact or continuity. At Kings Marsh, tutorial cover is given much higher priority. Tutors take all their tutorial and PSD sessions. In the event of absence, a system of 'attached' tutors has been devised to provide continuity. In addition, the allocation of tutors also impinges on academic concerns rather than the other way round. In the lower school, for instance, tutors are required to teach their tutor groups outside of their subject specialism in order to increase tutor–tutee contact time.

The extent to which the status of the pastoral dimension has been augmented is evident in the frequency of pastoral interruptions. At Elmfield, the subject lesson is seen as 'sacred'. While intrusion on pastoral time by academic concerns is commonplace, intrusion into the academic is not only rare, but highly resented. At Kings Marsh, there appears to be less intrusion into pastoral time and space, and far more intrusion of the pastoral into the academic, e.g.

'In designated counselling periods, you get extra frees as a tutor. You can take the child out of any lesson; there's never any conflict from the teacher.' (Jackie Carpenter, tutor and art teacher)

Even in the sixth form, PSD can take priority over 'specialist' subject time:

'They're told to go out of art to go to PSD.' (Jackie Carpenter)

It does not, of course, follow that staff will automatically take on board senior management's prioritization of tutorial work, or that PSD will be perceived by staff as an 'honour'. As at Elmfield, there is a fair amount of antipathy. Pastoral intrusion is still noted and resented by the academic. There may be less public criticism of 'pastoral [sic] nonsense', but this does not mean that it is not the subject of much contempt among some staff at coffee time.

Changes in nominal duties at senior level, and management insistence on the importance of the 'whole' child, are unlikely in themselves to challenge the identity and allegiance of the subject specialists as long as the academic is left to carry on unheeded.

In addition to prioritizing the pastoral, the dominance of the academic dimension has been challenged through attempts to diminish the importance, and modify the structure of, the subject department – weakening subject insulation and hierarchy. This strategy has been paralleled by a strengthening of the cohesion of senior management and the formulation of an alternative curricular principle to that of the stratificatory code of the academic.

CHALLENGING THE DOMINANCE OF THE ACADEMIC

At Elmfield, the bastion of academic specialization is the subject department. However, its internal stratification, insulation from other areas and relative self-determination are all features that have been challenged at Kings Marsh.

Strategies to weaken the power of departments have taken several directions. Firstly, the position of the head of the department, as the symbol of subject identity and academic authority, appears to have been substantially weakened. It has been necessary to displace, at least partially, these 'barons of education' (John Stephens, deputy headteacher). Many departments appear to have no titular heads. Where departmental heads have retired or moved on, they have not been replaced. There may be a 'key' person, but they carry neither the status nor resources of the traditional departmental head. Humanities, for instance, appears to have no head, either as a 'cluster',[1] or for individual subjects, geography, history and RE:

> 'I'm not really the head. I get a scale point for lower school humanities and geography, but no specific points. I'm the representative really.' (Matthew Harper)

The position of 'representative' marks a significant shift in authority. Rather than being 'in charge' as implied by departmental 'head', a 'representative' implies communicative agency only, the authority to negotiate and/or lobby, but not to control.

Science similarly lost its head when he was transferred to be head of Year 8. Pete Redman claims that he resigned his departmental headship because of the difficulty of coping with the headteacher's initiatives. Science remained, until recently, without a head:

> 'David Hartnell put pressure on the science department, for instance with changes to physics and biology and integrated science. I didn't want to go it alone, and it would have been. When the head of year post came up, David Hartnell at a review meeting felt I was better with kids than running the science department. I wasn't sure. When he suggests something, you do it. Life gets difficult if you don't... We didn't have a head of science. It was advertised but because of the development with TVEI it was a difficult beast and nobody applied who was capable of doing it. We belly-ached so much, David Hartnell appointed someone to be called a 'co-ordinator' – Keith Molton – but no one took curricular responsibility, though the head treated him as head of science and he took all the crap. He got one point, didn't get paid and didn't get any free time ... a lot of lobbying went on. After constant nagging we eventually got one.' (Pete Redman)

The term 'co-ordinator', like 'representative', again implies a substantial weakening of hierarchy. The status of the subject as reflected through the amount of free time allotted to its specialists has also been diminished. At Elmfield, the Head of Physics and science co-ordinator has 13 free periods, while the science co-ordinator at Kings Marsh, through not having the designation of 'head', receives no extra time allocation. This contrasts with the extra frees that are designated 'counselling time' for tutors.

While the case of the science department might illustrate the power of the headteacher to 'channel' certain teachers in particular, and somewhat untypical, directions, it also illustrates the strength of some departments to resist managerial moves. Science staff *did* succeed in pressuring the head-teacher into appointing a science 'head', even if only with the modified designation of 'co-ordinator'. But even here there is doubt from the science staff over the nature and reasons behind the particular appointment:

> 'The head promotes heads of department who are useless. We're still waiting for Gillett to earn his money.' (Bernie Hall)

There is a clear sense of antagonism in these comments that indicates a polarization of interest around the departmental academic side and the integrative pastoral side. This appears most pronounced in those subjects that could be said to constitute the academic 'core'. This polarization becomes evident as the threat of integration increases. It might also suggest that the boundary between the academic and the pastoral has not been eroded, so much as redrawn.

An apparent weakening of the strength of the department is also evident in changes in the way the school budget is allocated. At Elmfield, depart-ments are allotted an annual budget which they then distribute according to their own priorities. At Kings Marsh there is no such annual allocation. Financial representations have to be made to senior management, who then set their own priorities. Despite academic specialists' attempts to overturn this strategy through complaints that it is costly and ineffective – inasmuch as it militates against careful budgeting because there is no longer the incentive for departments to be thrifty – they have in this case been unsuccessful.

Similar indicators of attempts to weaken the power of subject depart-ments can be seen through the establishment of a School Policy Advisory Group:

> After consultation with the Senior Management Team I have decided to accept their advice and reduce the number of people invited to attend what was the old Heads of Department Meeting. (Memo on notice board from David Hartnell, headteacher)

Although four departments are explicitly represented (maths, English, CDT and modern languages), the nine other members of the group attend in different capacities, either as year heads or as unspecified senior teachers through which departments can be represented indirectly. This representa-tion might reflect both the extent to which some subject departments have had their power base eroded, and the extent to which four others have retained subject-based executive power.

The substantially weakened position of the head of department can be seen through incorrect and confused identifications. At Elmfield there is little ambiguity of academic position – departmental heads are clearly recognized by staff and pupils. At Kings Marsh, senior academic identity tends to be not so visible. For example, Cynthia Greene and Nigel Taylor, both drama teachers, spend some time discussing who is head of the drama department. Staff often seem to have to think twice over who heads departments. Pupils' identifications are also often inaccurate. Again, though, there is less uncertainty over some departments. Neither staff nor pupils were unsure about who was in charge of maths or modern languages.

Not only has there been a relative weakening of the subject department, and a diminution of both the symbolic and real influence of the departmental head, but there has also been alteration of the criteria that underpin staff hierarchies – both within the management structure of the school as a whole and within individual departments.

At Elmfield, differentiation and stratification of teachers relates to subject-specialist status. With the significant exception of the pastoral deputy, senior post-holders in the management and departmental structure hold specialist subject degrees. Staff with 'applied', 'vocational' qualifications (BEds or CertEds) are positioned lower down the departmental hierarchy and are commonly found within the pastoral team. At Kings Marsh, specialist knowledge and certification do not seem to be as significant in providing the basis for differentiation among staff. The headteacher started his career as a PE teacher; as did all his deputies. Although Mr Hartnell later took a degree in economics, none of his deputies had 'specialist' qualifications at the time of their appointment. Being a PE teacher does not carry the high-status connotations of other subject areas – a reflection of the brawn–brain dichotomy of knowledge. It is surely significant that the headteacher composes his senior management team out of those similarly classified as 'unintellectual' within the dominant values of the academic tradition. It is also worth noting that the head of Years 9, 10 and 11 also happens to be an ex-PE teacher, as does one of his assistants. It could be argued that in attempting to integrate the curriculum, the need for senior management to achieve consensus disqualifies staff whose identity stems from subject specialization. Early socialization into subject specialism, and the concomitant connection between academic status and authority, renders them both unsuitable for, and potentially dangerous in, senior positions. At Kings Marsh, seniority in management may actually relate to *lack* of academic status.

It may at first appear as if the loosening of the connection between specialist degree and senior managerial position could contribute to a more 'open' structure that might enhance and widen career opportunity. This is not necessarily the case. At Kings Marsh, the importance of achieving ideological consensus, at least within senior management, and the resultant homogeneity of this group in terms of background and sporting interest, have resulted in a particularly masculine ethos. Those female staff in senior positions give their gender as the main criterion behind their appointment. These positions seem to have been obtained 'by default' rather than 'earned':

'I started to have a role in senior management when they looked around for experienced women.' (Gwen Langfield)

'They wanted more females.' (Jenny Jordan)

While at Elmfield there is a similar disparity between men and women in managerial positions, there are several women who head departments. Although they may be 'low-status' departments, such as HE or RE, these women are nevertheless able to attend heads of department meetings and allocate their own budget. At Kings Marsh, the erosion of departmental power has resulted in an even greater disparity, with a conspicuous lack of women in policy-making positions. The School Policy Advisory Group, for instance, which replaced the old Heads of Department Group, is composed of eleven men and only two women.

If academic status is not commensurate with seniority in the management structure of Kings Marsh, neither does it necessarily correlate with hierarchical position within subject departments. Although at Kings Marsh position within departments is often related to academic identity, this is not always the case. It is possible, if not to 'head', then at least to 'co-ordinate' departments. Several departmental co-ordinators, such as Matthew Harper of the humanities cluster, have 'vocational' teaching qualifications rather than the more academically acceptable specialist degree and post-graduate teaching certificate.

If subject specialist status does not necessarily imply academic responsibility, neither is the subject in which one was trained necessarily related to the subject which one teaches. Subject status is not, therefore, perceived as fixed and permanent, but changeable. This occurs not only when teachers have to contribute to integrated courses, but also on a wider basis. Many staff teach outside their area of initial specialism. Christopher Lloyd, for instance, started his career as a PE teacher and now only teaches English. Jonathan Murray, again trained as a PE/outdoor pursuits teacher, teaches only maths. James Owen, yet another ex-PE teacher, was soon given a complete science timetable.

At Elmfield, staff with low academic specialist status teach outside their areas to cover lessons which those of higher academic status will not teach. These Elmfield teachers, however, are always contained in the 'lowest' streams, 'low' in terms of both age and perceived ability; the first years, and the non-examination groups. At Kings Marsh this connection between the 'able' specialist teacher and the 'able' pupil is not as strong. 'Out of subject' teachers appear to teach at all levels, from top GCSE groups and into the sixth form. Conversely, teachers with high academic status are obliged to teach low-status students. This can be the cause of resentment among subject specialists who consider both their own and their academic colleagues' sensitivities to be somehow violated through having to share their subject with insensitive, reluctant pupils:

'It's unfair on him [Richard Holland, Head of Modern Languages]. How can you ask a man like him, deeply interested and absorbed in the language and culture, to try and teach it to some of these kids? I mean it's not fair.' (Simon Darby, dance teacher)

The diminished role of the heads of departments and the changed authority basis for senior posts raise theoretical issues over the location and concentration of control within secondary schools: does integration threaten or strengthen centralized control? Bernstein (1977) argues that the erosion of boundaries strengthens horizontal relations between staff, thereby threatening the control of the head, while the regulation of knowledge through a collection code 'points to oligarchic control of the institution' (p. 103). Musgrove, on the other hand, argues that integration will lead to centralization of power within the hands of the head:

> Headmasters who wish to reduce their subordinates' power and increase their own will be wise to abolish subjects and integrate the curriculum. For subjects are centres of power. They are also centres of authority. They help to make up the pluralism of power which is a crucial check on the power of headmasters, principals and vice-chancellors. Autocratic heads of schools and colleges will decry subject boundaries and initiate policies of integration and hybridization. They will be in the forefront of the progressives who attack such obvious and easy targets as 'narrow specialization' and the 'compartmentalization of knowledge'... They will discredit the very concept of a boundary. It is already one of the most disgraceful concepts in education. And in removing boundaries they will remove important and legitimate defences of those within them. Integrated curricula are powerless curricula, wide open to centralized control. They present no effective curb on the will of the man at the top. (Musgrove, 1971, p. 69)

Although there is little evidence from Elmfield to support Musgrove's assertion of 'pluralism' within a subject-based curriculum, it does appear that, at Kings Marsh, the diminution of departmental power has been a significant feature of the ability of the headteacher to introduce, albeit limited, change to the organization of the curriculum.

It is not the case, however, that integrated curricula are 'powerless' in that they offer 'no effective curb on the will of the man at the top'. Integrated curricula must have some shared principle to which all members of staff concede – 'some relational idea, a supra-content concept' (Bernstein, 1977, p. 101). Although the head and senior management may be influential in expressing and prioritizing this principle, they too must adhere to it. The reasons why decisions are made must be visible and explicit: 'the administration and specific acts of teaching are likely to shift from the relative invisibility to visibility' (Bernstein, 1977, p. 104). In order for this to happen, the integration must be structured through a relational concept.

THE INTEGRATIVE CONCEPT

It is hard to identify any single term that could be said to constitute the integrative concept or relational idea. There are, though, two key themes which frequently crop up as significant features of managerial vocabulary – 'professionalism', and 'active learning'. The concept of 'professional' was identified in Chapter 3, as one of the main strands underlying the discourse of pastoral care. 'Active learning' is another integral element of a pedagogy that stresses 'self', a key dimension of the pastoral discourse. The adoption of these principles as a relational concept for the curriculum could be interpreted as an indicator of the extent to which the pastoral, when it is no longer tightly bounded, tends to subsume other curricular categories.

The references to professionalism occur not only in rhetorical statements about school policy but also as a means of evaluating teachers' practices. At staff meetings the headteacher outlines aspects of professional conduct which should be adhered to. Some teachers report being accused of 'unprofessional conduct' by senior management.

'Professionalism' is an interesting concept and has significance in a variety of contexts. At Kings Marsh, the emphasis on professionalism can be interpreted as a means of weakening the scholarly tradition embodied in the collection code. Although much has been written of the relationship between the professionalization of teaching and the growth of occupational control (e.g. Ozga and Lawn, 1981), it is a complex term with a number of connotations, often contradictory. There is one interpretation of the concept 'professional' which puts it in contrast not to that of the 'layman', but to that of 'gentleman' (Wiener, 1981). Thus while the idea of the 'expert' educator may be used to differentiate from the 'inexpert', e.g. the parent, it also can be seen to stand in opposition to the 'scholar'. The 'professional' relationship between the teacher and the student implies a consensual code of conduct – governed by notions of 'sound practice' rather than 'intellectual authority'. The call for teaching staff to be 'professionals' can therefore be seen as a threat to teachers who identify themselves in terms of their academic prowess. The authority that previously stemmed from the erudition of the scholar is usurped by the good practice of the technocrat.

Just as this model of professionalism denies the intellectual authority of the scholar, so the concept 'active learning' challenges both the insularity and exclusiveness of the disciplines. It also has implications for pupil–teacher relations through rejecting perceptions of the pupil as passive learner. It emphasizes the ambiguity of what counts as 'learning' and 'knowledge'. It also usually has cross-curricular dimensions, which will be considered later in the chapter.

Such integrative ideas, however, need to be made explicit and available to all staff – not just senior management. There must be mechanisms for disseminating and gauging support, for socializing staff into the relational concept to prevent fallback into traditional academic values. At Elmfield there are few occasions when the staff assemble for meetings. Meetings are almost always exclusively departmental or pastoral. At Kings Marsh, there is a staff meeting every morning which teachers must attend. Where there are PSD and tutor meetings, again all staff are expected to attend. These meetings provide an important channel for disseminating, and socializing the staff into, the superordinate principle.

The extent to which teachers are successfully socialized will determine the extent to which integration is achieved throughout the curriculum. Not only will integration involve erosion of boundaries and weakening of subject hierarchy, but it must be based on principles that are conceded at all levels to be legitimate. Although academic status may no longer be the principal criterion for hierarchical position, it does not mean that there is no differentiation, rather that such differentiation is underlain by different principles. The extent to which these principles are seen as legitimate is problematic at Kings Marsh. Seniority of position does not necessarily imply seniority of authority.

At Elmfield, status within the academic and the pastoral is assigned on explicit criteria. For the academic, specialist academic qualifications provide the basis for screening and positioning. Within the pastoral side, there is, as discussed, more ambiguity over differentiation. However, it is still possible to relate pastoral responsibility to some publicly conceded criteria – whether of pastoral certification or personal attributes. At the time of Elmfield's amalgamation, when the primacy of the specialized collection code was asserted, those who were transferred were quite clear about the basis of the decision, even if they felt it to be unjustified.

At Kings Marsh, there appear to be no public, explicit criteria underpinning hierarchical position. With the arrival of Paul Hartnell, several staff were moved out of their positions of either pastoral or academic responsibility. Alex Parish, who had been acting Head of English, was given joint responsibility of the library with Frank Weeks, who had been assistant head of house. Mavis Andrews, who had also been assistant head of house, was transferred to examinations. These tended to be the 'older, long-serving staff', who 'weren't tending to get amongst the rest of the staff' (Christopher Lloyd). Henderson, a deputy headteacher, was seconded, according to staff, 'for standing up to the head' (Pete Redman). Vera Reynolds, for example, appears to have been considered 'unsuitable' to be given the responsibility of tutoring or teaching PSD:

> 'John (Stephens) put up a list for people to sign if they wanted to be on the course. We signed and then found he'd already decided who he wanted to be in his team anyway so it didn't seem worth bothering.'

The criteria upon which such decisions are made appear to be unarticulated. It is likely that staff promotions, demotions and transfers are related to the extent to which candidates are seen to support the relational principle. As Bernstein (1977) says, integrated codes 'may require a high level of ideological consensus, and this may affect the recruitment of staff' (p. 107). The problem is, however, that ideological consensus does not currently constitute a publicly legitimate means of positioning. And where staff appear to be positioned according to this criterion, it is not made explicit. Bernstein's claim that the insularity of the collection code results in a degree of 'conspiracy theory' among staff (Bernstein, 1977, p. 103) is not borne out by the data available from Kings Marsh and Elmfield.

The reasons behind staff allocation are quite visible at Elmfield, which can be characterized as representing the collection code. Apart from isolated incidents, or perceived pastoral encroachment, there is little evidence of conspiracy theory amongst staff about senior management. It is at Kings Marsh that conspiracy theory is most clearly articulated. The invisible, but suspected, criteria for promotion are widely seen as partisan and unfair, particularly by those on the academic side:

'It's not what you know, it's who you know.'

'You've got to be one of their team.'

In the following quote, it is clear that seniority is not seen to be commensurate with 'authority'.

'Henderson [the deputy head who was seconded] was an intellectual, so they got rid of him. The head's got a school management team that are very thick. I mean they're none of them what I would call intellectual. The main qualification is to be a football referee... The way he talks to some staff. It's awful. I mean most of them are his intellectual superiors, yet he talks to them like a manager to his football team. I mean, John's a nice enough chap – but he took two bashes to get his MEd. Gwen, she's very good at her job, but she only finished an in-service BEd three years ago.' (Bernie Hall)

Authority is seen to reside in the 'intellect', indicated by academic qualifications. Although senior staff may be either 'a nice enough chap' or even 'very good at her job', these qualities are not seen to provide adequate bases for authority. Where management is not invested with 'authority', it is unlikely that a management-led attempt to redefine the order of school knowledge will gain general consensus. The strong subject socialization of some academic staff may make them resistant to effective resocialization within a different knowledge code. And staff who do not concede to the new ideas constitute a source of danger and subversion. As Bernstein (1977) points out, this is a major problem for schools attempting to restructure themselves through an integrated code: 'Where such ideologies are not shared, the consequences will become visible and threaten the whole at every point' (p. 107).

INNOVATION AND RESISTANCE

Although the strength of the academic may make integration problematic, it does not mean that there has been no change at Kings Marsh. The underlying principles of the pastoral combined with a weakening of the structure of the academic have resulted in knock-on effects throughout the curriculum. Blurring the boundary between the pastoral and the academic will result in a blurring of the boundary between components of the academic.

Since David Hartnell's arrival at Kings Marsh, there have been moves to initiate 'active learning' across the curriculum. Curricular initiatives – TVEI, CPVE, BTEC, the OCEA project – that all tend to express the value of cross-curricular learning and 'experiential' pedagogies have been quickly seized upon.[2]

While at Elmfield it is possible to identify features of 'active learning' contained within tutor work and EPR programmes, at Kings Marsh attempts have been made to broaden its impact. As Jenny Jordan (assistant head of Years 9/10/11) says 'Active learning is the buzzword here.'

'We're practically devising active learning situations. In HE we had ideas. The kids had placards pretending to be nuts and pulses, physically moving around. In science, there was an idea about first years pretend-ing to be light waves. In maths, they did number patterns.' (Christopher Lloyd, head of Years 9/10/11 and Head of PSD)

As with the tutor work, these initiatives are not always taken on board as enthusiastically as their initiators intend. Subject identity can cause resis-tance:

'I don't like doing it [role play]. I'm not a drama teacher.'

Resistance to such intrusion can be seen in the distancing and status scep-ticism seen at Elmfield:

'Staff call it "rocking in pairs". They say "Not rocking in pairs again." A lot are positive; some say "What a load of cobblers".' (Christopher Lloyd)

Although resistance to such initiatives can be found, it is less publicly artic-ulated than at Elmfield. Neither is it the case that the division between resistors and initiators falls as unambiguously either side of the pastoral–academic boundary as at Elmfield. At Kings Marsh, academic specialists also take on board the ideology of 'active learning':

'We use any medium in terms of material, drawing on different areas of experience, drawn by whoever's free at the time – it's that sort of curriculum. It's delivered in a holistic nature. Not knowledge driven – process driven, student access driven. It's active learning enshrined as part of a motivational approach. They should be able to access programmes of study at any level that they want.' (Mark Lear on economic awareness)

It is important to note that the 'student-driven' nature of such approaches marginalizes subject boundaries and teacher specialization. It also raises issues about the whole business of timetabling. As Mark Lear continues:

'The problem is, how do you do lesson plans?'

Community studies is also a cross-curricular initiative. It is interesting to contrast community studies at Elmfield with community studies at Kings Marsh.

At Elmfield, community studies is a timetabled non-examination option for 'less able' pupils, usually girls, who are going into the 'caring profes-sions'. At Kings Marsh, community studies is not bounded within subject categorization. Although it has a 'community tutor', Graham George, his role is to feed in to other areas rather than 'specialize' within his own:

'I'd never want "community studies" as a timetabled subject – I'd resist that tooth and nail. It's for extending the richness of existing subjects. More often subjects do it themselves. The maths department have been doing things on areas. "Let's do houses" – inviting three people, solici-tors, estate agents, the building society. For some subjects, community education is not going to be a major part. Some see no relevance ... for example, physics. I keep a close eye on a subject. I might say, for example, "Have you considered ...?" Some say, "It's not part of my job."

I find out from talking informally to kids. I have contact with kids of most ages.'

It is important to note that by remaining free of timetable demarcation community studies is thereby able to survey and intervene in the academic. So aware is Mr George of the dangers that containment might bring to community studies, that he recognizes even his demarcated presence as a sign of failure:

'I'm not making inroads – because I'm still an extra person on the staff. I've always wanted an integrated approach.'

Limited subject integration is also a feature of Kings Marsh. Unlike at Elmfield, where integrated science is aimed at the lower streams, all pupils take it at Kings Marsh.

'Forget biology – nobody specializes any more.'

Although the science department has not been able to resist these particular policies of senior management, many science staff still identify themselves through their specialism. Even where there may be integration at the level of formal designation, insulation may continue at the level of classroom transmission.

While 'like' subjects are integrated, so are some that are 'unlike'. Art, for instance, has been dissociated from its aesthetic orientation and has been integrated with technology. It is taught in modular units that cover a variety of topics: 'visual awareness', 'technology and society', 'materials'. There is extensive team-teaching, and teachers are expected to teach outside their subject specialism. Within the 'aesthetics' cluster, integration has also occurred. Drama, music and textiles have combined to work around themes such as 'fear'. These integrations can cause problems for staff:

'The overlap of areas is getting confused. It's hard to teach across areas. It's outside my area of understanding.' (Jackie Carpenter, Art)

'It'll only work if you have "aesthetic" teachers. We're not sure how to do it. You tend to think – that'll be the music input, what is the drama input?' (Mandy Price, Drama)

Despite the problems articulated by teachers concerning integration, staff socialization can be considered successful to the extent that perceived failure of integrated courses is usually expressed in terms of problems of training and experience, rather than in terms of any fundamental incompatibility. The mutually exclusive nature of subject specialisms is not given the same emphasis as at Elmfield. Teachers are also more likely to take on board 'social' issues rather than distance themselves from them:

'We always do social themes – but then that's every teacher's goal.' (Mandy Price, Drama)

An example of this boundary crossing is provided by the comments of science teacher, Keith Molton, posted on a graffitied science poster:

'I would like everyone to notice that this poster advertising the senseless destruction of the rain forests has been vandalized by some ill-informed and vulgar graffiti... Many of you will expect me to remove this damaged poster, but I shall leave it as a monument to the ignorant views which, unfortunately, dominate the management of our planet.'

It is inconceivable that this kind of incident would have been treated in this way at Elmfield. Such misbehaviour would have been seen as the province of the pastoral staff, an act of indiscipline, unrelated to and outside the remit of 'science'. The explicit connection between syllabus content, social issue and graffiti indicates the success with which some curricular boundaries have been weakened at Kings Marsh.

It is possible, therefore, to claim that there has been some pastoral–academic integration at Kings Marsh and that the related weakening of the collection code has resulted in ambiguity for some staff over their curricular identity. But to what extent does increased ambiguity in terms of staff identity contribute to a weakening of pupil classification and stratification?

As subject status does not provide the sole basis for staff differentiation, there is a relaxation of the early screening procedures that differentiate pupils. As John Stephens says:

'We blur edges. The curriculum doesn't discriminate. You can't stream kids – maybe eventually but not early.'

If it is the case that 'With specialized education the sheep have to be very quickly separated from the goats and the goats are invested with the attributes of pollution' (Bernstein, 1977, p. 82), then integration, even if only limited, might promote greater flexibility between educational categories, diminishing the rigid demarcation between successes and failures.

At Kings Marsh there is mixed-ability teaching in all subjects until the start of the third year. This is much later than at many schools, particularly for subjects such as maths, where, as at Elmfield, formal screening begins at the point of entry. Although there is 'remedial' identification and provision at Kings Marsh, there is no policy of segregation. Pupils are generally taught within their tutor groups with 'in-class' support being provided. Where exclusion is used it only takes place during English classes, whereas at Elmfield exclusion occurs across the academic curriculum and becomes the all-encompassing dimension of the pupil's educational identity. In many subjects, including at A-level, modular courses have been introduced, in an attempt to 'broaden' the intake. Inclusivity is aimed at rather than exclusivity. Neither is there any formal celebration of the academic through prize-giving, as at Elmfield. The weakening of the boundaries between subjects has also resulted in erosion of subject hierarchy.

At Elmfield, particular subjects are invested with high status that provide the means for differentiating pupils. Linguistic ability is the perceived determinant of general ability and constitutes the basis of banding. This not only reinforces the importance of languages as indicators of ability, but also invests German with the status of being 'difficult'. At Kings Marsh, all pupils may take German from the first year. The choice of language is based on personal preference rather than perceived ability. German at

Kings Marsh is therefore not invested with the attributes of its Elmfield counterpart. It does not constitute, as at Elmfield, the means by which the 'sheep' are separated from the 'goats'. Because subjects are not used to differentiate pupils in the lower school, there are no 'timetable fillers'. Economic awareness, for instance, which has similarities with citizenship at Elmfield, is compulsory for all pupils during their first three years.

The integration and 'dilution' of high-status subjects, particularly science specialisms, has also been matched by the disappearance of traditionally low-status subjects aimed at the lower streams. Rural science and environmental science have both been dropped as 'options' at Kings Marsh in recent years.

Not only has the hierarchy between subjects been weakened, thus eliminating one means through which pupils are categorized, but there has also been an attempt to blur the distinction between high-status 'pure' subject collections and lower-status 'mixed' subject collections.

The move away from the 'specialized' aspect of the collection code, where some subjects are seen to have 'natural' affinities with others, is reflected in the sixth-form prospectus. According to Bernstein, the need to keep educational identity 'pure' within the specialized collection code means that ambiguous combinations are avoided. Mixed, or 'impure', combinations, 'although formally possible, very rarely substantively exist, for pupils are not encouraged to offer – neither does timetabling usually permit – such a combination' (Bernstein, 1977, p. 91). At Kings Marsh, sixth formers who are thinking of specializing in science are advised to consider mixed combinations: 'The division between arts and sciences is not as rigid as you may think. Often a combination of arts and science subjects may provide you with a more suitable, interesting and relevant course' (6th Form booklet). The mixing of categories is not only recommended, but also, for some pupils, unavoidable. Timetabling actually prevents the more traditionally 'pure' and unambiguous collections of subjects from being followed. At A-level, for instance, English clashes with Art. Art also clashes with Theatre Studies and Geography. It is not possible, therefore, to take A-level Theatre Studies with either English or Art.

It is also likely that reduction in academic differentiation of pupils and teachers will affect the relationship between teacher and taught. Integration through weakening the insulation between, and hierarchy within, subjects changes the structuring of transmissions and the authority relations within the classroom:

> If the underlying theory of pedagogy under collection is didactic, then under integration the underlying theory is likely to be self-regulatory. Such a change in emphasis and pedagogy is likely to transform the teacher-pupil–lecturer-student authority relations, and in particular increase the status and thus the rights of the pupil or student. (Bernstein, 1977, p. 83)

It should of course be remembered that although Kings Marsh has made steps towards integration, the curriculum still contains distinct academic areas. However, the move towards the incorporation of 'active learning' within these areas, as well as within the pastoral, could be expected to make a mutual experience of the 'learning situation' more valued than the one-way transmission of bodies of knowledge. The extent to which this is the case is extremely difficult to establish. As at Elmfield, lessons are difficult to access for research – a reflection in itself of the extent to which Kings Marsh has not succeeded in establishing the 'openness' of a fully integrated code.

It is significant, however, that the word 'student' as opposed to 'pupil' is frequently used by both senior management and other staff. Although the word 'student' still retains the status of 'learner', it evokes different connotations. While the term 'pupil' is exceedingly narrow, 'student', maybe through association with tertiary education, implies greater autonomy over the learning situation and expectations of associated behavioural styles of a higher level of sophistication. It also conveys more of a sense of 'client'. As discussed in Chapter 3, the professional–client relation is a key aspect of pastoral care rather than of the academic tradition.

THE LIMITS OF INTEGRATION

From the data and interpretations given above, it might appear that the erosion of the pastoral–academic boundary has led to a restructuring of curriculum practices which will eventually lead to a new regime no longer characterized by differentiation and stratification on academic criteria. However, such a conclusion would be hard to sustain.

That there has been a loss of insularity and consequent weakening of the academic through the erosion of the pastoral–academic boundary at Kings Marsh is undeniable. However, the boundary is maintained inasmuch as there is still a demarcated timetable. And although there has been some integration, it tends to be 'at the fringes' of the academic curriculum. Cross-curricular schemes are mainly operating only in those areas that already have a more ambiguous subject identity – those constructed along the arts/humanities and technology/vocational dimensions. The academic 'core' at Kings Marsh has retained its insularity, and hence its hold on educational identity. It is also possible to suggest that its dominance has actually been increased as a result of partial integration. The 'loss' of subjects at the margins of the academic has resulted in a greater definition for those that remain intact. The academic becomes more streamlined and stands in clearer opposition than hitherto.

There is certainly no evidence to suggest that students are less differentiated and stratified. Indeed, such partial integration seems to result in pupils' educational identities being even more unambiguously defined than at Elmfield. Although there is no formal public screening and resultant segregation of pupils in the lower years, at 'options' stage (the end of Year 9) Kings Marsh operates a process of 'sifting' in which the resultant categories of pupils are more visibly demarcated than at Elmfield. At Elmfield, pupils are screened and segregated at a very early stage, in terms of both general 'bands' and particular 'sets':

A particular status in a given collection is made clear by streaming and/or a delicate system of grading. One nearly always knows the social significance of where one is, and, in particular, *who* one is, with each advance in the educational career. (Bernstein, 1977, p. 95; his emphasis)

For Elmfield pupils there is little ambiguity over which category they belong to, and this category is assigned early. However, as the pupil progresses through the school, this categorization becomes less visible. At 'options' stage, a range of subjects at a range of levels allows for a remixing of categories. This remixing may be possible within the collection code simply because pupils' academic identity has already been established. Even in the sixth form, although there are two 'classes' of pupils, CPVE and A-level, these classes are mixed for tutor times, and they share rooms and resources.

At Kings Marsh the lack of early categorization contrasts with a marked differentiation of pupils at the start of Year 10. Pupils are then divided into 'GCSE students' and 'BTEC students'. These 'BTEC students' constitute a far more visible collective category than their Elmfield counterparts. They have 'BTEC lessons', in 'BTEC groups', with 'BTEC teachers'. Even in other areas, such as art or PSD where the pupil categories are mixed, they are given a BTEC identity:

'I've got seven BTEC students in my group.'

'In my art class, half of them are BTEC students and the other half normal. It's a very difficult group.'

To be a 'BTEC student' is therefore to be given a distinct and differentiated identity, defined in opposition to the hidden referent of 'normal'.

At A-level this differentiation again remains more visible than at Elmfield. As at Elmfield, there are both CPVE students and A-level students. But at Kings Marsh they are segregated for most of their 'non-academic' time as well – tutorial and PSD sessions. They have different tutors and tutor rooms.

In conclusion, even at Kings Marsh, the academic domain still constitutes the cornerstone of educational identity. Its continuing dominance in the face of coherent and continuing attempts to erode it from a united senior management group reveals the strength of resistance it can muster. This raises all kinds of issues concerning the ability of curricular modes to reformulate and reproduce themselves.

From the data available at Kings Marsh, it is clear that curriculum 'control' is not simply a case of managerial decision-making. And if it does not lie in the hands of senior management, it can hardly be argued that it emanates from teachers lower down the hierarchy. Although they may resist managerial moves, they could not do so without drawing on a wider and deeper resource. Nor can it be argued that external assessment procedures are the sole cause of the failure of educational innovations.[3] While the structure and degree of specialization in school examinations reflect the power of higher education to continue to define what counts as 'proper' school knowledge (Whitty, 1985), it also reflects/reinforces a deeply held conviction that school subjects are the *only* valid way of organizing the curriculum. The potency of this conviction is generated through opposition. The authority invested in the academic domain does not stem from individual capability or external constraint. It is derived from the 'non-academicness' attributed to other forms of knowledge. The boundary surrounding the academic at Kings Marsh has been eroded at its weakest points, notably those where there may be ambiguity in a subject. Although such a blurring of boundaries signals some loss to the academic, it may only be peripheral and superficial. Indeed, it is possible to argue that such partial integration has resulted in a redrawing of the boundary within which the academic is reformulated as more sharply defined, and therefore more powerful, than ever.

NOTES

1. At Kings Marsh, the word 'faculty' is avoided as too rigid and demarcatory. Subjects are put together as 'clusters'.
2. In addition, and unlike at Elmfield, staff at Kings Marsh appear to engage with the contemporary debates around educational policy. At the time of the fieldwork, the timetable had already been restructured to ease the introduction of the core and foundation subjects in the National Curriculum even though it was to be some time before this became necessary at this level. Several members of staff were liaising with each other on the ways in which the cross-curricular elements could be incorporated. Indeed, shortly after my fieldwork finished I heard that the school was seriously considering grant-maintained status.
3. Integrated science, for instance, is no longer a non-examination, or 'foundation', course. It offers many pupils the equivalent of two GCSEs. But this equivalence is only nominal. A double integrated science GCSE does not have the same academic cachet as two specialist science GCSEs.

CHAPTER 9

The pastoral and the academic: curriculum theory and professional practice

At the beginning of this book, I argued that a critical analysis of pastoral care has potentially important implications for curriculum theory and professional practice. This chapter, through reviewing and extending arguments developed in earlier chapters, considers some of these implications. Discussion of the limits and possibilities of pastoral care is especially important in the light of the current policy context. The National Curriculum, in particular, would appear to present advocates of pastoral care with new challenges to their attempts to transform students' experience of schooling. And while there is no simple relationship between the realms of curriculum theory and professional practice, unless those involved with pastoral care take on board the political dimensions of the context into which it has been inserted, any attempts to change the curriculum will surely falter.

PASTORAL CARE AND CURRICULUM THEORY

This book has argued that research into the emergence, expansion and significance of pastoral care reveals processes and outcomes which are complex and contradictory. These processes render any simple and uni-dimensional accounts of curricular change and continuity unsatisfactory. This section considers some of the complexities which have emerged in this analysis and which need to be taken on board if theorizations of curricular change are to achieve some degree of explanatory adequacy.

More specifically, the task of analysing pastoral care has highlighted the importance of dealing with the complex construction of the curriculum as a whole, rather than focusing on individual elements in isolation. It has also revealed the need for theorizations of curricular change to link broader socio-historical context with more immediate circumstance. In addition, this analysis of pastoral care demonstrates that the *intrinsic* features of innovations should be explored, rather than simply seen as channels for external forces. Finally, any satisfactory understanding of the significance of curricular change and continuity should not interpret the outcomes of interventions as arising out of their imputed functions, whether these are attributed to institutional imperatives or professional agendas.

Curricular elements and relationships

As we have seen, many educational commentators and analysts have expressed opinions about pastoral care. These are often hostile, stressing its 'social engineering' or 'social control' attributes. Sometimes they can be more favourably disposed towards pastoral care, holding out for its reforming potential. In all these cases, however, pastoral care is presented as a discrete element, and the significance of its oppositional relationship with the academic side of the curriculum overlooked. Yet it is only through looking at this opposition that we can make sense of the emergence of pastoral care at all – let alone begin to explore its significance.

Pastoral care is not something that has been 'tacked on' to a collection of school subjects. Indeed, the compartmentalization of social, personal and moral issues within the pastoral domain has only been made possible by a reformulation of the academic dimension. Similarly, the incorporation and expansion of pastoral care within secondary schools needs to be understood in terms of its complex relationship with school subjects.

It is through problematizing the demarcation between the pastoral and the academic that it is possible to see that the distinction between the two dimensions does not lie in their attributes of morality or value-neutrality, but in their *contrasting* underlying principles. Furthermore, it is these contrasts which account for the tension, conflict and contradictory outcomes of pastoral care. In short, the case of pastoral care reveals the importance of moving beyond the analysis of isolated curricular elements and focusing on 'the principle by which certain periods of time and their contents are brought into a special relationship with each other' (Bernstein, 1977, p. 79).

Broad trends and immediate circumstances

Problematizing the classification of pastoral care also directs attention to the socio-historical conditions which surround its emergence and expansion. However, in focusing on these conditions it is clear that we need to accommodate both general trend and fine-grained detail. Neither on its own offers adequate explanation.

For instance, accounts which relate the growth of pastoral care to the development of capitalism are not only theoretically problematic, but are empirically weak. Such 'grand theories' cannot account for the specificities which surround the emergence of pastoral care. Why is it only a feature of secondary education? And why did it spread so rapidly in the 1960s and 1970s?

On the other hand, less grand accounts which look only at immediate circumstances are similarly unsatisfactory. The rapid and extensive institutionalization of pastoral care during the introduction of comprehensive schools has to be more than coincidental. Yet no specific feature of secondary school reorganization can explain the reformulation of the academic or the institutional tensions which heralded the appearance of pastoral care. What is needed is an explanatory framework which can encompass long-term social process without ignoring detail.

Of course, there is nothing original in such a request. As Bernstein (1977) argues: 'All would agree that an exciting sociological account should be comparative and historical and should reveal the relationships between structural features and interactional practices in a context of change' (p. 159). While the task of obtaining such an account is not simple, what has become clear from this study is the inadequacy of understanding change solely in terms of external forces. It is not only, as we have seen, difficult to decide which conditions are most significant and which merely peripheral, but it is also hard to understand change in the absence of any analysis of what it is that is changing.

External conditions and internal properties

As Donald (1985) argues, the explication of change requires more than the identification of the conditions through which it is signified. We need to know not just when it occurred, but why it took that particular form. In addressing these issues, we should look at internal dynamics as much as at external forces. For instance, in relation to the institutional appearance of pastoral care, we need to know what it was about the academic domain that made such an oppositional category possible. We need to explore what possibilities pastoral care made available.

Although the relationship between external force and intrinsic property is complex, the institutional incorporation of pastoral care in the 1960s and 1970s shows that one cannot be reduced to the other. This book has argued that pastoral care developed in response to the need to resolve tensions embodied within the new system of schooling. However, a key aspect of this resolution lay not just in external imperatives but in the developing discourse and features of pastoral care itself. The pastoral emphasis on the 'whole child' provided a means by which the segregative, hierarchical academic dimension and the integrative egalitarianism of the comprehensive spirit could be reconciled.

The importance of looking at the intrinsic properties of educational discourses means moving beyond many theories of social and cultural reproduction. Most of these 'are concerned only to understand how external power relations are *carried* by the system, they are not concerned with the description of the carrier, only with a diagnosis of its pathology' (Bernstein, 1990, p. 172, his emphasis). Rather than read off curricular changes from the wider social setting as so much of the sociology of education has done, it might be more appropriate to empirically explore them as representations in their own right – to focus on underpinnings rather than overbearance.

Functions and consequences

Just as we cannot explain the emergence of pastoral care in terms of external forces, neither should we infer that its consequences bear any relation to functions. This discrepancy has been evident in many places in this book, in relation to: the growing tension between the pastoral and the academic; the consequences of curricular integration; and the messages which emanate from the pastoral–academic boundary.

For instance, the claim that pastoral care arose in response to the need to reconcile problems within comprehensive schooling should not be taken to indicate that it *does* in fact accommodate academic interests. Such an assumption would make no sense of the evident tension and antagonism between the pastoral and the academic, nor of the concern expressed by advocates of the subject-centred curriculum that pastoral care encroaches on the 'real business' of schooling. Pastoral care provides a clear example of how discourses can extend beyond authorial control (Donzelot, 1979). Far from accommodating and servicing the academic, the discourse of pastoral care now poses a challenge. It has undergone expansion, sophistication and professionalization. Drawing from alternative ideologies of schooling, the discourse of pastoral care embodies a pedagogy that stands in opposition to that which prevails within the academic dimension of the curriculum.

Just as one cannot read off the significance of pastoral care from institutional imperatives, neither can one presume that its outcomes will bear any relation to the intentions of its practitioners. As we saw in Chapter 6, the pastoral attempt to reward personal effort is subverted by the oppositional relationship that exists between the pastoral and the academic. The pastoral intention of counteracting the harsh differentiation of academic achievement rebounds. Similar contradictory outcomes are evident in the attempted integration between the pastoral and the academic at Kings Marsh. As discussed in Chapter 8, although integration has blurred the boundaries of some school subjects, it seems to have contributed to a greater coherence and insulation of the academic dimension at its 'core'. Indeed, the removal of pupil segregation procedures in the early years may result in more clear-cut and unambiguous demarcations of educational identity being established later on.

It is important to note that these processes should again not be accounted for solely in terms of external forces. Dale (1989), for instance, claims that the irreconcilable contradictions felt at 'every level of the education system, from national policy making to PTA meetings' (p. 49) stem from the irreconcilable contradictions of state and capital. In the case of pastoral care, however, contradictory outcomes emanate from the tensions and contradictions inherent in their oppositional pedagogic principles as much as from the irresolvable demands of capitalism.

PASTORAL CARE AND PROFESSIONAL PRACTICE

It might appear as if the account of pastoral care provided in this book offers little scope for teachers to use pastoral care as a means of reforming the curriculum. Indeed, it has been argued not only that pastoral care has been marginalized by school subjects, but that even concerted efforts to reduce the negative consequences of academic stratification have rebounded. The case of Kings Marsh offers little hope to prospective integrationists either. It is suggested that partial integration may strengthen the academic core even further. Moreover, analysis of pastoral practices suggests that pedagogic limitations are likely to render pastoral care at worst reproductive, and at best ineffective.

It is true that this book is not optimistic about the potential of pastoral care to reform the curriculum, certainly as it is currently structured. However, neither should it be read as wholly pessimistic. While advocates might be naïve to claim that pastoral care holds endless possibilities for curriculum change, they are surely correct in recognizing that its non-subject-based structure and lack of assessment procedures lend it more opportunities than other areas of the curriculum. It is certainly hard to see how school subjects can provide space for alternative and critical educational practices. As a number of studies have revealed (e.g. Layton, 1973; Whitty, 1985), reformist and radical intentions tend to be sacrificed in the struggle to gain academic respectability. Initial missionary enthusiasm is successively replaced by a process of emergent specialization and then, ultimately, full establishment as a tradition into which students are initiated – 'their attitudes approaching passivity and resignation, a prelude to disenchantment' (Layton, 1972, p. 11). As Goodson (1983) argues, the process of 'becoming a school subject' involves the marginalization of pedagogic or utilitarian values.

Pastoral care cannot travel down this route. It does not strive for academic respectability, and has few objectives other than pedagogic and utilitarian ends. However, while the shape and content of pastoral care mean that it will not share the same fate as subject-based reform movements, it is not at all clear what potential it has, and how this might be realized. The next section considers the possibilities of pastoral care as currently constituted, and future strategies in the context of the curriculum, and more specifically, in the context of the National Curriculum.

Pastoral care as egalitarian education

It has been argued in this book that the boundary between the pastoral and the academic serves to uphold the dominance of school subjects. It endorses discipline-based claims to impartiality and exclusivity that give the academic dimension the authority to differentiate and stratify staff and students. These arguments might lead one to suggest that pastoral care offers a 'potential code for egalitarian education' (Bernstein, 1977, p. 110). However, although it is possible only to conjecture on the consequences of a pastorally inspired curriculum, it seems unlikely that it would remove differentiation and stratification.

While a diminution of the power of school subjects will result in a reformulation of the foundations upon which educational identities are currently constructed, it does not follow that academic criteria constitute the only possible means of differentiation and stratification. Although pastoral care is underpinned by contrasting principles to those of the academic, it too is rule-governed. And these rules would have to be acquired. As Bernstein argues:

> In any pedagogic relationship the transmitter has to learn to be a transmitter and the acquirer has to learn to be an acquirer. When you go to the doctor you have to learn how to be a patient. It is no good going to the doctor and saying 'I feel really bad today, everything is really grey.' He says, 'Don't waste my time,' because he has many patients. 'Where's

the pain? How long have you had it? What kind of pain is it? Is it acute? Is it sharp? Is it persistent?' After a bit you learn how to talk to your doctor. He teaches you to be an acquirer. (Bernstein, 1990, p. 65)

If a curriculum were to be based on principles of a pastoral nature, school children would have to learn to be 'tutees' rather than 'pupils'. There would be a fundamental change in the structuring of school space and time and a concomitant reduction in the insulation, and therefore the power, of the academic. In instances where such integration extended beneath the surface, it may be that failure to meet academically defined criteria would no longer constitute educational ineptitude. In fact it may be that submission to academic authority might be perceived as a sign of incompetence: children who hold their arms around their work might be 'insecure', those who sit in silence to listen might be 'withdrawn', and those who ask for extra work might be 'obsessive'. In order to be competent tutees, students must understand the rules of the pastoral pedagogic encounter, and these rules are not universally available or accessible. Tutees must know how to present themselves as 'individuals'; they must know which bits they should disclose to their tutors and which bits should remain hidden. They cannot withdraw entirely. For many pupils their inability to acquire the rules may result in them being categorized as 'non-cooperative' and 'badly adjusted'. Of invisible pedagogy in general, Bernstein claims that it 'is likely to create a pedagogic code intrinsically more difficult, initially at least, for disadvantaged social groups ... to read and control' (1990, p.79). If Bernstein is correct then it seems unlikely that any curriculum integrated on pastoral principles would result in any significant difference in existing patterns of stratification amongst pupils.[1]

However, the inability of pastoral care to redistribute educational outcomes does not mean that it has no potential to change students' experience of schooling. Indeed, if interrupting entrenched patterns of inequality is the only criterion of successful interventions, then it is hard to think of any educational practices which score well. Pastoral care may contribute to other forms of empowerment through providing students with alternative and critical learning opportunities which challenge prevailing practices and social structures.

Pastoral care and pupil empowerment

For schools to provide critical learning experiences, Whitty (1985) argues that it is necessary for them to afford opportunities through which students can make meaningful connections between school knowledge and everyday knowledge. One strategy would be to formulate

an approach to social and political education that is neither merely 'relevant' in a narrow sense nor merely 'academic' in its content. Rather, it would need to make sense to pupils in terms of their actual or potential experience outside the classroom but also involve critical reflection upon that experience and involvement in the strategies that might change it. (Whitty, 1985, p. 164)

At that time, Whitty claimed that it was areas such as community studies and humanities programmes that held out the most promise for such an approach. However, this research, and subsequent policy developments, indicate that these are not likely to be fruitful areas. As we have seen at Elmfield, subjects such as community studies are frequently targeted at less able students. This only further endorses the association between relevance and lack of academic status. Integrated humanities is a higher-status academic area, but this means it experiences the tension between relevance and academic respectability more acutely. Moreover, while the introduction of the subject-dominated and tightly timetabled National Curriculum, together with its various assessment procedures, may not have debarred alternative and innovative curriculum projects, it has made their occurrence less likely. As Whitty and Kirton (1995) argue, it 'heralded a curriculum straitjacket from which even the most committed progressive humanities teacher might find it difficult to escape' (p. 12). And although subsequent modifications to the National Curriculum (Dearing, 1993) provide more scope for manoeuvre, it is hard to foresee the introduction of extensive programmes of academic integration in the current climate of educational conservatism and cultural restorationism (Ball, 1993).

It may be that pastoral care provides a more appropriate vehicle for pupil empowerment. Indeed, some of its pedagogic principles already offer opportunities for students to begin to make meaningful and critical connections. For instance, pastoral care attempts to break down the barriers between school and pupil knowledge. As we saw in Chapters 3 and 5, it takes as its starting point the experience of the student. Also, while it is certainly the case that there are stereotype-affirming messages in pastoral transmissions, these may be less pervasive than those found in other areas of the curriculum. Given that pastoral care is not based on principles which uphold the impregnability of school knowledge, it could be argued that it provides a channel for these same distorted messages to be exposed and counteracted. Indeed, the principles of the pedagogy invite challenges to stereotyping.

There are, as we have seen, a number of difficulties with pastoral care which would need to be addressed. Two, in particular, seem to be important but also intractable. One relates to the structuring of pastoral pedagogy and the other to the oppositional relationship between pastoral care and the academic domain.

As I have argued in Chapter 5, the principles of pastoral pedagogy are limiting. In challenging such stereotyping and asking students to make meaningful connections between their own experiences, it is necessary to move beyond liberal humanism, in which prejudices are presented as divorced from the economic, political and social basis of their construction. In order to do this, pastoral care may have to be based on modified pedagogic principles. It would certainly have to move beyond analogy, metaphor and parable as the key learning devices.

Even more problematic, however, is the oppositional relationship between the academic and the pastoral. As we have seen, so long as the academic domain can contain and marginalize pastoral concerns, subject specialisms will be able to preserve their territory. Furthermore, it has also been argued that the existence of the pastoral–academic boundary provides an oppositional basis from which the academic can generate even more of the exclusivity from which it partly derives its authority.

Although it is hard to see how pastoral care alone can escape from this self-defeating position, it may be more powerful if it forms alliances with other marginalized and ambiguous elements of the curriculum. The curriculum is constructed along not one continuum of opposition, but many. There are, for instance, connections to be made between pastoral care and aspects of vocational education. Inasmuch as the discourse of pastoral care rejects any narrow classification and fragmentation of 'individuals', and stresses the importance of intrinsic self-fulfilment over extrinsic reward, it could be argued that the two areas exist in opposition. However, vocational education, like pastoral care, challenges the social order of academic disciplines. As presently conceived, it too is based on 'experientialism in which there is no concept of knowledge' (Spours and Young, 1990, p. 60). As Ball demonstrates, advocates of these approaches, which he terms 'vocational progressivism', have reacted against the 'narrow, abstract, academic, élitist nature of knowledge and teaching predominant in British schools since the nineteenth century' (1990, p. 102).

The National Curriculum might also offer scope for alliances. In some ways it will undoubtedly constrain pastoral care provision. Allder (1992) claims that the pressures of the National Curriculum, together with changes in school management, are likely to threaten many middle-management pastoral posts. Indeed, she questions whether pastoral care staff have any future in comprehensive schools. But the National Curriculum also offers opportunities. As discussed below, pastoral care might be able to exploit some of the tensions within it.

Pastoral care and the National Curriculum

Although many claim that the National Curriculum represents the 'reconstitution of subjects' (Goodson, 1990) and is essentially 'traditionalist' and 'academist' (Coulby, 1989), this is only partly true. While the emphasis on 'core' and 'foundation subjects' does underscore the dominance of the subject-centred approach, guidance from the National Curriculum Council (NCC, 1989) argues the necessity of cross-curricular elements. These are classified as: cross-curricular themes, including 'health education' and 'citizenship'; cross-curricular dimensions, such as 'equal opportunities', 'preparation for life' and 'personal and social education'; and cross-curricular skills, for instance 'communication' and 'problem-solving'.

Although these cross-curricular elements have been overlooked in subsequent guidance and legislation, they are nonetheless likely to be a source of tension within the curriculum. There is, for instance, nothing to stop the core and foundation subjects being written around the cross-curricular themes. And although such an occurrence is likely, at best, to be rare, given the radical shift in curriculum design that this would entail and the consolidation of power embedded within the insularity of subjects, cross-curricular elements provide official recognition of the limitations of educating through subjects. As Whitty *et al.* point out, they were partly a response to criticisms of the narrowly subject-based curriculum as being an inadequate preparation for the world beyond school. In a sense, the invention of cross-curricular themes was predicated on the belief that pupils needed to be able to synthesise learning from a range of different subjects and apply this to life beyond the school. (Whitty *et al.*, 1994, p. 34)

There are useful connections between cross-curricular elements and pastoral care. Firstly, they cover many areas that are frequently deemed to fall within the remit of pastoral care. Secondly, they share a similar approach to learning. Many of the areas that are now classified as cross-curricular elements, such as health education and careers education and guidance, are 'associated with innovative pedagogical practice – process-based, skills-based and issue-based approaches' (Halpin and Whitty, 1992, p. 108), in other words drawing on the rules of invisible pedagogy that underlie pastoral care.

They also suffer the same problems of marginalization and compartmentalization. Whitty *et al.* (1994) show that although the various cross-curricular themes were distributed differently throughout the curriculum, there was generally very little synthesis between the more experiential approaches of the cross-curricular elements and the knowledge-led subjects. They attribute this absence to differences in the discursive features of cross-curricular themes and school subjects. This echoes the contrast between the pedagogic principles of the pastoral and the academic identified in this book. Discussion of the potential which PSE might hold for pupil empowerment also raises dilemmas which confront pastoral care: 'The issue is whether PSE could be "reconstituted" without either becoming another conventional subject or dissolving the pedagogic context altogether' (Whitty *et al.*, 1994, p. 38).

The parallels between cross-curricular themes and pastoral care might not only provide the basis for useful comparison, but also afford points of common interest which could be used to obtain greater control over the academic subject-centred domain. It should, of course, be remembered that these common interests will probably share a common ownership. Teachers who support learning in cross-curricular contexts, be they pastorally based or National Curriculum inspired, are not likely to have high academic status. And diminishing the power of subject specialists will require more than missionary zeal and shared commitment.

CONCLUSION

This book has focused on the development, practice and significance of pastoral care. In brief, it has suggested that the oppositional relationship between pastoral care and school subjects protects and perpetuates the authority of the academic domain as the cornerstone of educational identity. However, this argument rests on a number of simplifications which need more fine-grained analysis.

For instance, the relationship between the pastoral and the academic is not the only opposition through which educational identities are produced.

Within this analysis, there has also been a tendency to homogenize and reify the 'pastoral' and the 'academic'. And while I have argued that the internal dynamics of the pedagogic discourses should be considered in their own right, they are, of course, located in a wider social context. The pastoral and academic domains are not free-standing. They are also social communities which are inevitably interwoven with social interests.

Thus, while the 'conventional wisdom' of pastoral care has long since been debunked (Best *et al.*, 1977), further critical explorations are badly needed. In relation to pastoral care, we are still some way from answering the question posed at the beginning of this book: 'How does this management of knowledge institute a complex pattern of cultural difference?' (Donald, 1985, p. 238).

NOTE

1. The extent to which such integration would selectively benefit fractions of the middle class is an issue, however. If Bernstein (1990) is correct in his social class assumptions of visible and invisible pedagogies, children of parents who stand in direct relation to symbolic production and indirect relation to 'material' production will be relatively advantaged by such an integrated curriculum, over and above their middle-class counterparts who stand in a direct relation to 'material' production.

APPENDIX 1

Elmfield School

STAFF LIST

		Main academic subject specialism	Key pastoral/ administrative responsibility
CH	Miss C. Howard		Headteacher
MA	Mr Martin Alcock	CDT	Deputy Headteacher
GA	Mr Graham Anstey	Head of History and Humanities Faculty Co-ordinator	Year 8 tutor
PB	Miss Pauline Bradley	Maths (probationer)	
CB	Miss Caroline Britain	French and German	Year 10 tutor
EC	Miss Eileen Chandler	Housecraft and Head of Needlework	Year 8 tutor
LC	Mrs Linda Chappell	Girls' PE	Year 9 tutor
TC	Mr Tim Cornish	Head of Geography	Year 10 tutor
MC	Mrs Margaret Costello	Head of German and Modern Language Faculty Co-ordinator	Year 9 tutor
JC	Miss Joyce Cox	Art	Year 10 tutor
SD	Mrs Susan Daniels	Geography	Director of Sixth Form
CD	Mr Colin Derrick	English	Year 9 tutor
BD	Mr Bob Dewar	Head of Boys' PE	Year 11 tutor
AD	Mr Andrew Diamond	Head of Biology	Year 10 tutor
BD	Mrs Birgit Drake	German	Sixth-form tutor
PE	Mr Philip Easterbrook	English	Deputy Head
GE	Mr Gareth Evans	Head of Physics and Science Faculty Co-ordinator	Year 11 tutor
LE	Miss Louise Ewan	Head of Music	Sixth-form tutor
PF	Mrs Penny Ferguson	Head of HE and Creative Faculty	Year 11 tutor
AG	Mrs Anna Gardener	Science	Year 10 tutor
BG	Mrs Barbara Gibson	Maths	Year 9 tutor

		Main academic subject specialism	Key pastoral/ administrative responsibility
VG	Miss Valerie Goddard	French	Year 8 tutor
JH	Mrs Julia Harding	English	Sixth-form tutor
TH	Mr Tony Haskins	Commerce, Economics, Law	Year 10 tutor
RH	Mr Reg Hawker	Science	Head of Year 9
PH	Mr Patrick Hillman	Head of CDT	Year 11 tutor
SH	Mrs Sarah Hughes	History and French	Year 8 tutor
BH	Mr Basil Hunt	Maths	Head of Year 7 and teacher in charge of lower school
NJ	Mr Neil Jennings	Head of French	Year 9 tutor
JK	Mrs Janice Kemp	RS	Year 7 tutor
RK	Mr Roger Knowles	CDT	Year 11 tutor
IL	Mr Ian Loveless	English and Head of Remedial Education	Year 7 tutor
AM	Mr Alec MacDonald	Head of Chemistry	Year 11 tutor
HM	Mrs Helen Madden	Maths	Deputy Headteacher
MM	Mrs Maureen McColl	History	Head of Year 10 and teacher in charge of upper school
RM	Mr Ron Morris	Science	Year 11 tutor
JN	Mrs Judith Norton	Typing and General Studies	Year 10 tutor
DP	Mrs Dorothy Parfitt	Drama	Year 9 tutor
HP	Mr Henry Perrett	Geography	Head of Year 11
WP	Mr William Perry	English Faculty Co-ordinator	Year 10 tutor
RP	Mr Ray Pimm	Boys' PE	
IP	Mrs Irene Platt	Geography and Careers Head of Careers	
SR	Mr Simon Reed	Science, CPVE, EPR	Sixth-form tutor
UR	Mrs Una Roberts	Head of Girls' PE	Year 7 tutor
GR	Mrs Gwen Robertson	HE	Sixth-form tutor
JS	Miss Jane Schroder	Sociology, Business Studies and Head of Sociology and Citizenship	Sixth-form tutor
RS	Ms Rebecca Scoggins	Maths (probationer)	
PS	Mr Paul Seymour	Head of Maths and Faculty of Maths Co-ordinator	Year 10 tutor
AS	Mr Alistair Silcox	CDT	Year 8 tutor
SS	Mrs Shirley Skinner	Computer Studies and Head of Computers	Year 11 tutor
KS	Mr Kevin Smart	Art, CDT	Year 8 tutor
BS	Mrs Brenda Stone	Science (HE), PT Supply	
JT	Mrs Jean Taylor	RS and Community Studies and Head of RE	Year 7 tutor
CT	Mrs Carol Thompson	Maths, PT Supply	
WT	Mrs Wendy Tozer	English	Year 7 tutor

		Main academic subject specialism	*Key pastoral/ administrative responsibility*
MU	Mrs Marilyn Upton	English	Year 9 tutor
MV	Mrs Marjorie Voisey	PT Home Economics	
MW	Mrs Mary Wade	Maths	Year 8 tutor
SW	Mr Steve Woods	PE, Maths, Geography	Head of Year 8
BC	Mrs Brenda Champion	Education Welfare Officer	
ES	Ms Eleanor Simpson	Educational Psychologist	

Kings Marsh School

STAFF LIST

		Main academic subject specialism	Key pastoral/ administrative responsibility
DH	Mr David Hartnell	PE/Economics	Headteacher
MA	Mrs Mavis Andrews	Textiles	
FA	Mr Frank Arnold	Maths	Year 11 tutor
EB	Mrs Evelyn Barnes	Languages	Year 12 tutor
HB	Mrs Heather Booth	Special Needs	Year 8 tutor
DB	Mr David Briars	English	Year 10 tutor
SB	Ms Stella Bromley	Business Studies, Humanities	Year 10 tutor
JC	Ms Jackie Carpenter	Art	Year 10 tutor
AC	Miss Anne Clements	Languages	Year 11 tutor
NC	Mr Nigel Coles	Business Studies	Year 10 tutor
MC	Mrs May Cox	Business Studies	Year 9 tutor
SD	Dr Simon Darby	Head of Dance	
BD	Mr Brian Dowling	Head of English	Year 13 tutor
PD	Mr Peter Duffy	CDT	
BF	Mr Brian Findlow	CDT	Year 10 tutor
CF	Mr Chris Flavin	PE	Year 9 tutor
GF	Mrs Gillian Ford	Head of Maths	Year 10 tutor
JF	Mr Jack Ford	Head of BTEC	Deputy Head
PF	Mr Patrick Foster	Science	Year 7 tutor
GG	Mr Graham George	Community Education Officer	
MG	Mr Mike Gillett	Head of Science	Year 7 tutor
TG	Mr Tom Glover	Head of Business Studies	Year 13 tutor
SG	Mrs Sue Goldsmith	Maths	Year 9 tutor
CG	Ms Cynthia Green	Drama/Dance	Year 8 tutor
JG	Mr James Gwynn	English	Year 8 tutor
BH	Mr Bernie Hall	Head of Careers	
MH	Mr Matthew Harper	Humanities	Year 9 tutor

		Main academic subject specialism	Key pastoral/ administrative responsibility
CH	Miss Carole Hawk	Maths	Year 9 tutor
SH	Mrs Sue Hegarty	CPVE	Year 12 tutor
JH	Ms Julie Hemmings	Acting Head of PE	Year 7 tutor
RH	Mr Richard Holland	Head of Languages	
BJ	Mrs Barbara Jones	Head of HE	Year 10 tutor
JJ	Ms Jenny Jordan	English	Assistant Head of Years 9/10/11
RK	Mrs Rachel Keene	PE	Assistant Head of Years 9/10/11
PK	Mrs Paula King	English	
FK	Mr Fred Knowles	Special Needs	Year 9 tutor
GL	Mrs Gwen Langfield	Head of Special Needs	Deputy Head
ML	Mr Mark Lear	Economics	Year 11 tutor
RL	Mr Ronald Leigh	Maths	Year 9 tutor
CL	Mr Christopher Lloyd	English and Head of PSD	Head of Years 9/10/11
JMc	Mrs Jane McCann	Head of Art	Year 8 tutor
HM	Mr Hugh Mason	Business Studies	Year 12 tutor
NM	Mr Neil Metcalf	Head of CDT	Year 11 tutor
MM	Mrs Maureen Milton	Special Needs	Year 7 tutor
LM	Miss Lucy Mitchell	HE	Year 7 tutor
KM	Mr Keith Molton	Science	Year 10 tutor
JM	Mr Jonathan Murray	Maths	Year 9/10/11 tutor
SN	Mrs Sally Newman	HE	Year 9 tutor
DN	Mrs Doreen Norman	Science	Year 11 tutor
JO	Mr James Owen	Science	
AP	Mr Alex Parish	English	
RP	Mrs Ruth Pearce	Maths	Year 8 tutor
MP	Mrs Mandy Price	Head of Drama and Aesthetics Co-ordinator	Head of Year 8
PR	Mr Peter Redman	Science	Head of Year 7
VR	Miss Vera Reynolds	Humanities	
SR	Ms Sarah Richards	Languages	Year 11 tutor
MS	Ms Martine Schmidt	Languages	Year 7 tutor
DS	Mr David Scott	CDT	Year 13 tutor
RS	Mr Roger Simpson	Science	Year 12 tutor
ES	Mrs Eileen Spencer	Music	
JS	Mr John Stephens		Deputy Head
RT	Mr Ron Taplin	Geography	Year 8 tutor
NT	Mr Nigel Taylor	Drama	Head of Year 11/12
DT	Mr Dennis Thomas	Computer Studies	Year 11 tutor
PT	Mr Paul Thorne	Art	Year 11 tutor
SW	Mr Stuart Warner	Humanities	Year 12 tutor
JW	Mrs Joy Warren	Languages	
CW	Mrs Christine Watford	Special Needs	
FW	Mr Frank Weeks	Humanities	
NW	Mr Nelson Wheeler	Electronics	Year 12 tutor
EW	Miss Elaine White	Science	Year 13 tutor

References

Adatto, C.P. (1958) Ego reintegration observed in analysis of late adolescence. *International Journal of Psychoanalysis*, **39**, 172.

Allder, M. (1992) Is there a future for pastoral care staff in our comprehensive schools? *Pastoral Care in Education*, **10**(1), 3–7.

Allen, R. (1843) An account of St Mark's College, Chelsea, Report of the Committee of Council on Education for 1842–3 in Gosden, P.H.J.H. (ed.), *How They Were Taught*, pp. 290–303. Oxford: Basil Blackwell.

AMMA (1988) Pastoral symphony. *Report*, **10**(5), 1–2.

Anyon, J. (1979) Ideology and United States history textbooks. *Harvard Educational Review*, **49**(3), 361–86.

Apple, M.W. (1979a) *Ideology and Curriculum*. London: Routledge and Kegan Paul.

Apple, M.W. (1979b) What correspondence theories of the hidden curriculum miss. *Review of Education*, Spring, 101–12.

Aries, P. (1975) *Centuries of Childhood*. London: Jonathan Cape.

Atkinson, P. (1985) *Language, Structure and Code*. London: Methuen.

Atkinson, P., Davies, B. and Delamont, S. (eds) (1995) *Discourse and Reproduction: Essays in Honor of Basil Bernstein*. New Jersey: Hampton Press.

Baldwin, J. and Wells, H. (1979) *Active Tutorial Work Books 1 and 2*. Oxford: Basil Blackwell in association with Lancashire County Council.

Baldwin, J. and Wells, H. (1980) *Active Tutorial Work Books 3 and 4*. Oxford: Basil Blackwell in association with Lancashire County Council.

Baldwin, J. and Wells, H. (1981) *Active Tutorial Work Book 5*. Oxford: Basil Blackwell in association with Lancashire County Council.

Ball, S.J. (1981) *Beachside Comprehensive: A Case Study of Secondary Schooling*. Cambridge: Cambridge University Press.

Ball, S.J. (1986) Relations, structures and conditions in curriculum change: a political history of English teaching 1970–85. In Goodson, I. (ed.), *International Perspectives in Curriculum History*, pp. 17–45. London: Routledge.

Ball, S.J. (1990) *Politics and Policy Making in Education*. London: Routledge.

Ball, S.J. (1993) Education, Majorism and 'the Curriculum of the Dead'. *Curriculum Studies*, **1**(2), 195–214.

Ball, S.J. and Bowe, R. (1992) Subject departments and the 'implementation' of National Curriculum policy: an overview of the issues. *Journal of Curriculum Studies*, **24**(2), 97–115.

Ball, S.J. and Lacey, C. (1980) Subject disciplines as the opportunity for group action: a measured critique of subject subcultures. In Woods, P. (ed.), *Teacher Strategies: Explorations in the Sociology of the School*, pp. 147–77. London: Croom Helm.

Bamford, T.W. (1967) *Rise of the Public Schools*. London: Nelson.

Bamford, T.W. (1970) *Thomas Arnold on Education*. Cambridge: Cambridge University Press.

Bandura, A. and Walters, R.H. (1959) *Adolescent Aggression: A Study of the Influences of Child-training Practice and Family Interrelationships*. New York: Ronald Press.

Bantock, G.H. (1980) *Dilemmas of the Curriculum*. Oxford: Martin.

Barnes, A.R. (1970) Ruffwood School, Kirkby, Liverpool. In Halsall, E. (ed.), *Becoming Comprehensive: Case Histories*, pp. 229–47. Oxford: Pergamon Press.

Bates, A.W. (1970) The administration of comprehensive schools. In Monks, T.G. (ed.), *Comprehensive Education in Action*, pp. 25–59. Windsor: NFER.

Beasley, K. and Quicke, J. (1989) Curriculum approach to mental handicap in a comprehensive school. *Pastoral Care in Education*, **7**(1), 13–18.

Benn, C. and Simon, B. (1970) *Half Way There: Report on the British Comprehensive School Reform*. London: McGraw Hill.

Bernbaum, G. (1977) *Knowledge and Ideology in the Sociology of Education*. London: Macmillan.

Bernstein, B. (1977) *Class, Codes and Control*, Vol. 3, 2nd edn. London: Routledge and Kegan Paul.

Bernstein, B. (1992) Code theory and research, unpublished paper; published in Spanish as *Code Theory and Research for the Sociology of Education*. Barcelona, El Roure (1993).

Bernstein, B. (1995) Code theory and its positioning: a case study in misrecognition. *British Journal of Sociology of Education*, **16**(1), 3–20.

Best, R., Jarvis, C. and Ribbins, P. (1977) Pastoral care: concept and process. *British Journal of Educational Studies*, **25**(2), 124–35.

Best, R., Jarvis, C. and Ribbins, P. (eds) (1980) *Perspectives on Pastoral Care*. London: Heinemann Educational.

Best, R., Ribbins, P., Jarvis, C. and Oddy, D. (1983) *Education and Care*. London: Heinemann Educational.

Bisseret, N. (1979) *Education, Class, Language and Ideology*. London: Routledge and Kegan Paul.

Blackburn, K. (1975) *The Tutor*. London: Heinemann Educational.

Blackburn, K. (1980) The tutor: a developing role. In Best, R., Jarvis, C. and Ribbins, P. (eds), *Perspectives on Pastoral Care*, pp. 56–67. London: Heinemann Educational.

Bloom, B.S. (ed.) (1956) *Taxonomy of Educational Objectives*, Book 1. New York: David McKay Company.

Board of Education (1927) *The Education of the Adolescent* (The Hadow Report). London: HMSO.

Bond, J. (1984) It's who you are, not what you do that makes a difference. *Pastoral Care in Education*, **2**(2), 129–35.

Bourdieu, P. (1971) Systems of education and systems of thought. In Young, M.F.D. (ed.), *Knowledge and Control*, pp. 189–207. London: Collier Macmillan.

Bourdieu, P. (1976) The school as a conservative force. In Dale, R., Esland, G. and MacDonald, M. (eds), *Schooling and Capitalism*, pp. 110–18. London: Routledge and Kegan Paul.

Bowes, M. (1987) Care and control: a challenge for I.N.S.E.T. *Pastoral Care in Education*, **5**(3), 183–9.

Bowles, S. and Gintis, H. (1976) *Schooling in Capitalist America*. London: Routledge and Kegan Paul.

Browning, O. (1969) Memories of sixty years at Eton, Cambridge and elsewhere. Extracts in Gosden, P.H.J.H., *How They Were Taught*. Oxford: Basil Blackwell.

Bryant, P.H.M. (1936) *Harrow*. London: Blackie and Son.

Burgess, R.G. (1983) *Experiencing Comprehensive Education: A Study of Bishop McGregor School*. London: Methuen.

Burgess, R.G. (1989) The politics of pastoral care. In Walker, S. and Barton, L. (eds), *Politics and the Process of Schooling*, pp. 7–30. Milton Keynes: Open University Press.

Button, L. (1981) *Group Tutoring for the Form Teacher*. London: Hodder and Stoughton.

Buzzard, T. (1983) Option choice: no choice. *Pastoral Care in Education*, **1**(1), 36–40.

Carleton, J. (1965) *Westminster School*. London: Hart-Davis.

Chadwick, J. (1986) The relationship between the pastoral, academic and disciplinary aspects of the school and the future for pastoral care. In Wooster, A. and Hall, E. (eds), *Perspectives on Pastoral Care*, pp. 5–17. Nottingham: University of Nottingham School of Education.

Cicourel, A.V. and Kitsuse, J.I. (1963) *The Educational Decision-Makers*. New York: Bobbs-Merrill.

Climo, J. (1970) Three into one: Glossop School, Derbyshire. In Halsall, E. (ed.), *Becoming Comprehensive: Case Histories*, pp. 95–110. Oxford: Pergamon Press.

Clinstie, O.F. (1935) *A History of Clifton College 1860–1934*. Bristol: Arrowsmith.

Cobbe, F.P. (1904) *The Life of Frances Power Cobbe as Told by Herself*. Quoted in Gosden, P.H.J.H., *How They Were Taught*, pp. 60–9. Oxford: Basil Blackwell.

Collins, H.M. (1985) *Changing Order: Replication and Induction in Scientific Practice*. London: Sage.

Corbishley, P. and Evans, J. (1980) Teachers and pastoral care: an empirical comment. In Best, R., Jarvis, C. and Ribbins, P. (eds), *Perspectives on Pastoral Care*, pp. 201–24. London: Heinemann Educational.

Coulby, D. (1989) The National Curriculum. In Bash, L. and Coulby, D., *The Education Reform Act: Competition and Control*, pp. 54–71. London: Cassell.

Craft, M. (1980) School welfare roles and networks. In Best, R., Jarvis, C. and Ribbins, P. (eds), *Perspectives on Pastoral Care*, pp. 32–49. London: Heinemann Educational.

Dale, R. (1989) *The State and Education Policy*. Milton Keynes: Open University Press.

Daniels, H.J.J. (1988) An enquiry into different forms of special school organization, pedagogic practice and pupil discrimination. *CORE* **12**(2). Fiche 2, F7.

Daniels, H.J.J. (1989) Visual displays as tacit relays of the structure of pedagogic practice. *British Journal of Sociology of Education*, **10**(2), 123–40.

Davies, B. (1994) Durkheim and sociology of education. *British Journal of Sociology of Education*, **15**(1), 3–26.

Davies, B. (1995) Bernstein on classrooms. In Atkinson, P., Davies, B. and Delamont, S. (eds), *Discourse and Reproduction: Essays in Honor of Basil Bernstein*, pp. 137–58. New Jersey: Hampton Press.

Davies, K. (1974) History is about chaps. *Times Educational Supplement*, 29 November.

Davis, R. (1967) *The Grammar School*. Harmondsworth: Penguin.

Dearing, R. (1993) *The National Curriculum and Its Assessment, Final Report*. London: Schools Curriculum and Assessment Authority.

Diaz, M. (1984) A Model of Pedagogic Discourse with Special Application to Columbian Primary Level. Unpublished PhD thesis, University of London.

Donald, J. (1985) Beacons of the future: schooling, subjection and subjectification. In Beechey, V. and Donald, J. (eds), *Subjectivity and Social Relations*, pp. 214–49. Milton Keynes: Open University Press.

Donzelot, J. (1979) *The Policing of Families: Welfare versus the State*. London: Hutchinson.

Dooley, S.K. (1980) The relationship between the concepts 'pastoral care' and 'authority'. In Best, R., Jarvis, C. and Ribbins, P. (eds), *Perspectives on Pastoral Care*, pp. 16–24. London: Heinemann Educational.

Duncan, C. (1988) *Pastoral Care: An Antiracist/Multicultural Perspective*. Oxford: Basil Blackwell.

Eastgate, C. (1982) Curricular guidance at 14+: teacher and pupil perspectives. MA Thesis (unpublished), University of London, Institute of Education.

Edwards, R. (1969) *The Secondary Technical School*. London: University of London Press.

Edwards, T. (1980) Schooling for change: function, correspondence and cause. In Barton, L., Meighan, R. and Walker, S. (eds), *Schooling, Ideology and the Curriculum*, pp. 67–80. Lewes: Falmer Press.

Eggar, T. (1991) Speech given at Leeds Polytechnic 16 July, reported in *The Guardian*, 17 July.

Elkin, S.J. (1992) Classroom organization: an unorthodox view. *Pastoral Care in Education*, **10**(1), 39–42.

Elliott, J. (1983) A curriculum for the study of human affairs: the contribution of Lawrence Stenhouse. *Journal of Curriculum Studies*, **15**(2), 105–23.

English, P. (1991) The Tao of pastoral care. *Pastoral Care in Education*, **9**(3), 17–26.

Farley, R. (1960) *Secondary Modern Discipline*. London: Adam and Charles Black.

Ferguson, J. (1990) Lesbian and gay issues in the wake of HIV and AIDS. *Pastoral Care in Education*, **8**(3), 17–22.

Flew, A. (1976) *Sociology, Equality and Education*. London: Macmillan.

Follett, J. (1986) The concept of pastoral care: a genealogical analysis. *Pastoral Care in Education*, **4**(1), 3–10.

Ford, J. (1969) *Social Class and the Comprehensive School*. London: Routledge and Kegan Paul.

Foucault, M. (1980) Truth and power. In Gordon, C. (ed.), *Power/Knowledge: Selected Interviews and Other Writings 1972–77 by Michel Foucault*, pp. 109–33. Brighton: Harvester Press.

Foucault, M. (1982) The subject and power. In Dreyfus, H. and Rabinow, P. (eds), *Michel Foucault: Beyond Structuralism and Hermeneutics*, pp. 208–26. Brighton: Harvester Press.

Gibson, R. (1977) Bernstein's classification and framing: a critique. *Higher Education Review*, **9**(2), 23–45.

Gibson, R. (1984) *Structuralism and Education*. London: Methuen.

Giddens, A. (1984) *The Constitution of Society*. Cambridge: Polity Press.

Gitelson, M. (1948) Character synthesis: the psychotherapeutic problem of adolescence. *American Journal of Orthopsychiatry*, **18**, 422–31.

Gleeson, D. and Whitty, G. (1976) *Developments in Social Studies Teaching*. London: Open Books.

Goodson, I.F. (1983) *School Subjects and Curriculum Change*. London: Croom Helm.

Goodson, I.F. (1988) *The Making of the Curriculum*. Lewes: Falmer Press.

Goodson, I.F. (1990) Curriculum reform and curriculum theory: a case of historical amnesia. In Moon, B. (ed.), *New Curriculum – National Curriculum*, pp. 47–56. London: Hodder and Stoughton in association with The Open University.

Gordon, P. and Lawton, D. (1978) *Curriculum Change in the Nineteenth and Twentieth Centuries*. London: Hodder and Stoughton.

Grumet, M. (1981) Restitution and reconstruction of educational experience: an autobiographical method for curriculum theory. In Lawn, M. and Barton, L. (eds), *Rethinking Curriculum Studies*, pp. 115–30. London: Croom Helm.

Haigh, G. (1975) *Pastoral Care*. London: Pitman.

Halpin, D. and Whitty, G. (1992) Secondary education after the Reform Act, Unit S1–2, Course EP228, *Frameworks for Teaching*. Milton Keynes: Open University.

Halsall, E. (ed.) (1970) *Becoming Comprehensive: Case Histories*. Oxford: Pergamon Press.

Halsey, A.H., Heath, A.F. and Ridge, J.M. (1980) *Origins and Destinations: Family, Class and Education in Modern Britain.* Oxford: Clarendon Press.

Hamblin, D. (1978) *The Teacher and Pastoral Care.* Oxford: Blackwell.

Hamilton, D. (1988) Some observations on progressivism and curriculum practice. In Green, A.G. and Ball, S.J. (eds), *Progress and Inequality in Comprehensive Education*, pp. 23–38. London: Routledge.

Hargreaves, A. (1989) *Curriculum Assessment and Reform.* Milton Keynes: Open University Press.

Hargreaves, D.H. (1980) The occupational culture of teachers. In Woods, P. (ed.), *Teacher Strategies: Explorations in the Sociology of the School*, pp. 125–48. London: Croom Helm.

Hargreaves, D.H. (1982) *The Challenge for the Comprehensive School.* London: Routledge and Kegan Paul.

Harker, R. and May, S.A. (1993) Code and *habitus*: comparing the accounts of Bernstein and Bourdieu. *British Journal of Sociology of Education*, **14**(2), 169–78.

Hewitson, J.N. (1969) *The Grammar School Tradition in a Comprehensive World.* London: Routledge and Kegan Paul.

Hine, R.J. (1975) Political bias in school physics. *Hard Cheese*, 4/5.

HMI (1989) *Pastoral Care in Secondary Schools: An Inspection of Some Aspects of Pastoral Care in 1987–1988.* London: DES.

Hoffman, M. (1975) Assumptions in sex education books. *Educational Review*, **27**(3), 211–20.

Hogan, D. (1981) Capitalism, liberalism and schooling. In Dale, R., Esland, G., Fergusson, R. and MacDonald, M. (eds), *Education and the State* Vol. I: *Schooling and the National Interest*, pp. 31–45. Lewes: Falmer Press.

Hopper, B. (1986) Pastoral care – or control? In Wooster, A. and Hall, E. (eds), *Perspectives on Pastoral Care*, pp. 55–65. Nottingham: University of Nottingham School of Education.

Hughes, P.M. (1980) Pastoral care: the historical context. In Best, R., Jarvis, C. and Ribbins, P. (eds), *Perspectives on Pastoral Care*, pp. 25–32. London: Heinemann Educational.

Hunt, A. (1972) On the tyranny of subjects. In Rubinstein, D. and Stoneman, C. (eds), *Education for Democracy*, 2nd edn, pp. 26–33. Harmondsworth: Penguin.

Hurn, R. (1978) *The Limits and Possibilities of Education.* Boston: Allyn and Bacon.

IAAMSS (Incorporated Association of Assistant Masters in Secondary Schools) (1963) *General Education in Grammar Schools.* Cambridge: Cambridge University Press.

Independent Schools Information Service (ISIS) (1994) *Annual Census.* London: ISIS.

Jackson, B. and Marsden, D. (1967) *Education and the Working Class.* London: Routledge and Kegan Paul.

Jeffrey, I. (1974) Integrating art into society. In Holly, D. (ed.), *Education or Domination?* pp. 126–47. London: Arrow.

Jenkins, C. (1989) The Professional Middle Class and the Origins of the

New Education Fellowship 1920–50. PhD Thesis, University of London.

Kay, J.P. (1970) *The Training of Pauper Children in London: Poor Law Commission*. Manchester: E.J. Morton.

Keddie, N. (1971) Classroom knowledge. In Young, M.F.D. (ed.), *Knowledge and Control: New Directions for the Sociology of Education*, pp. 133–60. London: Collier-Macmillan.

King, R. (1969) *Values and Involvement in a Grammar School*. London: Routledge and Kegan Paul.

King, R. (1976) Bernstein's sociology of the school: some propositions tested. *British Journal of Sociology*, **27**, 430–43.

King, R. (1981a) Bernstein's sociology of the school – a further testing. *British Journal of Sociology*, **32**, 259–65.

King, R. (1981b) Secondary schools: some changes of a decade. *Educational Research*, **23**, 173–6.

King, R. (1983) *The Sociology of School Organization*. London: Methuen.

Kitzinger, C. (1989) Liberal humanism as an ideology of social control: the regulation of lesbians. In Shotter, J. and Gergen, K.J. (eds), *Texts of Identity*, pp. 82–98. London: Sage.

Lacey, C. (1970) *Hightown Grammar: The School as a Social System*. Manchester: Manchester University Press.

Lakoff, G. and Johnson, M. (1980) *Metaphors We Live By*. Chicago: University of Chicago Press.

Lang, P. (1977) It's easier to punish us in small groups. *Times Educational Supplement*, 6/5.

Lang, P. (1983) How pupils see it. *Pastoral Care in Education*, **1**(3), 164–75.

Lang, P. (1984) Pastoral care: some reflections on possible influences. *Pastoral Care in Education*, **2**(2), 136–47.

Lang, P. (1985) Taking the consumer into account. In Lang, P. and Marland, M. (eds), *New Directions in Pastoral Care*, pp. 169–86. Oxford: Basil Blackwell.

Layton, D. (1972) Science as general education. *Trends in Education*, **25**, January, 11–15.

Layton, D. (1973) *Science for the People: The Origins of the School Science Curriculum in England*. London: George Allen and Unwin.

Lowe, R. (1988) *Education in the Post-War Years*. London: Routledge.

Lyons, G. (1981) *Teacher Careers and Career Perception*. Windsor: NFER.

Mack, E.C. (1938) *Public Schools and British Opinion*. London: Methuen.

Maher, P. and Best, P. (1985) Preparation and support for pastoral care: a survey of current provision. In Lang, P. and Marland, M. (eds), *New Directions in Pastoral Care*, pp. 50–66. Oxford: Basil Blackwell.

Marland, M. (1974) *Pastoral Care*. London: Heinemann Educational.

Marland, M. (1980) The pastoral curriculum. In Best, R., Jarvis, C. and Ribbins, P. (eds), *Perspectives on Pastoral Care*, pp. 151–70. London: Heinemann Educational.

Marsden, W.E. (1987) *Unequal Educational Provision in England and Wales*. London: Woburn Press.

May, M. (1981) Innocence and experience: the evolution of the concept of juvenile delinquency in the mid-nineteenth century. In Dale, R., Esland, G., Fergusson, R. and MacDonald, M. (eds), *Education and the State* Vol. II: *Politics, Patriarchy and Practice*, pp. 269–84. Lewes: Falmer Press.

McLaughlin, C., Lodge, G. and Watkin, C. (1991) *Gender and Pastoral Care.* Oxford: Basil Blackwell.

McNamara, E. (1992) Motivational interviewing: the gateway to pupil self-management. *Pastoral Care in Education,* **10**(3), 22–9.

Meighan, R. (1986) *A Sociology of Educating,* 2nd edn. London: Cassell.

Millerson, G. (1964) *The Qualifying Associations: A Study in Professionalization.* London: Routledge and Kegan Paul.

Millstein, B. (1972) *Women's Studies – Women in History.* New York: New York Board of Education.

Monks, T.G. (ed.) (1968) *Comprehensive Education in England and Wales.* Windsor: NFER.

Mosely, J. (1988) Some implications arising from a small-scale study of a circle-based programme initiated for the tutorial period. *Pastoral Care in Education,* **6**(2), 2–10.

Musgrave, P.W. (1970) A model for the analysis of the development of the English educational system from 1860. In Musgrave, P.W. (ed.), *Sociology, History and Education,* pp. 15–29. London: Methuen.

Musgrave, P.W. (1973) *Knowledge, Curriculum and Change.* London: Angus and Robertson.

Musgrove, F. (1964) *Youth and the Social Order.* London: Routledge and Kegan Paul.

Musgrove, F. (1968) Curriculum objectives. *Journal of Curriculum Studies,* **1**(1), 5–18.

Musgrove, F. (1971) *Patterns of Power and Authority in English Education.* London: Methuen.

Nash, R. (1972) History as She Is Writ, *New Society,* 3 August, 230–32.

National Curriculum Council (1989) *Circular Number 6: The National Curriculum and Whole Curriculum Planning.* York: NCC.

Neill, S. (1988) Non-verbal communication: its significance for the pastoral specialist. *Pastoral Care in Education,* **6**(4), 7–14.

O'Hear, A. (1991) *Education and Democracy: Against the Educational Establishment.* London: Claridge Press.

Ozga, J. and Lawn, M. (1981) *Teachers, Professionalism and Class.* Lewes: Falmer Press.

Partridge, J. (1968) *Life in a Secondary Modern School.* Harmondsworth: Penguin.

Pearson, G.J.J. (1958) *Adolescence and the Conflict of Generations.* New York: Norton.

Pedley, R. (1963) *The Comprehensive School.* Harmondsworth: Penguin.

Pepper, B., Myers, K. and Coyle/Dawkins, R. (eds) (1984) *Sex Equality and the Pastoral Curriculum.* London: ILEA.

Phares, E.J. (1976) *Locus of Control in Personality.* Morristown, NJ: General Learning.

Potter, J. and Wetherell, M. (1987) *Discourse and Social Psychology.* London: Sage.

Pring, R. (1972) Knowledge out of control. *Education for Teaching*, **89**, 19–28.

Pring, R. (1975) Bernstein's classification and framing of knowledge. *Scottish Educational Studies*, **7**(1), 67–74.

Quicke, J. (1987) The disability curriculum. *Journal of Pastoral Care in Education*, **5**(2), 114–23.

Raymond, J. (1985) *Implementing Pastoral Care in Schools.* London: Croom Helm.

Redican, B. (1985) Subject teachers under stress. In Walford, G. (ed.), *Schooling in Turmoil*, pp. 215–43. London: Croom Helm.

Reynolds, D. and Sullivan, M. (1981) The comprehensive experience. In Barton, L. and Walker, S. (eds), *Schools, Teachers and Teaching*, pp. 121–38. Lewes: Falmer Press.

Reynolds, D. and Sullivan, M. with Murgatroyd, S. (1987) *The Comprehensive Experiment: A Comparison of the Selective and Non-selective Systems of School Organization.* London: Falmer.

Ribbins, P.M. (1985) Editorial: three reasons for thinking more about schooling and welfare. In Ribbins, P. (ed.), *Schooling and Welfare*, pp. 1–6. Lewes: Falmer Press.

Ribbins, P. and Best, R. (1985) Pastoral care: theory, practice and the growth of research. In Lang, P. and Marland, M. (eds), *New Directions in Pastoral Care*, pp. 14–49. Oxford: Basil Blackwell.

Ribbins, P.M. and Ribbins, P.A. (1983) The conversation of care. *Educational Review*, **35**(1), 59–68.

Richardson, E. (1973) *The Teacher, the School and the Task of Management.* London: Heinemann Educational.

Riseborough, G.F. (1984) Teacher careers in comprehensive schooling: an empirical study. In Hargreaves, A. and Woods, P. (eds), *Classrooms and Staffrooms*, pp. 245–57. Milton Keynes: Open University Press.

Rose, N. (1989) Individualizing psychology. In Shotter, J. and Gergen, K.J. (eds), *Texts of Identity*, pp. 119–32. London: Sage.

Rotter, J.B. (1966) Generalised expectancies for internal versus external control of reinforcement. *Psychological Monographs*, **80**(1), 1–28.

Sadler, P. (1989) RO-RO: role on–role off. *Pastoral Care in Education*, **7**(3), 26–30.

Sadovnik, A. (ed.) (1994) *Pedagogy and Knowledge: Commentaries on the Sociology of Basil Bernstein.* New York: Ablex Press.

Sarup, M. (1982) *Education, State and Crisis: A Marxist Perspective.* London: Routledge and Kegan Paul.

Schools Council (1970) *Cross'd with Adversity: The Education of Socially Disadvantaged Children in Secondary Schools.* Working Paper 27. London: Evans/Methuen.

Shaw, J. (1981a) In loco parentis: a relationship between parent, state and child. In Dale, R., Esland, G., Fergusson, R. and MacDonald, M. (eds), *Education and the State* Vol. II: *Politics, Patriarchy and Practice*, pp. 257–68. Lewes: Falmer Press.

Shaw, J. (1981b) Family, State and Compulsory Education, Unit 13, Block

15, Course E353, *Education, Welfare and Social Order*. Milton Keynes: Open University.

Shield, G.W. (1970) Mexborough Grammar School, Yorkshire. In Halsall, E. (ed.), *Becoming Comprehensive: Case Histories*, pp. 189–202. Oxford: Pergamon Press.

Sikes, P.J. (1984) Teacher careers in the comprehensive school. In Ball, S.J. (ed.), *Comprehensive Schooling: A Reader*, pp. 227–47. Lewes: Falmer Press.

Simon, B. (1974) *The Two Nations and the Educational Structure 1780–1870*. London: Lawrence and Wishart.

Simon, B. (1975) Introduction. In Simon, B. and Bradley, J. (eds), *The Victorian Public School*, pp. 1–18. Dublin: Gill and Macmillan.

Spours, K. and Young, M. (1990) Beyond vocationalism: a new perspective on the relationship between work and education. In Moon, B. (ed.), *New Curriculum – National Curriculum*, pp. 57–70. London: Hodder and Stoughton in association with The Open University.

Steedman, C. (1982) *The Tidy House*. London: Virago.

Stone, L.J. and Church, J. (1975) Adolescence as a cultural invention. In Esman, A.H. (ed.), *The Psychology of Adolescence*, pp. 7–11. New York: International Universities Press.

Tattum, D. (1982) *Disruptive Pupils in Schools and Units*. Chichester: Wiley.

Tattum, D. (1984) Pastoral care and disruptive pupils: a rhetoric of caring. *Pastoral Care in Education*, **2**(1), 4–15.

Tattum, D. (1985) Control and welfare: towards a theory of constructive discipline in schools. In Ribbins, P. (ed.), *Schooling and Welfare*, pp. 43–60. Lewes: Falmer Press.

Taylor, M. (1980) The language of pastoral care. In Best, R., Jarvis, C. and Ribbins, P. (eds), *Perspectives on Pastoral Care*, pp. 225–51. London: Heinemann Educational.

Thewlis, J. (1988) Progress and the radical educational press. In Green, A.G. and Ball, S.J. (eds), *Progress and Inequality in Comprehensive Education*, pp. 247–68. London: Routledge.

Turner, G. (1984) Assessment in the comprehensive school: what criteria count? In Broadfoot, P. (ed.), *Selection, Certification and Control*, pp. 67–82. Lewes: Falmer Press.

Tyler, W. (1988) *School Organization: A Sociological Perspective*. London: Croom Helm.

Vulliamy, G. (1976) What counts as school music? In Whitty, G. and Young, M.F.D. (eds), *Explorations in the Politics of School Knowledge*, pp. 19–34. Driffield: Nafferton.

Walford, G. (1986) *Life in Public Schools*. London: Methuen.

Walkerdine, V. (1984) Developmental psychology and the child-centred pedagogy: the insertion of Piaget into early education. In Henriques, J., Holloway, W., Urwin, C., Venn, C. and Walkerdine, V. (eds), *Changing the Subject: Psychology, Social Regulation and Subjectivity*, pp. 153–202. London: Methuen.

Walkerdine, V. (1987) Sex, power and pedagogy. In Arnot, M., and Weiner, G. (eds), *Gender and the Politics of Schooling*, pp. 166–74. London:

Hutchinson Education.

Walkerdine, V. (1989) Femininity as performance. *Oxford Review of Education*, **15**(3), 267–79.

Wall, W.D. (1968) *Adolescents in School and Society*. Slough: NFER.

Wardle, D. (1976) *English Popular Education 1780–1975*. Cambridge: Cambridge University Press.

Wexler, P. (1982) Structure, text and subject. In Apple, M.W. (ed.), *Cultural and Economic Reproduction in Education*, pp. 275–303. London: Routledge and Kegan Paul.

Whitty, G. (1985) *Sociology and School Knowledge; Curriculum Theory, Research and Politics*. London: Methuen.

Whitty, G. and Kirton, A. (1995) From learning reform to curriculum reform: curriculum reform and integrated Humanities in England. In Inui, A. and Ohta, M. (eds), *Koza Koko Kyoiku Kaikaku: Gakko-zukuri no soten (High School Education Today)*. Tokyo: Rodojunpa-sha.

Whitty, G., Rowe, G. and Aggleton, P. (1994) Discourse in cross-curricular contexts: limits to empowerment. *International Studies in Sociology of Education*, **4**(1), 25–42.

Wiener, M.J. (1981) *English Culture and the Decline of the Industrial Spirit 1850–1980*. Cambridge: Cambridge University Press.

Williams, R. (1983) *Keywords*. London: Fontana.

Williamson, B. (1974) Continuities and discontinuities in the sociology of education. In Flude, M. and Ahier, J. (eds), *Educability, Schools and Ideology*, pp. 3–14. London: Croom Helm.

Williamson, D. (1980) Pastoral care or pastoralization? In Best, R., Jarvis, C. and Ribbins, P. (eds), *Perspectives on Pastoral Care*, pp. 171–81. London: Heinemann Educational.

Willis, P. (1977) *Learning to Labour*. Farnborough: Saxon House.

Wolpe, A. (1988) *Within School Walls*. London: Routledge and Kegan Paul.

Woods, N.E. (1983) The Structure and Practice of Pastoral Care at Oakfield School. MEd Dissertation (unpublished), University of Birmingham.

Young, M.F.D. (ed.) (1971a) *Knowledge and Control: New Directions for the Sociology of Education*. London: Collier-Macmillan.

Young, M.F.D. (1971b) Introduction. In Young, M.F.D. (ed.), *Knowledge and Control*, pp. 1–19. London: Collier-Macmillan.

Young, M.F.D. (1976) The schooling of science. In Whitty, G. and Young, M.F.D. (eds), *Explorations in the Politics of School Knowledge*, pp. 47–61. Driffield: Nafferton.

Name index

Subject index